256

FAT QUARTER QUILT BLOCKS™

Edited by Jeanne Stauffer & Sandra L. Hatch

HOUSE of
WHITE
BIRCHES

PUBLISHERS
SINCE 1947

W9-ASP-209

256 Fat Quarter Quilt Blocks

Copyright © 2005 House of White Birches, Berne, Indiana 46711

EDITORS	Jeanne Stauffer, Sandra L. Hatch
ART DIRECTOR	Brad Snow
PUBLISHING SERVICES MANAGER	Brenda Gallmeyer
ASSOCIATE EDITOR	Dianne Schmidt
ASSISTANT ART DIRECTOR	Nick Pierce
COPY SUPERVISOR	Michelle Beck
COPY EDITORS	Nicki Lehman, Beverly Richardson
GRAPHIC ARTS SUPERVISOR	Ronda Bechinski
GRAPHIC ARTISTS	Debby Keel, Edith Teegarden
PRODUCTION ASSISTANTS	Cheryl Kempf, Marj Morgan
TECHNICAL ARTIST	Connie Rand
PHOTOGRAPHY	Tammy Christian, Don Clark, Christena Green, Matthew Owen
PHOTO STYLISTS	Tammy Nussbaum, Tammy M. Smith
CHIEF EXECUTIVE OFFICER	John Robinson
PUBLISHING DIRECTOR	David J. McKee
EDITORIAL DIRECTOR	Vivian Rothe
MARKETING DIRECTOR	Dan Fink

Printed in China
First Printing: 2005
Library of Congress Control Number: 2004116729
Hardcover ISBN: 1-59217-075-7
Softcover ISBN: 1-59217-076-5

1 2 3 4 5 6 7 8 9

WELCOME

Quilters love collecting two things: fabric and quilt patterns. You can never have too much fabric or too many quilt patterns.

It doesn't matter what kind of quilts you love to make. If you are like most quilters, you are always looking for fabric and quilt patterns that are unique, something you haven't seen before.

With that in mind, we selected 256 block designs that are original or at least uncommon. All can be made from fat quarters. We've included easy-to-use instructions for all 256 blocks since we know that many quilters will not have seen or stitched these blocks before.

We also added 20 fun projects for you to make, using several of the block designs in this book. Since the block designs are all 12 inches square, you can easily interchange one block for another. Whether you use the same block for an entire quilt or create a sampler by using a variety of blocks, you'll enjoy stitching these quick and easy quilts and quilted projects.

Before you start your first project, read the How to Use This Book section on pages 6 and 7. You will find tips for using the templates and for using a rotary cutter to cut some pieces without the use of templates.

With the addition of the 256 blocks in this book, you'll add lots of block-design choices to your growing pattern collection. So take a look at your stash of fat quarters, or plan a trip to your favorite quilt shop. It's time to quilt!

Warm regards,

Jeanne Stauffer

Sandra L. Hatch

CONTENTS

HOW TO USE THIS BOOK

The 256 block designs given in this book are all 12" square. Each block is made up of templates labeled with R (rectangle), S (square), T (triangle) and Z (all other shapes). A template labeled S3 may be found in the section of square templates with the S3 label.

To extend the life of this book, we recommend tracing the templates for your chosen block from the book onto template plastic. Transfer all information to the template including the pattern letter and number and grain line. Keep templates in a zippered bag inside this book for future use. You may photocopy the templates, glue to cardboard and cut them out, but if using this method, be sure the copier reproduces the pattern exactly. To check, lay the paper copy on the book pattern. If it is a different size, the copier is not accurate. You should then trace the patterns from the book onto paper.

A grain line is marked on each template. The grain line means that the piece should be cut with that line on the straight of grain. Some T (triangle) templates are marked with two arrows. These templates may be placed with either grain line on the straight of grain. If the triangle's longest edge lies along the outside edges of a block, then the straight of grain would be on that edge as shown in Figure 1. If the shorter sides of the triangle lie along the outside edge of the block, then it would be cut with the short side on the straight of grain as shown in Figure 2.

The projects in this book were made with one or more of the 256 block designs given. Each project includes cutting and piecing instructions to complete the project as shown. In some cases, other blocks from the book may be substituted for those used.

You may prefer to make a quilt using just one block design, or mix and match using many designs. Some blocks are easier than others. Harder blocks include those with set-in pieces or pieces with narrow points and angles.

Each block is shown whole and then broken apart into units to aid in the piecing process. Instructions are written with what we think are the easiest unit breakdowns. Most blocks have center, side and corner units, or center and side rows.

If you are making multiple blocks using the same block design, it is possible to use a rotary cutter, ruler and mat to cut the pieces for some designs. For example, if you are making the Alaska block with the S2 square, it measures 3½" with the seam allowance. Cut a 3½" by fabric width strip and subcut it into 3½" squares as shown in Figure 3. You can get 12 S2 squares from one 42" width-of-fabric strip.

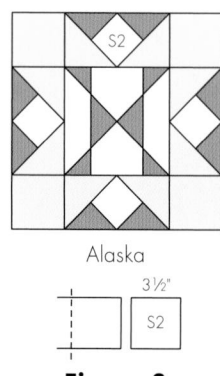

Alaska

Figure 3

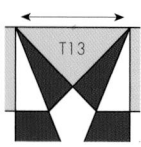

Figure 1

Figure 2

If there are triangles in your block, such as Mrs. Cleveland's Choice, measure the triangle sides, including the seam allowance, and cut a strip that width. For example, T23 is 2⅛" along the short sides. Cut a 2⅛" by fabric width strip and subcut the strip into 2⅛" squares. You can cut (19) 2⅛" squares from a 42" width of fabric. Cut each square in half on one diagonal to make 38 T23 triangles from one fabric width as shown in Figure 4.

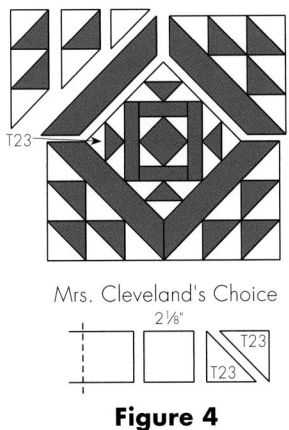

Mrs. Cleveland's Choice

Figure 4

Rectangles may be cut in the same manner; cut a strip the size of the longest edges of the rectangle across the fabric width, then subcut the strip into the proper widths. For example, for R6 in Nine-Patch Plaid, cut a 6½" by fabric width strip, and then subcut the strip into 2½" segments. You can cut 16 R6 rectangles from a 42" width-of-fabric strip.

Other shapes may also be rotary-cut. Simply measure the template side that includes the grain-line arrow and cut a fabric-width strip that size.

If your pattern calls for a reversed piece, that means that the piece is cut with one side of the template up, then the template is flipped over and it is cut again. For example, T16 and T16R in Optical Illusion can be cut from a 4½" by fabric width strip as shown in Figure 5.

Blocks are shown using light, medium and dark fills. Some designs require more than one light, medium or dark. In those cases, we have added lightest and

darkest or dark 1, dark 2, etc., to the instructions to help designate the colors.

The blocks are shown in alphabetical order beginning on page 72. All templates are given starting on page 136 of the book.

If you need basic quiltmaking instructions, there are many books available to help you out. This book is intended to be a pattern book with a library of block-design choices to add to your growing pattern collection. ■

Figure 5

DESIGN BY **TOBY LISCHKO**

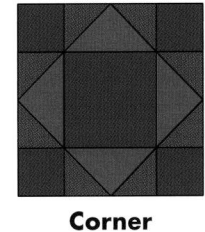

Corner
8" x 8" Block

Diamonds Galore
12" x 12" Block

DIAMONDS GALORE

Fat quarters in red, blue, green and cream provide the contrast in the blocks of this pretty quilt.

PROJECT SPECIFICATIONS

Skill Level: Intermediate
Quilt Size: 64" x 64"
Block Size: 12" x 12"
Number of Blocks: 16

MATERIALS

- 6 green fat quarters (dark 1)
- 6 cream fat quarters (light)
- 8 blue fat quarters (dark 2)
- 12 red fat quarters (dark 3)
- ½ yard red tonal for binding
- Backing 70" x 70"
- Batting 70" x 70"
- All-purpose thread to match fabrics
- Quilting thread
- Basic tools and supplies

INSTRUCTIONS

Note: Block piecing instructions are given on page 84. Rotary-cutting sizes are given here for both block and setting pieces. If you prefer to cut the block pieces with templates, the letter/number label for each piece is given to identify the template that may be used. Block templates may be found by letter/number in the template section beginning on page 136.

CUTTING

Step 1. From each blue, cut eight 4¾" x 4¾" dark 2 S22 squares, two 25/8" x 25/8" dark 2 S2 squares and two 2½" x 12½" B strips.

Step 2. Using the T28 template, cut two T28 and two T28R pieces from each blue.

Step 3. Using the T44 template, cut two T44 pieces from each blue.

Step 4. From each of four blues, cut four 2½" x 2½" S19 squares and one 4½" x 4½" S14 square.

Step 5. From each of four greens, cut six 4¼" x 4¼" squares.

Step 6. From each of the remaining two green fabrics, cut four 4¼" x 4¼" squares and four 2⅞" x 2⅞" squares.

Step 7. Cut the 4¼" x 4¼" squares on both diagonals to make 128 dark T33 triangles. Cut the 2⅞" x 2⅞" squares on one diagonal to make 32 T11 triangles.

Step 8. Cut a total of 32 T38 and 32 T28R pieces and 16 T44 pieces from green fabrics.

Step 9. From each of eight reds, cut eight 3⅞" x 3⅞" squares and four 4¼" x 4¼" squares.

Step 10. Cut the 3⅞" x 3⅞" squares on one diagonal to make 128 dark 3 T7 triangles. Cut the 4¼" x 4¼" squares on both diagonals to make 128 dark T33 triangles.

Step 11. From each of the remaining four reds, cut one 5¼" x 5¼" square, four 2½" x 12½" A strips and four each T28 and T28R pieces.

Step 12. Cut the 5¼" x 5¼" squares on both diagonals to make 16 T18 triangles.

Step 13. Cut 32 cream squares each 3⅞" x 3⅞" and 4¼" x 4¼".

Step 14. Cut the 3⅞" x 3⅞" squares in half on one diagonal to make 64 light T7 triangles. Cut the 4¼" x 4¼" squares in half on both diagonals to make 128 light T33 triangles.

Step 15. Cut a total of 32 light T28 and 32 T28R pieces from cream fabric.

Step 16. Cut seven 2¼" by fabric width strips red tonal for binding.

COMPLETING THE TOP

Step 1. Complete 16 Diamonds Galore blocks referring to the instructions on page 84. **Note:** *Use same-fabric green and blue pieces in each block. Use one red for the center T7 pieces and T33 pieces and another red for the block corner T7 pieces in each block.*

Step 2. Arrange the blocks in four rows of four blocks each; join blocks in rows. Press seams in adjacent rows in opposite directions. Join the rows to complete the pieced center; press seams in one direction.

Step 3. Sew a green T28 and T28R triangle to the angled sides of a blue T44 triangle as shown in Figure 1; press seams toward T28 and T28R. Repeat for 16 blue T44 units. Repeat with blue T28 and T28R pieces and green T44 pieces to make 16 green T44 units, again referring to Figure 1.

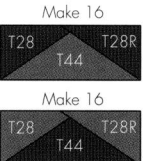

Figure 1

Step 4. Sew a cream T28 triangle to a red T28 triangle to make a red T28 unit as shown in Figure 2; repeat for 16 units. Repeat with cream and red T28R triangles to make 16 red T28R units. Repeat with cream T28 and T28R and green T28 and T28R triangles to make 16 each green T28 and T28R units, again referring to Figure 2. Press seams toward green and red pieces.

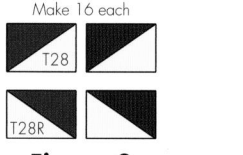

Figure 2

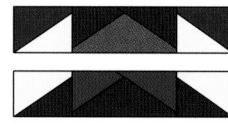

Figure 3

Step 5. Sew a red T28 and T28R unit to opposite ends of a blue T44 unit as shown in Figure 3; repeat for 16 units. Repeat with a green T28 and T28R unit on opposite ends of a green T44 unit, again referring to Figure 3; press seams toward T28 and T28R units.

Step 6. Join the two units with A and B strips to make a border unit as shown in Figure 4; press seams toward A and B strips. Repeat for 16 border units.

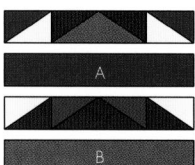

Figure 4

Step 7. Sew a T11 triangle to the two short sides of a T18 triangle as shown in Figure 5; press seams toward T11 pieces. Repeat for 16 T11-18 units.

Figure 5

Step 8. Sew a T11-18 unit to opposite sides of an S5 square to make a center unit as shown in Figure 6; press seams toward S14. Repeat for four units.

Figure 6

Step 9. Sew an S19 square to each end of each remaining T11-18 unit as shown in Figure 7; press seams toward S19. Repeat for eight side units.

Figure 7

Step 10. Sew a side unit to opposite sides of a center unit to complete one corner block as shown in Figure 8; press seams away from center unit. Repeat for four Corner blocks.

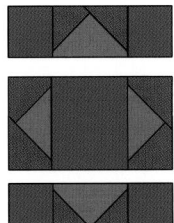

Figure 8

Step 11. Join four border units to make a side border strip as shown in Figure 9; press seams open. Repeat for four side border strips.

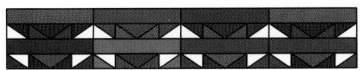

Figure 9

Step 12. Sew a side border strip to two opposite sides of the pieced center; press seams toward strips.

Step 13. Sew a Corner block to each end of the remaining side border strips. Repeat for two border strips; press seams open.

Step 14. Sew a border strip to the top and bottom of the pieced center; press seams toward strips to complete the pieced top.

COMPLETING THE QUILT

Step 1. Sandwich batting between the completed top and prepared backing piece; pin or baste layers together to hold flat.

Step 2. Quilt as desired by hand or machine.

Step 3. When quilting is complete, remove pins or basting; trim batting and backing edges even with quilt top.

Step 4. Join binding strips on short ends to make one long strip; press seams open.

Step 5. Fold binding strip in half with wrong sides together along length; press.

Step 6. Sew binding strip to quilt top with raw edges even, mitering corners and overlapping ends. Turn binding to the back side; hand- or machine-stitch in place to finish. ■

Diamonds Galore
Placement Diagram
64" x 64"

DESIGN BY **JUDITH SANDSTROM**

Primrose Cluster 1
12" x 12" Block

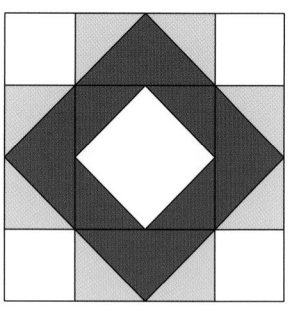

Primrose Cluster 2
12" x 12" Block

PRIMROSE CLUSTER

Two different blocks with common pieces combine to make this lap-size quilt.

PROJECT SPECIFICATIONS

Skill Level: Beginner
Quilt Size: 45" x 57"
Block Size: 12" x 12"
Number of Blocks: 12

MATERIALS

- 2 each orange, yellow and purple fat quarters
- 2 each of 3 dark green fat quarters
- ¾ yard tan tonal
- ⅞ yard light green tonal
- 1 yard white tonal
- Backing 51" x 63"
- Batting 51" x 63"
- All-purpose thread to match fabrics
- Quilting thread
- Basic tools and supplies

INSTRUCTIONS

Note: *Block piecing instructions are given on page 116. Rotary-cutting sizes are given here for both block and setting pieces. If you prefer to cut the block pieces with templates, the letter/number label for each piece is given to identify the template that may be used. Block templates may be found by letter/number in the template section beginning on page 136.*

CUTTING

Step 1. Cut one 4¾" by fabric width strip white tonal; subcut strip into six 4¾" lightest S22 squares.

Step 2. Cut two 3⅞" by fabric width strips white tonal; subcut strips into (14) 3⅞" squares. Cut each square in half on one diagonal to make 28 lightest T7 triangles.

Step 3. Cut five 3½" by fabric width strips white tonal; subcut two of the strips into (24) 3½" lightest S5 squares. Cut the remaining strips into (14) 3½" x 6½" A rectangles and four more 3½" lightest S5 squares.

Step 4. Cut two 7¼" by fabric width strips light green tonal; subcut strips into (10) 7¼" squares. Cut each square on both diagonals to make 40 medium T32 triangles. Set aside two triangles for another project.

Step 5. Cut three 3⅞" by fabric width strips light green tonal; subcut strips into (24) 3⅞" squares. Cut each square on one diagonal to make 48 medium T7 triangles.

Step 6. Cut one 7¼" x 22" strip from each of the three dark greens; cut two 7¼" squares from each strip. Cut each square in half on both diagonals to make eight darkest T32 triangles from each fabric.

Step 7. Cut one 4¾" x 22" strip from each of the three dark greens; cut two 4¾" darkest S22 squares from each strip.

Step 8. Cut two 3⅞" x 22" strips from each of the

three dark greens; subcut strips into eight 3⅞" squares of each fabric. Cut each square in half on one diagonal to make 16 darkest T7 triangles from each fabric.

Step 9. Cut four 2" x 2" C squares and eight 2" x 6½" B rectangles total dark greens.

Step 10. Cut three 3⅞" x 22" strips each orange, yellow and purple; subcut strips into (12) 3⅞" squares each fabric. Cut each square in half on one diagonal to make 24 dark T7 triangles each fabric.

Step 11. Cut eight 2" x 6½" B rectangles each orange, yellow and purple.

Step 12. Cut two 3⅞" by fabric width strips tan tonal; subcut strips into (12) 3⅞" squares. Cut each square in half on one diagonal to make 24 light T7 triangles.

Step 13. Cut six 2¼" strips tan tonal for binding.

Step 1. Complete six each Primrose Cluster 1 and Primrose Cluster 2 blocks referring to the instructions on page 116 and to the Placement Diagram for color combinations for each block.

Step 2. Join two Primrose Cluster 1 blocks with one Primrose Cluster 2 block to make a row as shown in Figure 1; press seams toward Primrose Cluster 1 blocks. Repeat for two rows.

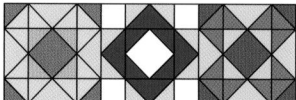

Figure 1

Step 3. Join two Primrose Cluster 2 blocks with one Primrose Cluster 1 block to make a row as shown in Figure 2; press seams toward Primrose Cluster 1 block. Repeat for two rows.

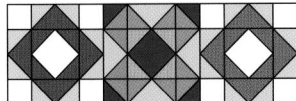

Figure 2

Step 4. Join the rows to complete the pieced center, referring to the Placement Diagram; press seams in one direction.

Step 5. Sew a lightest T7 triangle to each short side of a medium T32 triangle to make a T unit as shown in Figure 3; repeat for 14 units. Press seams toward lighter fabric.

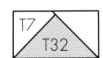

Figure 3

Step 6. Join two S5 squares, three A rectangles and four T units to make a side border strip as shown in Figure 4; repeat for two strips. Press seams toward A and S5. Sew a strip to opposite long sides of the pieced center; press seams toward strips.

Figure 4

Step 7. Join four A rectangles with three T units to make a strip as shown in Figure 5; repeat for two strips. Press seams toward A. Sew a strip to the top and bottom of the pieced center; press seams toward strips.

Figure 5

Step 8. Join nine B rectangles on short ends to a B side strip, referring to the Placement Diagram for color placement; press seams in one direction. Repeat for two strips. Sew a strip to opposite sides of the pieced center; press seams toward strips.

Step 9. Join seven B rectangles on short ends referring to the Placement Diagram for color placement; press seams in one direction. Add a C square to each end; press seams toward B. Sew a strip to the top and bottom of the pieced center; press seams toward strips to complete the top.

COMPLETING THE QUILT

Step 1. Sandwich batting between the completed top and prepared backing piece; pin or baste layers together to hold flat.

Step 2. Quilt as desired by hand or machine.

Step 3. When quilting is complete, remove pins or basting; trim batting and backing edges even with quilt top.

Step 4. Join binding strips on short ends to make one long strip; press seams open.

Step 5. Fold binding strip in half with wrong sides together along length; press.

Step 6. Sew binding strip to quilt top with raw edges even, mitering corners and overlapping ends. Turn binding to the back side; hand- or machine-stitch in place to finish. ■

Primrose Cluster
Placement Diagram
45" x 57"

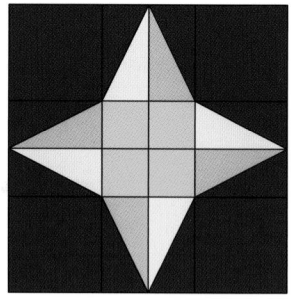

Star Light, Star Bright
12" x 12" Block

FIRST STAR

One block is the perfect size for a candle mat
or a small table centerpiece.

PROJECT SPECIFICATIONS

Skill Level: Beginner
Project Size: 12" x 12"
Block Size: 12" x 12"
Number of Blocks: 1

MATERIALS

- 1 each light, medium and dark yellow fat quarters
- 1 blue fat quarter (darkest)
- Backing 14" x 14"
- Batting 14" x 14"
- All-purpose thread to match fabrics
- Quilting thread
- Basic tools and supplies

INSTRUCTIONS

Note: *Block piecing instructions are given on page 125. Rotary-cutting sizes are given here for both block and setting pieces. If you prefer to cut the block pieces with templates, the letter/number label for each piece is given to identify the template that may be used. Block templates may be found by letter/number in the template section beginning on page 136.*

CUTTING

Step 1. Using template T16, cut four each T16 pieces from dark yellow and blue (darkest) fabrics, reverse

template and cut four each T16R pieces from light yellow and blue (darkest) fabrics.

Step 2. Cut four 2½" x 2½" S19 squares medium yellow.

Step 3. Cut four 4½" x 4½" S14 squares blue (darkest).

Step 4. Cut three 2¼" x 22" strips blue for binding.

COMPLETING THE PIECED TOP

Step 1. Piece one Star Light, Star Bright block referring to the instructions given on page 125.

COMPLETING THE TOPPER

Step 1. Sandwich batting between the completed top and prepared backing piece; pin or baste layers together to hold flat.

Step 2. Quilt as desired by hand or machine.

Step 3. When quilting is complete, remove pins or basting; trim batting and backing edges even with quilt top.

Step 4. Join binding strips on short ends to make one long strip; press seams open.

Step 5. Fold binding strip in half with wrong sides together along length; press.

Step 6. Sew binding strip to quilt top with raw edges even, mitering corners and overlapping ends. Turn binding to the back side; hand- or machine-stitch in place to finish. ■

Starry Lane A
12" x 12" Block

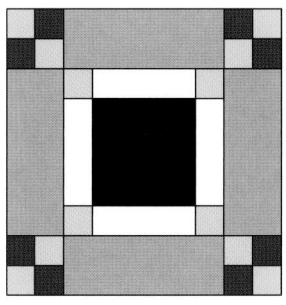

Starry Lane B
12" x 12" Block

STARRY LANE

Black, gray and white combine with yellow in this striking quilt made with two block patterns.

PROJECT SPECIFICATIONS

Skill Level: Intermediate
Quilt Size: 70" x 94"
Block Size: 12" x 12"
Number of Blocks: 35

MATERIALS

- 5 yellow fat quarters
- 8 white fat quarters
- 9 gray fat quarters
- 12 black fat quarters
- ½ yard yellow tonal
- 1¾ yards black print
- Backing 76" x 100"
- Batting 76" x 100"
- All-purpose thread to match fabrics
- Quilting thread
- Basic tools and supplies

INSTRUCTIONS

Note: Block piecing instructions are given on page 126. Rotary-cutting sizes are given here for both block and setting pieces. If you prefer to cut the block pieces with templates, the letter/number label for each piece is given to identify the template that may be used.

Block templates may be found by letter/number in the template section beginning on page 136.

CUTTING FOR STARRY LANE A

Step 1. Cut six 5½" x 22" strips black; subcut strips into (72) 1½" R34 rectangles.

Step 2. Cut (21) 4⅜" x 22" strips black; subcut strips into (144) 3" rectangles. Use template Z12 to cut 72 each Z12 and Z12R pieces from the rectangles. **Note:** *You may cut one end of the rectangles at a 45-degree angle to create the pieces without the template.*

Step 3. Cut six 3⅜" x 22" strips white; subcut strips into (36) 3⅜" squares. Cut each square in half on one diagonal to make 72 light T3 triangles.

Step 4. Cut six 1½" x 22" strips white; subcut strips into (72) 1½" S3 squares.

Step 5. Cut (11) 3" x 22" strips white; subcut strips into (72) 3" S15 squares.

Step 6. Cut six 6¼" x 22" strips gray; subcut strips into (18) 6¼" squares. Cut each square on both diagonals to make 72 T13 triangles.

Step 7. Cut six 3⅜" x 22" strips yellow; subcut strips into (36) 3⅜" squares. Cut each square in half on one diagonal to make 72 medium T3 triangles.

CUTTING FOR STARRY LANE B

Step 1. Cut (12) 1¾" x 22" strips black (dark); subcut strips into (136) 1¾" dark S20 squares. **Note:** *You may make three strip sets by joining one each black and yellow strips as in Step 8 of Completing the Top and Figure 2 to make 68 Four-Patch S20 units for blocks.*

Step 2. Cut (17) 1¾" x 22" strips yellow; subcut strips into (204) 1¾" medium S20 squares.

Step 3. Cut (17) 5" x 5" S28 squares black.

Step 4. Cut six 5" x 22" strips white; subcut strips into (68) 1¾" R39 rectangles.

Step 5. Cut (10) 7½" x 22" strips gray; subcut strips into (68) 3" R38 rectangles.

CUTTING TO COMPLETE THE QUILT

Step 1. Cut one 1¾" by fabric width strip each yellow tonal (E) and black print (F).

Step 2. Cut one 3" by fabric width strip black; subcut strip into eight 3" G squares.

Step 3. Cut seven 1¾" by fabric width strips yellow tonal; join strips on short ends to make one long strip. Subcut strip into two 84½" A and two 60½" C strips.

Step 4. Cut seven 4¼" by fabric width strips black print; join strips on short ends to make one long strip. Subcut strip into two 84½" B and two 60½" D strips.

Step 5. Cut nine 2¼" by fabric width strips black print for binding.

COMPLETING THE TOP

Step 1. Complete 17 Starry Lane B blocks and 18 Starry Lane A blocks referring to page 126.

Step 2. Join three A blocks with two B blocks to make a row referring to Figure 1; repeat for four rows. Press

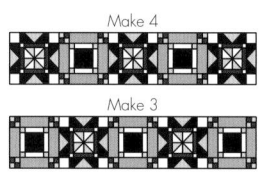

Make 4

Make 3

Figure 1

seams toward B blocks.

Step 3. Join three B blocks with two A blocks to make a row, again referring to Figure 1; repeat for three rows. Press seams toward B blocks.

Step 4. Join the rows referring to the Placement Diagram for positioning of rows; press seams in

one direction.

Step 5. Sew an A strip to a B strip with right sides together along the length; press seams toward B. Repeat for two strips.

Step 6. Sew an A-B strip to opposite long sides of the pieced center; press seams toward A-B.

Step 7. Sew a C strip to a D strip with right sides together along the length; press seams toward D. Repeat for two strips.

Step 8. Sew an E strip to an F strip with right sides together along length; press seams toward F. Subcut

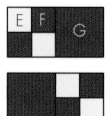

Figure 2

strip set into (16) 1¾" E-F segments.

Step 9. Join two E-F segments with two G squares to make a corner unit as shown in Figure 2; press seams

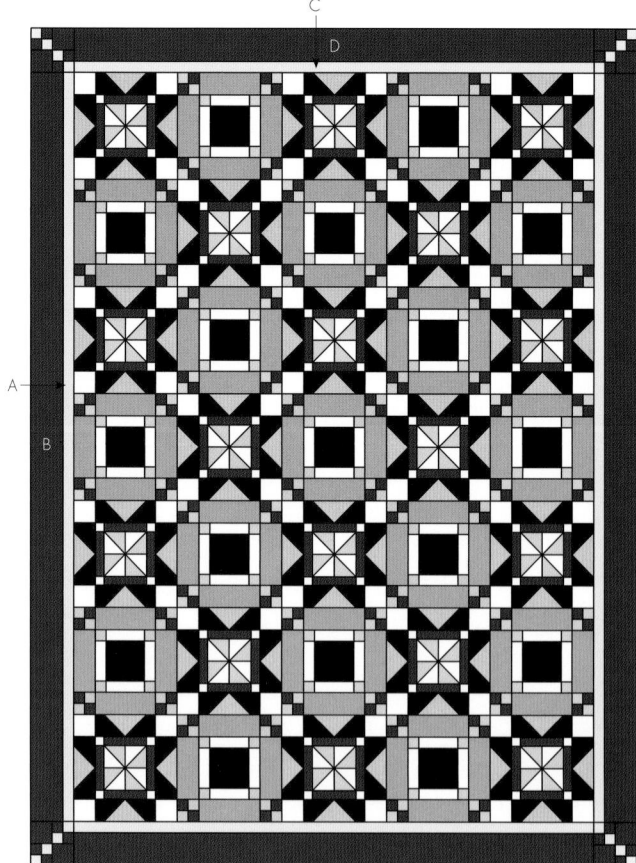

Starry Lane
Placement Diagram
70" x 94"

toward G. Repeat for four corner units.

Step 10. Sew a corner unit to each end of each C-D strip; press seams toward C-D. Sew these strips to the top and bottom of the pieced center to complete the top; press seams toward strips.

COMPLETING THE QUILT

Step 1. Sandwich batting between the completed top and prepared backing piece; pin or baste layers together to hold flat.

Step 2. Quilt as desired by hand or machine.

Step 3. When quilting is complete, remove pins or basting; trim batting and backing edges even with quilt top.

Step 4. Join binding strips on short ends to make one long strip; press seams open.

Step 5. Fold binding strip in half with wrong sides together along length; press.

Step 6. Sew binding strip to quilt top with raw edges even, mitering corners and overlapping ends. Turn binding to the back side; hand- or machine-stitch in place to finish. ■

No Place Like Home
12" x 12" Block

THERE'S NO PLACE LIKE HOME

A dark fabric used in all blocks and units
ties this scrappy plaid quilt together.

PROJECT SPECIFICATIONS

Skill Level: Beginner
Quilt Size: 56" x 70"
Block Size: 12" x 12"
Number of Blocks: 12

MATERIALS

- 16 assorted light-to-medium plaid homespun
  fat quarters
- 1⅞ yards burgundy plaid
- Backing 62" x 76"
- Batting 62" x 76"
- All-purpose thread to match fabrics
- Quilting thread
- Basic tools and supplies

INSTRUCTIONS

Note: Block piecing instructions are given on page
111. Rotary-cutting sizes are given here for both block
and setting pieces. If you prefer to cut the block pieces
with templates, the letter/number label for each piece
is given to identify the template that may be used.

*Block templates may be found by letter/number in the
template section beginning on page 136.*

CUTTING FOR BLOCKS

Step 1. Cut one 5¼" by fabric width strip burgundy
plaid; subcut strip into six 5¼" squares. Cut each square
on both diagonals to make 24 dark T8 triangles.

Step 2. Cut six 2½" by fabric width strips burgundy
plaid; subcut strips into (96) 2½" S19 squares.

Step 3. Cut one 5¼" x 5¼" square from each of 12
fat quarters; cut each square in half on both diagonals
to make four light T8 triangles from each fat quarter. Set
aside two triangles of each fabric for another project.

Step 4. Cut four 2½" x 4½" R11 rectangles from each
of the same 12 fat quarters.

Step 5. Cut four 2½" x 8½" R15 rectangles from each
of the same 12 fat quarters.

CUTTING FOR QUILT CONSTRUCTION

Step 1. Cut six 2½" by fabric width strips burgundy
plaid; subcut strips into (84) 2½" A squares.

Step 2. Cut one 4½" by fabric width strip burgundy

plaid; subcut strip into (14) 2½" E rectangles.

Step 3. Cut two 2⅞" x 2⅞" F squares burgundy plaid; cut each square in half on one diagonal to make four F triangles.

Step 4. Cut the following from each of 14 fat quarters for X units: one 2½" x 8½" B rectangle, three 2½" x 4½" C rectangles and four 2½" x 2½" D squares.

Step 5. Cut the following from each of the two remaining fat quarters for Y units: four 2½" x 4½" C rectangles, four 2½" x 2½" D squares and one 2⅞" x 2⅞" G square. Cut each G square in half on one diagonal to make G triangles.

Step 6. Cut (18) 2½" x 6½" H strips and (31) 2½" x 12½" I rectangles from the remainder of all fat quarters.

Step 7. Cut seven 2¼" by fabric width strips burgundy plaid for binding.

COMPLETING THE TOP

Step 1. Complete 12 No Place Like Home blocks referring to page 111, using the same plaid for the T8, R11 and R15 pieces in a single block.

Step 2. Arrange blocks in four rows of three blocks each. Join the three blocks with four I strips to make a block row as shown in Figure 1; repeat for four block rows. Press seams toward I.

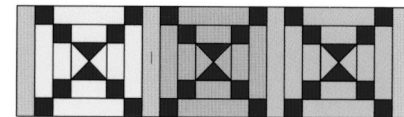

Figure 1

Step 3. Join three I strips with four A squares to make a sashing row; press seams toward I. Repeat for five sashing rows.

Step 4. Join block rows with sashing rows, beginning and ending with a sashing row, to complete the pieced center; press seams toward sashing rows.

Step 5. To complete an X unit, select one B, three C and four D pieces of one fat quarter. Sew A to D; repeat for two A-D units. Press seams toward A.

Step 6. Sew A to C; repeat for two A-C units. Press seams toward A.

Step 7. Mark a line from corner to corner on the wrong side of the remaining two D pieces; place D on E and stitch on the marked line as shown in Figure 2; trim seam to ¼" and press D to the right side, again referring to Figure 2. Repeat on the opposite end of E to complete a D-E unit as shown in Figure 3.

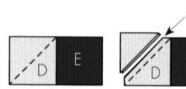
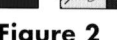

Figure 2   **Figure 3**

Step 8. Sew C to the D-E unit; press seam toward C. Sew an A-D unit to each end of the C-D-E unit and add B referring to Figure 4; press seams toward A-D units and B.

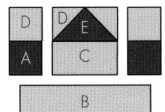

Figure 4

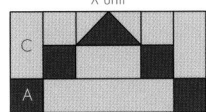

Figure 5

Step 9. Sew an A-C unit to the short ends of the pieced unit to complete an X unit as shown in Figure 5; repeat for 14 X units.

Step 10. To complete a Y unit, select one G and two each C and D pieces of one fat quarter. Sew F to G and add D as shown in Figure 6; press seams toward F and D. Sew A to D; press seams toward D.

Figure 6

Figure 7

Step 11. Join the D-F-G and A-D units and add C as shown in Figure 7; press seams toward A-D and C. Sew A to C; press seam toward A. Sew the A-D unit to the stitched unit to complete one Y unit as shown in Figure 8; press seam toward the A-D unit. Repeat for two Y units and two reversed Y units, again referring to Figure 8.

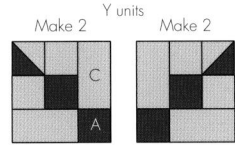

Figure 8

Step 12. Join four X units with five H strips to make a side border strip as shown in Figure 9; repeat for two strips. Press seams toward H.

Figure 9

Step 13. Sew a side border strip to opposite long sides of the pieced center; press seams toward the side border strips.

Step 14. Join one Y unit and one reversed Y unit with four H strips and three X units to make a strip as

shown in Figure 10; press seams toward H. Repeat for two strips. Sew a strip to the top and bottom of the pieced center to complete the pieced top; press seams toward strips.

Figure 10

COMPLETING THE QUILT

Step 1. Sandwich batting between the completed top and prepared backing piece; pin or baste layers together to hold flat.

Step 2. Quilt as desired by hand or machine.

Step 3. When quilting is complete, remove pins or basting; trim batting and backing edges even with quilt top.

Step 4. Join binding strips on short ends to make one long strip; press seams open.

Step 5. Fold binding strip in half with wrong sides together along length; press.

Step 6. Sew binding strip to quilt top with raw edges even, mitering corners and overlapping ends. Turn binding to the back side; hand- or machine-stitch in place to finish. ∎

There's No Place Like Home
Placement Diagram
56" x 70"

DESIGN BY **CONNIE RAND**

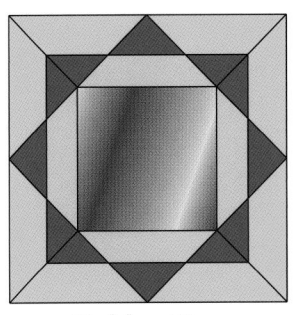

Golden Star
12" x 12" Block

GOLDEN STARS

Remember those two fat quarters of a pretty batik print you stashed away waiting until you found somewhere to use them? Dig them out and surround them with blue and gold!

PROJECT SPECIFICATIONS
Skill Level: Beginner
Quilt Size: 60" x 60"
Block Size: 12" x 12"
Number of Blocks: 9

MATERIALS
- 2 batik fat quarters
- 2 blue fat quarters
- 5 gold fat quarters
- ⅞ yard dark blue print for setting squares
- ⅞ yard gold print for borders
- 1½ yards blue marbled print
- Backing 66" x 66"
- Batting 66" x 66"
- All-purpose thread to match fabrics
- Quilting thread
- Basic tools and supplies

INSTRUCTIONS
Note: Block piecing instructions are given on page 96. Rotary-cutting sizes are given here for both block and setting pieces. If you prefer to cut the block pieces with templates, the letter/number label for each piece is given to identify the template that may be used. Block templates may be found by letter/number in the template section beginning on page 136.

CUTTING
Step 1. Cut nine 6½" x 6½" S21 squares batik.
Step 2. Prepare Z33 and Z22 templates.
Step 3. Cut 36 Z22 pieces gold.
Step 4. Cut 72 Z33 pieces gold.
Step 5. Cut six 2¾" x 22" strips blue; subcut strips into (36) 2¾" squares. Cut each square on one diagonal to make 72 T6 triangles.
Step 6. Cut three 3¼" x 22" strips blue; subcut strips into (18) 3¼" squares. Cut each square on one diagonal to make 36 T2 triangles.
Step 7. Cut four 12½" x 12½" A squares dark blue print.
Step 8. Cut two 18¼" x 18¼" squares blue marbled print; cut each square in half on both diagonals to make eight B triangles.
Step 9. Cut two 9⅜" x 9⅜" squares blue marbled print; cut each square in half on one diagonal to make four C triangles.
Step 10. Cut six 2" by fabric width strips gold print.

Join strips on short ends to make one long strip; press seams in one direction. Subcut strip into two 51½" D strips and two 54½" E strips.

Step 11. Cut six 3½" by fabric width strips blue marbled print. Join strips on short ends to make one long strip; press seams in one direction. Subcut strip into two 54½" F strips and two 60½" G strips.

Step 12. Cut six 2¼" by fabric width strips gold print for binding.

COMPLETING THE TOP

Step 1. Piece nine Golden Star blocks referring to the instructions on page 96.

Step 2. Arrange blocks with A squares and B and C triangles in diagonal rows as shown in Figure 1. Join in rows; press seams in one direction. Join rows, adding C triangles at corners; press seams in one direction to complete the top.

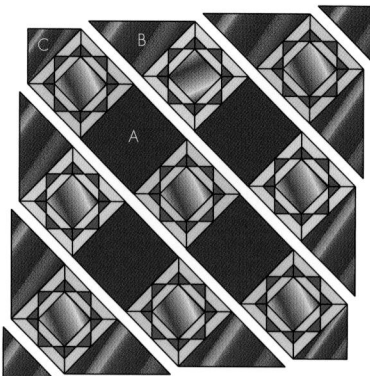

Figure 1

COMPLETING THE QUILT

Step 1. Sandwich batting between the completed top and prepared backing piece; pin or baste layers together to hold flat.

Step 2. Quilt as desired by hand or machine.

Step 3. When quilting is complete, remove pins or basting; trim batting and backing edges even with quilt top.

Step 4. Join binding strips on short ends to make one long strip; press seams open.

Step 5. Fold binding strip in half with wrong sides together along length; press.

Step 6. Sew binding strip to quilt top with raw edges even, mitering corners and overlapping ends. Turn binding to the back side; hand- or machine-stitch in place to finish. ■

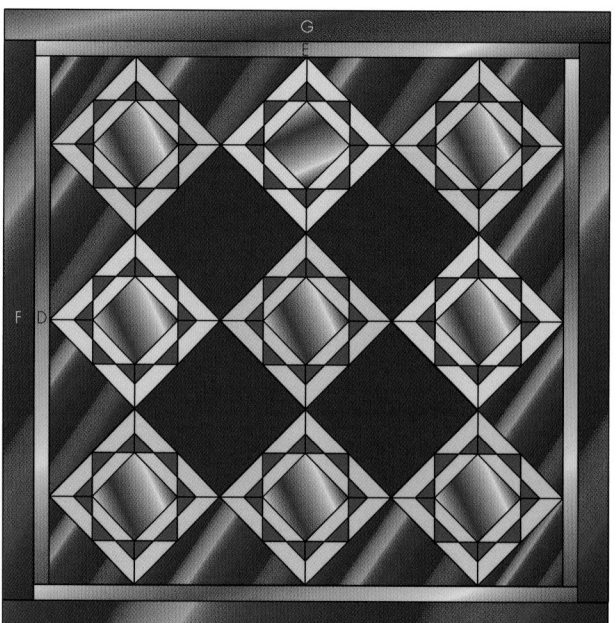

Golden Stars
Placement Diagram
60" x 60"

DESIGN BY **JUDITH SANDSTRUM**

Sedona Illusion
12" x 12" Block

SEDONA ILLUSIONS

Southwestern colors are inviting in this quick-to-stitch project.

PROJECT SPECIFICATIONS

Skill Level: Beginner
Project Size: 48" x 48"
Block Size: 12" x 12"
Number of Blocks: 4

MATERIALS

- 2 different tan fat quarters
- 2 each 3 different turquoise fat quarters
- ½ yard cream tonal
- 1 yard rust tonal
- 1 yard brown print
- Backing 54" x 54"
- Batting 54" x 54"
- All-purpose thread to match fabrics
- Quilting thread
- Basic tools and supplies

INSTRUCTIONS

Note: *Block piecing instructions are given on page 122. Rotary-cutting sizes are given here for both block and setting pieces. If you prefer to cut the block pieces with templates, the letter/number label for each piece is given to identify the template that may be used. Block templates may be found by letter/number in the template section beginning on page 136.*

CUTTING

Step 1. Cut two 4¾" x 22" strips from each different turquoise; subcut strips into eight 4¾" dark S22 squares each fabric.

Step 2. Cut four 7¼" x 7¼" turquoise squares total; cut each square in half on both diagonals to make 16 dark T32 triangles.

Step 3. Cut four 3½" x 6½" R21 rectangles and four 3⅞" x 3⅞" squares from each tan. Cut each square in half on one diagonal to make eight light T7 triangles each fabric.

Step 4. Cut four 3⅞" x 3⅞" squares cream tonal; cut each square in half on one diagonal to make eight lightest T7 triangles.

Step 5. Cut four 3⅞" x 3⅞" squares rust tonal; cut each square in half on one diagonal to make eight medium T7 triangles.

Step 6. Cut three 7¼" by fabric width strips brown print; subcut strips into (16) 7¼" squares. Cut each square in half on both diagonals to make 64 darkest T32 triangles.

Step 7. Cut four rust tonal (B) and eight cream tonal (A) 3½" x 12½" strips.

Step 8. Cut four 6½" x 6½" squares brown print for F.

Step 9. Cut two 2" x 33½" D strips and two 2" x 36½" E strips rust tonal.

Step 10. Cut one 3½" by fabric width strip brown print; subcut strip into nine 3½" C squares.

Step 11. Cut five 2¼" by fabric width strips rust tonal for binding.

COMPLETING THE PIECED TOP

Step 1. Piece four Sedona Illusion blocks referring to the instructions given on page 122.

Step 2. Join two blocks with one B and two A strips to make a row as shown in Figure 1; press seams toward A and B strips. Repeat for two rows.

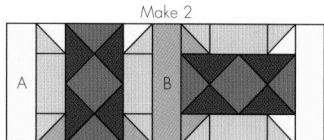
Figure 1

Step 3. Join two B strips with three C squares to make the center sashing row as shown in Figure 2; press seams toward B.

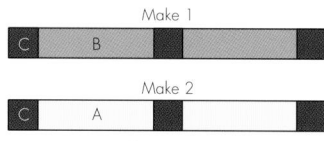
Figure 2

Step 4. Join the two block rows with the center sashing row referring to the Placement Diagram; press seams toward center sashing row.

Step 5. Join two A strips with three C squares to make a sashing row, again referring to Figure 2; press seams toward C. Repeat for two rows.

Step 6. Sew a sashing row to the top and bottom of the pieced center; press seams toward sashing rows.

Step 7. Sew a D strip to opposite sides and an E strip to the top and bottom of the pieced center; press seams toward D and E.

Step 8. Join five dark S22 squares with 12 darkest T32 and two dark T32 triangles to make a border strip as shown in Figure 3; press seams toward dark triangles. Repeat for four strips.

Figure 3

Step 9. Sew a border strip to opposite sides of the pieced center; press seams toward D strips.

Step 10. Sew an F square to each end of each remaining border strip; press seams toward F. Sew a strip to the top and bottom of the pieced center to complete the top; press seams toward E strips.

COMPLETING THE TOPPER

Step 1. Sandwich batting between the completed top and prepared backing piece; pin or baste layers together to hold flat.

Step 2. Quilt as desired by hand or machine.

Step 3. When quilting is complete, remove pins or basting; trim batting and backing edges even with quilt top.

Step 4. Join binding strips on short ends to make one long strip; press seams open.

Step 5. Fold binding strip in half with wrong sides together along length; press.

Step 6. Sew binding strip to quilt top with raw edges even, mitering corners and overlapping ends. Turn binding to the back side; hand- or machine-stitch in place to finish. ■

Sedona Illusions
Placement Diagram
48" x 48"

Harvesttime
12" x 12" Block

HARVESTTIME

Select autumn-color fabrics and a variety of tan fabrics to make this seasonal topper.

PROJECT SPECIFICATIONS

Skill Level: Beginner
Quilt Size: 48" x 48
Block Size: 12" x 12"
Number of Blocks: 12

MATERIALS

- 1 fat quarter brown tonal
- 1 fat quarter each green, gold, red, plum, rust and blue/green (dark)
- 7 cream/tan (light) fat quarters
- ½ yard tan plaid for binding
- Backing 54" x 54"
- Batting 54" x 54"
- All-purpose thread to match fabrics
- Quilting thread
- Basic tools and supplies

INSTRUCTIONS

Note: *Block piecing instructions are given on page 98. Rotary-cutting sizes are given here for both block and setting pieces. If you prefer to cut the block pieces with templates, the letter/number label for each piece is given to identify the template that may be used. Block templates may be found by letter/number in the template section beginning on page 136.*

CUTTING

Step 1. Cut two 5½" x 9½" R46 rectangles and two 4½" x 5½" R48 rectangles from each dark fabric.

Step 2. Cut four 7¼" x 7¼" A squares from one light fabric and two 7¼" x 7¼" A squares from each of the remaining light fabrics.

Step 3. Cut six 3⅞" x 3⅞" squares from each of six light and all dark fabrics; cut each square in half on one diagonal to make 12 T7 triangles each fabric.

Step 4. Using template Z39, cut 12 Z39 pieces brown tonal.

Step 5. Cut two 3½" x 3½" S5 squares from six of the light fabrics.

Step 6. Cut two 4⅜" x 4⅜" squares from each of six light fabrics; cut each square in half on one diagonal to make four T13 triangles from each light fabric.

Step 7. Cut five 2¼" by fabric width strips tan plaid for binding.

COMPLETING THE RUNNER TOP

Step 1. Piece 12 Harvesttime blocks referring to the instructions on page 98.

Step 2. Draw a diagonal line from corner to corner on the wrong side of eight A squares. Place a marked square right sides together with an unmarked A square in a different fabric.

Step 3. Sew ¼" on each side of the marked line as shown in Figure 1; cut apart on the marked line to make two A-A units, again referring to Figure 1. Open and press seam in one direction.

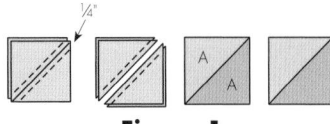

Figure 1

Step 4. Draw a line from unstitched corner to unstitched corner on the wrong side of eight of the A-A units. With seam lines matching, pair each of these units right sides together with an unmarked different-fabric A-A unit.

Step 5. Sew ¼" on each side of the marked line as shown in Figure 2; cut apart on the marked line. Open and press seam in one direction to complete the A units.

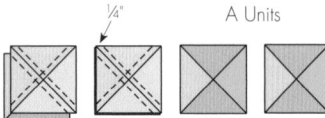

A Units

Figure 2

Step 6. Join four A units to make a row; press seams in one direction. Repeat for four rows. Join the rows; press seams in one direction.

Step 7. Join two Harvesttime blocks as shown in Figure 3 to make a row; repeat for two additional rows. Press seams in one direction.

Make 2

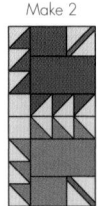

Figure 3

Step 8. Sew a two-block row to opposite sides of the pieced center; press seams toward blocks.

Step 9. Join four Harvesttime blocks as shown in Figure 4 to make a row; press seams in one direction. Repeat for two additional rows.

Make 2

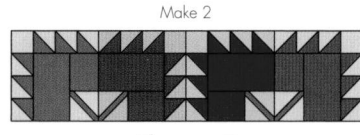

Figure 4

Step 10. Sew a four-block row to the pieced center row to complete the pieced top; press seams toward four-block rows.

COMPLETING THE RUNNER
Step 1. Sandwich batting between the completed top and prepared backing piece; pin or baste layers together to hold flat.
Step 2. Quilt as desired by hand or machine.
Step 3. When quilting is complete, remove pins or basting; trim batting and backing edges even with quilt top.
Step 4. Join binding strips on short ends to make one long strip; press seams open.
Step 5. Fold binding strip in half with wrong sides together along length; press.
Step 6. Sew binding strip to quilt top with raw edges even, mitering corners and overlapping ends. Turn binding to the back side; hand- or machine-stitch in place to finish. ■

Harvesttime
Placement Diagram
48" x 48"

Ice Crystals
12" x 12" Block

ICE CRYSTALS

Use a variety of white tonals to create the background of this pretty table runner.

PROJECT SPECIFICATIONS

Skill Level: Beginner
Project Size: 55¼" x 20"
Block Size: 12" x 12"
Number of Blocks: 3

MATERIALS

- 1 each light and medium blue fat quarters
- 2 dark blue fat quarters
- 5 white fat quarters
- Backing 61" x 26"
- Batting 61" x 26"
- All-purpose thread to match fabrics
- Quilting thread
- Basic tools and supplies

INSTRUCTIONS

Note: *Block piecing instructions are given on page 101. Rotary-cutting sizes are given here for both block and setting pieces. If you prefer to cut the block pieces with templates, the letter/number label for each piece is given to identify the template that may be used. Block templates may be found by letter/number in the template section beginning on page 136.*

CUTTING

Step 1. Cut three 2½" x 22" strips dark blue; subcut into (24) 2½" dark S19 squares.

Step 2. Cut two 5¼" x 5¼" squares each medium and dark blue; cut each square on both diagonals to make eight each medium and dark T18 triangles. Set aside two triangles of each fabric for another project.

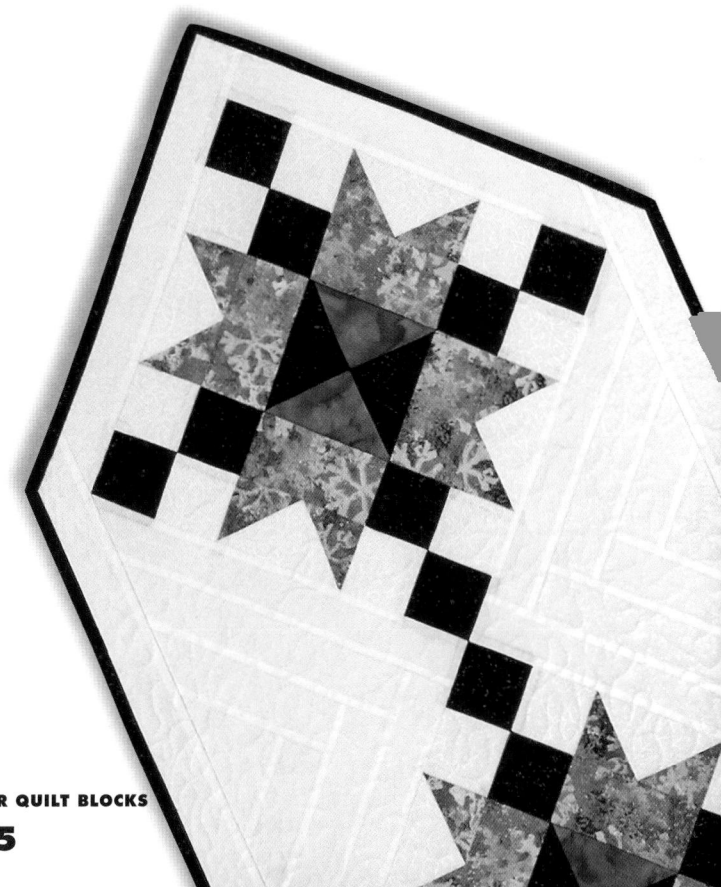

Step 3. Cut two 2⅞" x 22" strips light blue; subcut into (12) 2⅞" squares. Cut each square on one diagonal to make 24 light T11 triangles.

Step 4. Cut three 2½" x 22" strips light blue; subcut strips into (12) 4½" light R11 rectangles.

Step 5. Cut three 2½" x 22" strips from one white; subcut strips into 24 lightest S19 squares.

Step 6. Cut three 5¼" x 5¼" squares from the same white fabric; cut each square on both diagonals to make 12 lightest T18 triangles.

Step 7. Cut four 4½" x 4½" A squares white.

Step 8. Cut four 2"-wide rectangles white in each of the following lengths: 6" B, 7½" C, 9" D, 10½" E, 12" F and 13½" G.

Step 9. Cut two each 2" x 14" H strips and 2" x 16" I strips white.

Step 10. Cut four 2" x 22" strips white; join strips on short ends to make one long strip. Subcut strip into two 42" J strips.

Step 11. Cut eight 2¼" x 22" strips dark blue for binding.

COMPLETING THE PIECED TOP

Step 1. Piece three Ice Crystal blocks referring to the instructions given on page 101.

Step 2. Sew the B–G pieces to two sides of A in alphabetical order beginning on the right side edge referring to Figure 1 to piece a side unit; press seams away from A. Repeat for four side units.

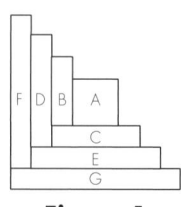

Figure 1   Figure 2

Step 3. Trim the ends of the side units as shown in Figure 2.

Step 4. Arrange the blocks with the side units in diagonal rows as shown in Figure 3; join to complete the pieced center. Press seams toward side units.

Step 5. Sew an H strip to one side of one end and I to the opposite side of the same end of the pieced center; press seams toward H and I. Trim ends even

with edge of pieced center as shown in Figure 4. Repeat on the other end.

Figure 3

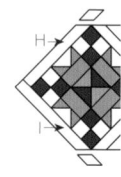

Figure 4   **Figure 5**

Step 6. Sew a J strip to opposite long sides of the pieced center; press seams toward J. Trim J ends, continuing angle of H/I ends as shown in Figure 5 to complete the pieced top.

COMPLETING THE TOPPER

Step 1. Sandwich batting between the completed top and prepared backing piece; pin or baste layers together to hold flat.

Step 2. Quilt as desired by hand or machine.

Step 3. When quilting is complete, remove pins or basting; trim batting and backing edges even with quilt top.

Step 4. Join binding strips on short ends to make one long strip; press seams open.

Step 5. Fold binding strip in half with wrong sides together along length; press.

Step 6. Sew binding strip to quilt runner with raw edges even, mitering corners and overlapping ends. Turn binding to the back side; hand- or machine-stitch in place to finish. ■

Ice Crystals
Placement Diagram
55¼" x 20"

Courthouse Steps Star
12" x 12" Block

Flying Geese Star
12" x 12" Block

BEYOND THE STARS

The 12 blocks in this quilt have different centers
but all have the same star frame.

PROJECT SPECIFICATIONS

Skill Level: Intermediate
Quilt Size: 64" x 78"
Block Size: 12" x 12"
Number of Blocks: 12

MATERIALS

- 1 medium brown fat quarter
- 1 dark brown fat quarter
- 1 light pink fat quarter
- 2 blue fat quarters
- 2 mauve fat quarters
- 2 each light, medium and dark green fat quarters
- 3 burgundy fat quarters
- 4 tan fat quarters
- 1⅓ yards blue print
- 1⅝ yards navy mottled
- 1⅞ yards cream tonal
- Backing 70" x 94"
- Batting 70" x 94"
- All-purpose thread to match fabrics
- Quilting thread
- Basic tools and supplies

INSTRUCTIONS

Note: *Instructions for individual blocks are given in*
alphabetical order starting on page 72. Rotary-cutting
sizes are given here for both block and setting pieces.
If you prefer to cut the block pieces with templates, the
letter/number label for each piece is given to identify
the template that may be used. Block templates may
be found by letter/number in the template section
beginning on page 136.

CUTTING COURTHOUSE STEPS STAR

Step 1. Cut one 2½" x 2½" burgundy S19 square.
Step 2. Cut (12) 1½" x 1½" burgundy S3 squares.
Step 3. Cut four 1½" x 2½" tan R41 rectangles.
Step 4. Cut four 1½" x 4½" tan R7 rectangles.
Step 5. Cut four 1½" x 6½" tan R16 rectangles.

CUTTING FLYING GEESE STAR

Step 1. Cut eight 2⅞" x 2⅞" squares from one tan;
cut each square on one diagonal to make 16
T11 triangles.
Step 2. Cut one 5¼" x 5¼" square each from mauve,
dark green, blue and dark brown; cut each square on
both diagonals to make four T18 triangles each fabric.
Set aside two triangles of each color for another project.

CUTTING FOUR-PATCH STAR

Step 1. Cut one 2½" x 22" strip each light and

Four-Patch Star
12" x 12" Block

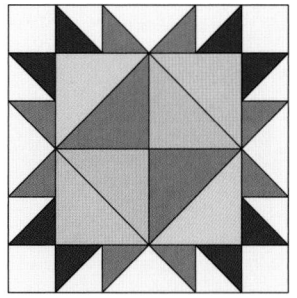

Half-Square Triangle Star
12" x 12" Block

Log Cabin Star
12" x 12" Block

Ohio Star-in-a-Star
12" x 12" Block

Pinwheel Star
12" x 12" Block

Quarter-Square Triangle Star
12"x 12" Block

Rail Fence Variation Star
12" x 12" Block

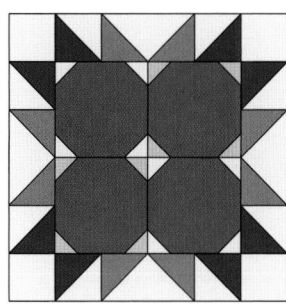

Snowball Star
12" x 12" Block

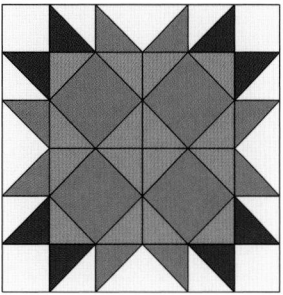

Square-in-a-Square Star
12" x 12" Block

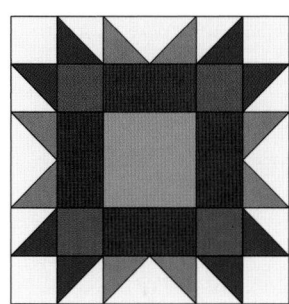

Uneven Nine-Patch Star
12" x 12" Block

dark green; subcut each strip into eight S19 squares.
Note: *If you would rather strip-piece these units, sew a light strip to a dark strip with right sides together along length; press seam toward dark strip. Subcut strip into 2½" units; join in four rows of two units each to complete the block center.*

CUTTING HALF-SQUARE TRIANGLE STAR

Step 1. Cut one 4⅞" x 4⅞" square each mauve (medium), one blue (dark) and one light green; cut each square on one diagonal to make two T19 triangles each fabric.

CUTTING LOG CABIN STAR

Step 1. Cut one 2⅞" x 2⅞" square each light pink (light) and mauve (medium). Cut each square on one diagonal to make two T11 triangles of each fabric; set aside one triangle of each fabric for another project.
Step 2. Cut the following rectangles: one 1½" x 2½" dark brown R41; one 1½" x 3½" medium brown R47; one dark green 1½" x 3½" R47; and one different dark green 1½" x 4½" R7.
Step 3. Cut the following rectangles: one 1½" x 4½" tan R7 (light); one 1½" x 5½" R34 from a different tan

(light); one 1½" x 5½" medium green R34; and one 1½" x 6½" R16 from another medium green.
Step 4. Cut the following rectangles: one 1½" x 6½" R16 from a third tan (light); and one 1½" x 7½" R45 from a fourth tan (light).
Step 5. Cut the following rectangles: one 1½" x 7½" light green R45; and one 1½" x 8½" R8 from another light green.

CUTTING OHIO STAR-IN-A-STAR

Step 1. Cut one 3⅜" x 3⅜" tan S29 square.
Step 2. Cut four 2½" x 2½" tan S19 squares.
Step 2. Cut one 5¼" x 5¼" tan square; cut the square on both diagonals to make four T18 triangles.

Step 3. Cut two identical 2⅞" x 2⅞" squares from burgundy (dark 1); cut each square on one diagonal to make four T11 triangles.

Step 4. Cut four 2⅞" x 2⅞" squares from a second burgundy (dark 2); cut each square on one diagonal to make eight T11 triangles.

CUTTING PINWHEEL STAR

Step 1. Cut eight 2⅞" x 2⅞" squares tan; cut each square on one diagonal to make 16 light T11 triangles.

Step 2. Cut two 2⅞" x 2⅞" squares each medium and dark browns and two different medium greens; cut each square in half on one diagonal to make four dark T11 squares each fabric.

CUTTING QUARTER-SQUARE TRIANGLE STAR

Step 1. Cut two 5¼" x 5¼" squares each mauve (medium) and burgundy (dark); cut each square on both diagonals to make eight each medium and dark T18 triangles.

CUTTING RAIL FENCE VARIATION STAR

Step 1. Cut two 2½" x 4½" R11 rectangles each light pink, mauve (medium) and medium green and dark green.

CUTTING SQUARE-IN-A-SQUARE STAR

Step 1. Cut four 3⅜" x 3⅜" blue S29 squares.

Step 2. Cut eight 2⅞" x 2⅞" squares medium brown; cut each square on one diagonal to make 16 T11 triangles.

CUTTING SNOWBALL STAR

Step 1. Cut four dark brown Z64 pieces.

Step 2. Cut four 1⅞" x 1⅞" squares each from two different light greens; cut each square on one diagonal to make eight T5 triangles of each fabric.

CUTTING UNEVEN NINE-PATCH STAR

Step 1. Cut one 4½" x 4½" medium green S14 square.

Step 2. Cut four 2¼" x 4½" dark green R11 rectangles.

Step 3. Cut four 2½" x 2½" dark brown S19 squares.

CUTTING FOR ALL BLOCKS & FINISHING

Step 1. Cut three 2½" by fabric width strips cream tonal; subcut strips into (48) 2½" S19 squares.

Step 2. Cut two 5¼" by fabric width strips cream tonal; subcut strips into (12) 5¼" squares. Cut each square on both diagonals to make 48 T18 triangles.

Step 3. Cut four 2⅞" by fabric width strips each cream tonal (light), navy mottled (dark) and blue print (medium); subcut strips into (48) 2⅞" squares each fabric. Cut each square on one diagonal to make 96 T11 triangles each from light, medium and dark fabric.

Step 4. Cut two 2½" by fabric width strips navy mottled; subcut strips into (28) 2½" A squares.

Step 5. Cut (22) 1¼" by fabric width B strips cream tonal.

Step 6. Cut (11) 1" by fabric width C strips navy mottled.

Step 7. Cut five 2½" by fabric width strips blue print; join strips on short ends to make one long strip. Subcut strip into two 58½" D strips and two 44½" E strips.

Step 8. Cut 110 assorted 2½" x 6½" F strips from the remaining fat quarters.

Step 9. Cut four 6½" x 6½" G squares navy mottled.

Step 10. Cut seven 2½" by fabric width strips blue print; join strips on short ends to make one long strip. Subcut strip into two 74½" H strips and two 60½" I strips.

Step 11. Cut eight 2¼" by fabric width strips navy mottled for binding.

COMPLETING THE TOP

Step 1. Complete one of each block referring to the instructions starting on page 72, finding blocks in alphabetical order. **Note:** *If you prefer to use other blocks in your sampler, you may choose any block to substitute for one or all of the blocks used in the quilt sample.*

Step 2. Sew a C strip between two B strips to make a strip set; press seams toward B. Repeat for 11 strip sets. Subcut strip sets into (31) 12½" B-C sashing strips as shown in Figure 1.

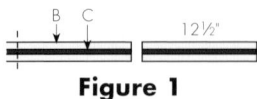

Figure 1

Step 11. Sew an H strip to opposite long sides of the pieced center; press seams toward H.

Step 12. Sew an A square to each end of each I strip; press seams toward A. Sew a strip to the top and bottom of the pieced center to complete the quilt top; press seams toward A-I strips.

COMPLETING THE QUILT

Step 1. Sandwich batting between the completed top and prepared backing piece; pin or baste layers together to hold flat.

Step 2. Quilt as desired by hand or machine.

Step 3. When quilting is complete, remove pins or basting; trim batting and backing edges even with quilt top.

Step 4. Join binding strips on short ends to make one long strip; press seams open.

Step 5. Fold binding strip in half with wrong sides together along length; press.

Step 6. Sew binding strip to quilt top with raw edges even, mitering corners and overlapping ends. Turn binding to the back side; hand- or machine-stitch in place to finish. ∎

Step 3. Arrange the pieced blocks in four rows with three blocks and four B-C sashing strips in each row, referring to the Placement Diagram for positioning of blocks. Join to complete rows; press seams toward B-C sashing strips.

Step 4. Join four A squares with three B-C sashing strips to make a sashing row referring to Figure 2; repeat for five sashing rows. Press seams toward B-C sashing strips.

Figure 2

Step 5. Join the block rows with the sashing rows to complete the pieced center; press seams toward sashing rows.

Step 6. Sew a D strip to opposite sides of the pieced center; press seams toward D.

Step 7. Sew an A square to each end of each E strip; press seams toward E. Sew an A-E strip to the top and bottom of the pieced center; press seams toward A-E.

Step 8. Join 31 F rectangles in random order to make an F side strip; repeat for two strips. Press seams in one direction. Repeat with 24 F rectangles to make an F top/bottom strip; repeat for two strips.

Step 9. Sew an F side strip to opposite long sides of the pieced center; press seams toward D strips.

Step 10. Sew a G square to each end of each F top/bottom strip; press seams toward F. Sew a strip to the top and bottom of the pieced center; press seams toward E strips.

Beyond the Stars
Placement Diagram
64" x 78"

Tropical Butterflies
12" x 12" Block

TROPICAL BUTTERFLIES

Make a butterfly design using the fabric-folding method.

PROJECT SPECIFICATIONS
Skill Level: Beginner
Quilt Size: 42" x 55"
Block Size: 12" x 12"
Number of Blocks: 12

MATERIALS
- 6 pastel fat quarters
- ½ yard blue print
- 1½ yards white/gold mottled
- Backing 48" x 61"
- Batting 48" x 61"
- All-purpose thread to match fabrics
- Quilting thread
- 1½ yards fusible web
- Basic tools and supplies

INSTRUCTIONS
Note: *Block piecing instructions are given on page 132. Rotary-cutting sizes are given here for both block and setting pieces. If you prefer to cut the block pieces with templates, the letter/number label for each piece is given to identify the template that may be used. Block templates may be found by letter/number in the template section beginning on page 136.*

CUTTING
Step 1. Cut (12) 12½" x 12½" A squares white/gold mottled; fold and crease to mark the horizontal and vertical center lines.
Step 2. Prepare a template for piece Z50 using pattern given on page 170.

Step 3. Cut two 8½" x 8½" squares from each pastel fat quarter and and (12) 8½" x 8½" squares fusible web; square to the wrong side of each fabric square. Fold each square in half and in half again with right sides together as shown in Figure 1.

Step 4. Place the Z50 template on a folded square as shown in Figure 2; cut out design. Open cut shape to

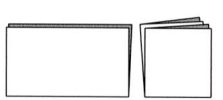

Figure 1   **Figure 2**

reveal the complete design; repeat for 12 Z50 shapes.

Step 5. Cut a total of (124) 2" x 3½" B rectangles from the six pastel fat quarters.

Step 6. Cut one 2" by fabric width strip blue print; subcut strip into (20) 2" B squares.

Step 7. Cut five 2¼" by fabric width strips blue print for binding.

COMPLETING THE TOP

Step 1. Complete 12 Tropical Butterflies blocks referring to page 132.

Step 2. Join four assorted B rectangles on the short ends to make a sashing strip; press seams in one direction. Repeat for 31 strips.

Step 3. Arrange the blocks in four rows of three blocks each; join blocks in rows with four sashing strips as shown in Figure 3; press seams toward strips.

Step 4. Join three sashing strips with four C squares to make a sashing row; press seams toward C. Repeat for five rows.

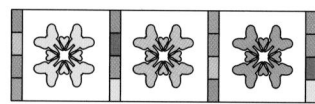

Figure 3

Step 5. Join the block rows with the sashing rows to complete the pieced center; press seams toward sashing rows.

COMPLETING THE QUILT

Step 1. Sandwich batting between the completed top and prepared backing piece; pin or baste layers together to hold flat.

Step 2. Quilt as desired by hand or machine.

Step 3. When quilting is complete, remove pins or basting; trim batting and backing edges even with quilt top.

Step 4. Join binding strips on short ends to make one long strip; press seams open.

Step 5. Fold binding strip in half with wrong sides together along length; press.

Step 6. Sew binding strip to quilt top with raw edges even, mitering corners and overlapping ends. Turn binding to the back side; hand- or machine-stitch in place to finish. ■

Tropical Butterflies
Placement Diagram
42" x 55"

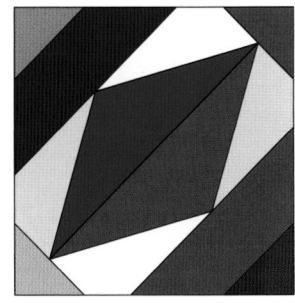

Shining Star
12" x 12" Block

SHINING STAR

The light background pieces really stand out in this pretty star-design quilt.

PROJECT SPECIFICATIONS
Skill Level: Intermediate
Quilt Size: 62" x 86"
Block Size: 12" x 12"
Number of Blocks: 24

MATERIALS
- 5 white fat quarters
- 5 light gray fat quarters
- 24 medium/dark jewel-tone fat quarters
- ⅝ yard black solid for binding
- 1¾ yards dark blue tonal
- Backing 68" x 92"
- Batting 68" x 92"
- All-purpose thread to match fabrics
- Quilting thread
- Rotary ruler with 45-degree-angle line
- Basic tools and supplies

INSTRUCTIONS
Note: *Block piecing instructions are given on page 122. Rotary-cutting sizes are given here for both block and setting pieces. If you prefer to cut the block pieces with templates, the letter/number label for each piece is given to identify the template that may be used. Block templates may be found by letter/number in the template section beginning on page 136.*

CUTTING
Step 1. Prepare templates for Z32, Z47 and T45 pieces.
Step 2. Cut two T45 pieces, three Z32 pieces and three 3⅞" x 3⅞" squares from each of the jewel-tones. Cut the squares in half on one diagonal to make T7 triangles. Set aside one triangle of each fabric for another project.
Step 3. Cut 48 Z47 pieces white and 48 Z47R pieces light gray fat quarters.
Step 4. Cut two 24½" by fabric width strips dark blue tonal; subcut strips into (10) 7½" A rectangles.
Step 5. Cut two 7⅞" x 7⅞" squares dark blue tonal; cut each square in half on one diagonal to make four B triangles.
Step 6. Cut eight 2¼" by fabric width strips black solid for binding.

COMPLETING THE TOP
Step 1. Complete 24 Shining Star blocks referring to page 122.
Step 2. Arrange blocks in six rows of four blocks each referring to Figure 1. Join blocks in rows; press seams in one direction. Join rows to complete the pieced top; press seams in one direction.
Step 3. Sew T7 to Z32 as shown in Figure 2; repeat for 24 units.

Figure 1

Figure 2

Step 4. Cut each end of each A rectangle at a 45-degree angle as shown in Figure 3.

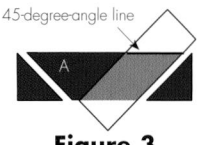

45-degree-angle line

Figure 3

Step 5. Sew a T7-Z32 unit to each angled end of A to make a border unit as shown in Figure 4; press seams away from A. Repeat for 10 units.

Figure 4   **Figure 5**

Step 6. Sew a T7-Z32 unit to B to make a corner unit as shown in Figure 5; press seam toward B. Repeat for four corner units.

Step 7. Join three border units as shown in Figure 6; press seams in one direction. Repeat for two strips. Sew a pieced strip to opposite long sides of the pieced center referring to the Placement Diagram for positioning of strips; press seams toward border strips.

Figure 6

Step 8. Join two border units and add a corner unit to each end to make a strip as shown in Figure 7; repeat for two strips. Press seams toward border units. Sew

a strip to the top and bottom of the pieced center to complete the pieced top; press seams toward strips.

Figure 7

COMPLETING THE QUILT

Step 1. Sandwich batting between the completed top and prepared backing piece; pin or baste layers together to hold flat.

Step 2. Quilt as desired by hand or machine.

Step 3. When quilting is complete, remove pins or basting; trim batting and backing edges even with quilt top.

Step 4. Join binding strips on short ends to make one long strip; press seams open.

Step 5. Fold binding strip in half with wrong sides together along length; press.

Step 6. Sew binding strip to quilt top with raw edges even, mitering corners and overlapping ends. Turn binding to the back side; hand- or machine-stitch in place to finish. ■

Shining Star
Placement Diagram
62" x 86"

DESIGN BY **KARLA SCHULZ**

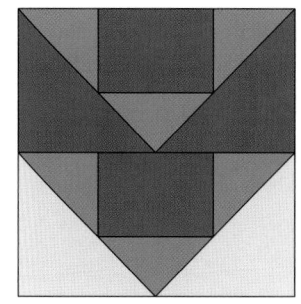

Vintage Memories
12" x 12" Block

VINTAGE MEMORIES

One block made with different fabrics creates
a quilt with variety.

PROJECT SPECIFICATIONS
Skill Level: Beginner
Quilt Size: 100" x 100"
Block Size: 12" x 12"
Number of Blocks: 36

MATERIALS
- 12 light fat quarters
- 12 medium fat quarters
- 12 dark fat quarters
- 2 yards border stripe
- 3 yards dark blue print
- Backing 106" x 106"
- Batting 106" x 106"
- All-purpose thread to match fabrics
- Quilting thread
- Basic tools and supplies

INSTRUCTIONS
Note: *Block piecing instructions are given on page
133. Rotary-cutting sizes are given here for both block
and setting pieces. If you prefer to cut the block pieces
with templates, the letter/number label for each piece
is given to identify the template that may be used.
Block templates may be found by letter/number in the
template section beginning on page 136.*

CUTTING

Step 1. Arrange fat quarters in 12 groups of one each light, medium and dark fabrics; each group yields three blocks.

Step 2. From each group, cut one 6⅞" x 22" light strip; subcut strip into three 6⅞" squares. Cut each square in half on one diagonal to make six light T39 triangles.

Step 3. From each group, cut three 4⅜" x 22" medium strips; subcut strips into nine 4⅜" squares. Cut each square in half on one diagonal to make 18 T13 triangles.

Step 4. From each group, cut one 6⅞" x 22" dark strip; subcut strips into three 6⅞" squares. Cut each square in half on one diagonal to make six dark T39 triangles.

Step 5. From each grouping, cut two 4" x 22" dark strips; subcut strips into six 5½" R10 rectangles.

Step 6. Cut (17) 4½" by fabric width strips dark blue print. Join strips on short ends to make one long strip; press seams in one direction. Subcut strips into two 72½" A strips, two 80½" B strips two 92½" E strips and two 100½" F strips.

Step 7. Cut nine 6½" by fabric width strips border stripe. Join strips on short ends to make one long strip; press seams in one direction. Subcut strips into two 80½" C strips and two 92½" D strips.

Step 8. Cut (10) 2¼" by fabric width strips dark blue print for binding.

COMPLETING THE TOP

Step 1. Complete 36 Vintage Memories blocks referring to page 133.

Step 2. Arrange and join six blocks to make a row as shown in Figure 1; repeat for six rows referring to the Placement Diagram for positioning of blocks. Press seams in one direction.

Figure 1

Step 3. Join the rows to complete the pieced center; press seams in one direction.

Step 4. Sew an A strip to the top and bottom and a B strip to opposite sides of the pieced center; press seams toward A and B strips.

Step 5. Sew a C strip to the top and bottom and a D strip to opposite sides of the pieced center; press seams toward C and D strips.

Step 6. Sew an E strip to the top and bottom and a F strip to opposite sides of the pieced center; press seams toward E and F strips.

COMPLETING THE QUILT

Step 1. Sandwich batting between the completed top and prepared backing piece; pin or baste layers together to hold flat.

Step 2. Quilt as desired by hand or machine.

Step 3. When quilting is complete, remove pins or basting; trim batting and backing edges even with quilt top.

Step 4. Join binding strips on short ends to make one long strip; press seams open.

Step 5. Fold binding strip in half with wrong sides together along length; press.

Step 6. Sew binding strip to quilt top with raw edges even, mitering corners and overlapping ends. Turn binding to the back side; hand- or machine-stitch in place to finish. ■

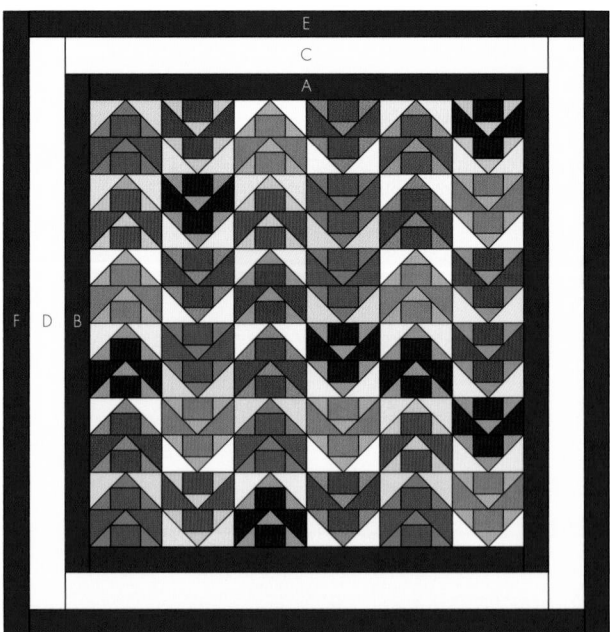

Vintage Memories
Placement Diagram
100" x 100"

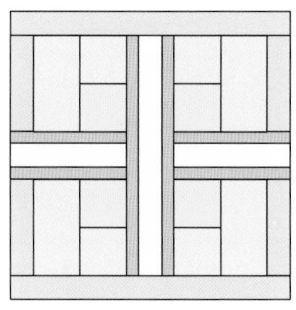

Woven Threads
12" x 12" Block

WOVEN THREADS

Pastel colors give this quilt a cottage look.

PROJECT NOTES

When making multiple blocks using a block pattern like Woven Threads, it is easier to use strip-piecing methods to save time. Instructions are given on page 135 for cutting and piecing one block, but here the instructions are written for making multiple blocks using quicker methods.

Because the block is stitched, then cut into fourths, and then sewn back together with strip-pieced units, the method of making this block is different here than in the block section of the book.

The woven look is created by turning the blocks when joining them in rows. What appears to be sashing really is part of the blocks. Have fun making your version of this interesting block. Fabrics with more contrast would take on a whole new look.

PROJECT SPECIFICATIONS

Skill Level: Intermediate
Quilt Size: 72" x 84"
Block Size: 12" x 12"
Number of Blocks: 20

MATERIALS

- 2 yellow fat quarters
- 6 pink fat quarters
- 7 blue fat quarters
- 1¼ yards white/green dot
- 2 yards light green tonal
- 2 yards large floral
- Backing 78" x 90"
- Batting 78" x 90"
- All-purpose thread to match fabrics
- Quilting thread
- Basic tools and supplies

INSTRUCTIONS

Note: *Block piecing instructions for one block are given on page 135.*

CUTTING

Step 1. Cut three 5" x 22" strips from each yellow; subcut strips into (10) 5" A squares each fabric.

Step 2. Cut five 2½" x 22" strips from each pink; subcut two strips into six 5" B rectangles each fabric and three strips into six 9" C rectangles each fabric.

Step 3. Cut two additional 2½" x 22" strips each from two pinks; subcut one strip into two 5" B rectangles each fabric and one strip into two 9" C rectangles each fabric. **Note:** *Each block uses two same-fabric B and C rectangles.*

Step 4. Cut nine 1½" x 22" strips from each of six blues; subcut three strips into six 9" D strips each fabric and six strips into six 12½" E strips each fabric.

Step 5. Cut six 1½" x 22" strips from the remaining blue fat quarter; subcut two strips into four 9" D strips

and four strips into four 12½" E strips. **Note:** *Each block uses two D and E strips of the same fabric.*

Step 6. Cut (22) 1" by fabric width F strips light green tonal.

Step 7. Cut (11) 1½" by fabric width G strips white/green dot.

Step 8. Cut (27) 1" by fabric width strips light green tonal for borders. Join strips on short ends to make one long strip; press seams in one direction. Subcut strip into two strips each in the following sizes: 60½" H, 49½" I, 63½" L, 52½" M, 80½" P, 69½" Q, 83½" T and 72½" U.

Step 9. Cut (14) 1½" by fabric width strips white/green dot. Join strips on short ends to make one long strip; press seams in one direction. Subcut strip into two strips each in the following sizes: 61½" J, 51½" K, 81½" R and 71½" S.

Step 10. Cut eight 8½" by fabric width strips large floral. Join strips on short ends to make one long strip; press seams open. Subcut strips into two 64½" N and two 68½" O strips.

Step 11. Cut eight 2¼" by fabric width strips light green tonal for binding.

COMPLETING THE BLOCKS

Step 1. Sew a G strip between two F strips to make a strip set; press seams toward F strips. Repeat for 11 strip sets. Subcut strip sets into (40) 5½" F-G units and (20) 10½" G-F units as shown in Figure 1.

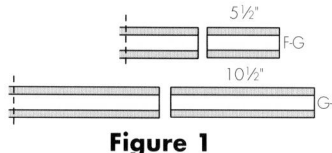

Figure 1

Step 2. To piece one block, select two same-fabric B and C rectangles. Sew B to opposite sides of A; press seams toward B.

Step 3. Sew C to the top and bottom of the A-B unit as shown in Figure 2; press seams toward C.

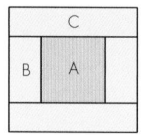

Figure 2

Step 4. Select two same-fabric D strips; sew a strip to the top and bottom of the pieced unit referring to Figure 3; press seams toward D.

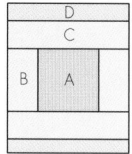
Figure 3

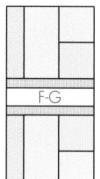
Figure 4

Step 5. Cut the pieced rectangle through the vertical and horizontal centers to make four 4½" x 5½" units as shown in Figure 4.

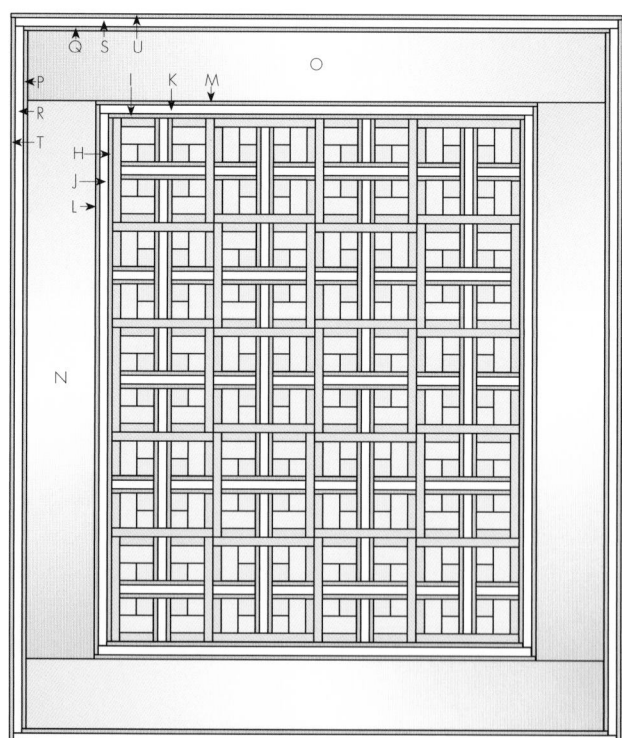

Figure 5

Step 6. Join two units with an F-G unit as shown in Figure 5; press seams toward F-G unit. Repeat for two joined units.

Woven Threads
Placement Diagram
72" x 84"

Step 7. Join the two units with a G-F unit as shown in Figure 6; press seams toward G-F unit.

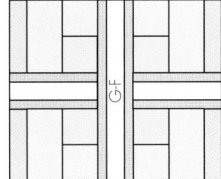

Figure 6

Step 8. Sew an E strip to opposite sides of the pieced unit to complete one block as shown in Figure 7; press seams toward E. Repeat for 20 blocks.

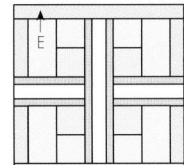

Figure 7

COMPLETING THE TOP

Step 1. Arrange and join four blocks to make a row, turning every other block as shown in Figure 8; repeat for five rows. Press seams in one direction. Join the rows to complete the pieced center; press seams in one direction.

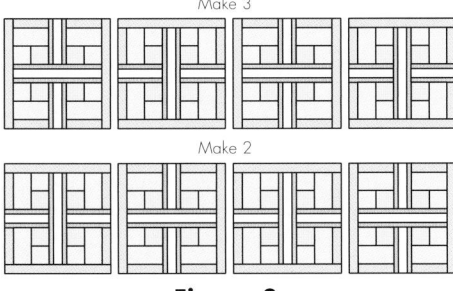

Make 3

Make 2

Figure 8

Step 2. Sew an H strip to opposite sides and an I strip to the top and bottom of the pieced center; press seams toward strips.

Step 3. Referring to the Placement Diagram for positioning of strips, repeat Step 2 with J and K, L and M, N and O, P and Q, R and S, and T and U strips; pressing seams toward newly added strip after stitching to complete the pieced top.

COMPLETING THE QUILT

Step 1. Sandwich batting between the completed top and prepared backing piece; pin or baste layers together to hold flat.

Step 2. Quilt as desired by hand or machine.

Step 3. When quilting is complete, remove pins or basting; trim batting and backing edges even with quilt top.

Step 4. Join binding strips on short ends to make one long strip; press seams open.

Step 5. Fold binding strip in half with wrong sides together along length; press.

Step 6. Sew binding strip to quilt top with raw edges even, mitering corners and overlapping ends. Turn binding to the back side; hand- or machine-stitch in place to finish. ■

DESIGN BY **CONNIE KAUFFMAN**

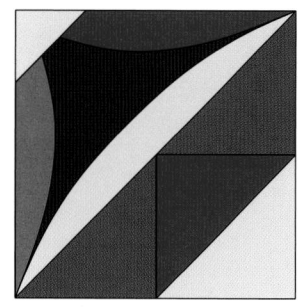

Golden Holiday
12" x 12" Block

GOLDEN HOLIDAY MAT

Add this pretty mat to your holiday decor this year.

PROJECT SPECIFICATIONS

Skill Level: Intermediate
Quilt Size: 36" x 36"
Block Size: 12" x 12"
Number of Blocks: 4

MATERIALS

- 1 cream/gold fat quarter
- 2 red fat quarters
- 2 green fat quarters
- Backing 42" x 42"
- Batting 42" x 42"
- All-purpose thread to match fabrics
- Quilting thread
- Basic tools and supplies

INSTRUCTIONS

Note: *Block piecing instructions are given on page 96. Rotary-cutting sizes are given here for both block and setting pieces. If you prefer to cut the block pieces with templates, the letter/number label for each piece is given to identify the template that may be used. Block templates may be found by letter/number in the template section beginning on page 136.*

CUTTING

Step 1. Cut one 12⅞" square from each green; cut each square in half on one diagonal to make four dark A triangles.

Step 2. Cut two 6⅞" squares from each green; cut each square in half on one diagonal to make four dark T39 triangles each fabric.

Step 3. Cut three 6⅞" squares from each red; cut each square in half on one diagonal to make six medium T39 triangles each fabric.

Step 4. Cut two 6⅞" squares cream/gold; cut each square in half on one diagonal to make four light T39 triangles.

Step 5. Cut two 3⅞" squares cream/gold; cut each square in half on one diagonal to make four light T7 triangles.

Step 6. Using template Z54, cut four light cream/gold Z54 pieces.

Step 7. Using template Z62, cut four medium red Z62 pieces. Reverse template and cut four medium Z62R pieces from second red.

COMPLETING THE TOP

Step 1. Complete four Golden Holiday blocks

Step 5. Center and stitch a T39 unit on each side of the pieced center; press seam toward the T39 units to complete the pieced top.

COMPLETING THE QUILT

Step 1. Place the pieced top right sides together with the prepared backing piece. Pin the batting piece to backing side of the pinned layers.

Step 2. Stitch all around the edges, leaving 8" open on one edge. Trim batting and backing edges even with the quilt top edge; turn right side out.

Step 3. Press edges flat and pull out all corners. Turn the opening edges to the inside ¼"; press. Hand-stitch opening closed.

Step 4. Quilt as desired by hand or machine to finish. ■

referring to the instructions on page 96 and Placement Diagram for color placement. **Note:** *Cut A triangles from two green fabrics. Follow the color placement of the two green and the two red fabrics in Figure 1 below, reversing the placement of the light and dark shades of each color.*

Step 2. Join two blocks to make a row referring to Figure 1; press seams toward one red fabric. Repeat for two rows.

Make 2

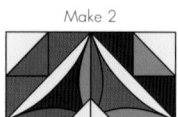

Figure 1

Step 3. Join the rows to complete the pieced center; press seam in one direction.

Step 4. Join one T39 triangle each red as shown in Figure 2; press seam in one direction. Repeat for four T39 units.

Make 2

Make 2

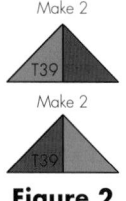

Figure 2

Golden Holiday Mat
Placement Diagram
36" x 36"

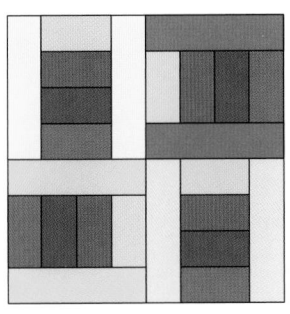

Spring Garden Path
12" x 12" Block

SPRING GARDEN PATH

The green pieces surrounded by floral pieces remind us of garden paths.

PROJECT SPECIFICATIONS

Skill Level: Intermediate
Quilt Size: 48" x 48"
Block Size: 12" x 12"
Number of Blocks: 16

MATERIALS

- 7 small-scale floral fat quarters
- 8 green fat quarters
- ½ yard green tonal for binding
- Backing 54" x 54"
- Batting 54" x 54"
- All-purpose thread to match fabrics
- Quilting thread
- Basic tools and supplies

INSTRUCTIONS

Note: *Block piecing instructions are given on page 124. Rotary-cutting sizes are given here for both block and setting pieces. If you prefer to cut the block pieces with templates, the letter/number label for each piece is given to identify the template that may be used.*

Block templates may be found by letter/number in the template section beginning on page 136.

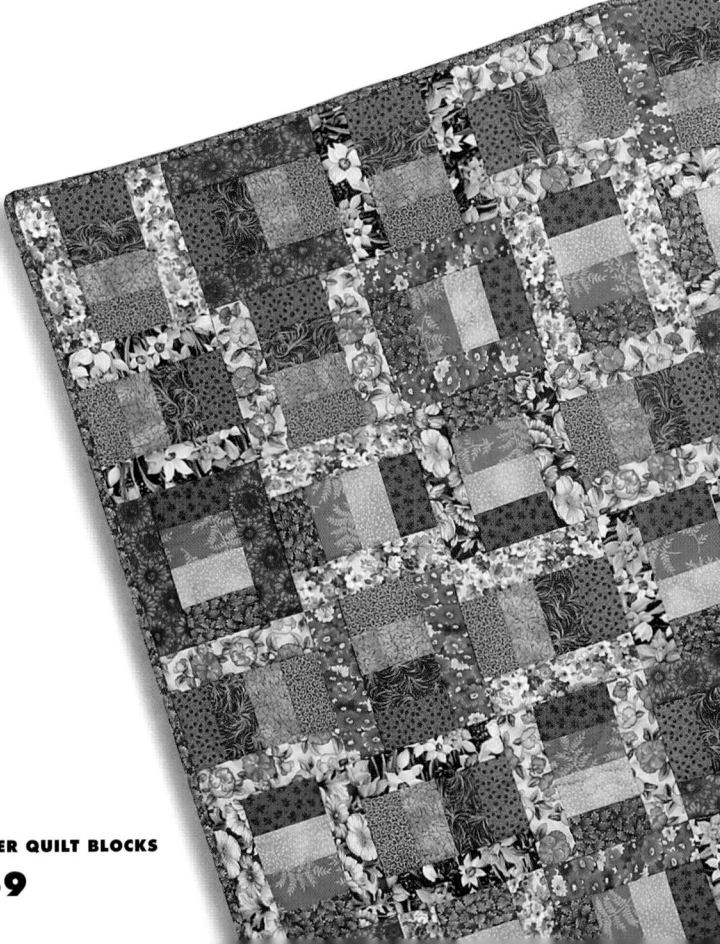

CUTTING

Step 1. Cut six 2" x 22" strips from each green; subcut strips into (256) 3½" R44 rectangles. **Note:** *For optional quick-piecing method for multiple blocks, do not cut strips into R44 rectangles.*

Step 2. Cut two 6½" x 22" strips each floral; subcut strips into (128) 2" R33 rectangles (64 same-fabric pairs).

Step 3. Cut five 2¼" by fabric width strips green tonal for binding.

OPTIONAL QUICK-PIECING FOR BLOCKS

Step 1. Join one 2"-wide strip each four different greens with right sides together along length; press seams in one direction. Repeat to make 12 strip sets.

Step 2. Subcut strip sets into (64) 3½" segments as shown in Figure 1.

Figure 1

Step 3. Sew identical R33 rectangles to each long side of one segment referring to Figure 2; press seams toward R33. Repeat with all segments.

Figure 2

Step 4. Join four pieced units as shown in Figure 3 to complete one block; repeat for 16 blocks. Press seams in one direction.

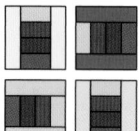

Figure 3

COMPLETING THE TOP

Step 1. Complete 16 Spring Garden Path blocks referring to the instructions on page 124.

Step 2. Join four blocks to make a row referring to Figure 4; press seams in one direction. Repeat for four rows.

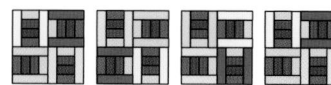

Figure 4

Step 3. Join the rows referring to the Placement Diagram to complete the pieced center; press seams in one direction.

COMPLETING THE QUILT

Step 1. Sandwich batting between the completed top and prepared backing piece; pin or baste layers together to hold flat.

Step 2. Quilt as desired by hand or machine.

Step 3. When quilting is complete, remove pins or basting; trim batting and backing edges even with quilt top.

Step 4. Join binding strips on short ends to make one long strip; press seams open.

Step 5. Fold binding strip in half with wrong sides together along length; press.

Step 6. Sew binding strip to quilt top with raw edges even, mitering corners and overlapping ends. Turn binding to the back side; hand- or machine-stitch in place to finish. ■

Spring Garden Path
Placement Diagram
48" x 48"

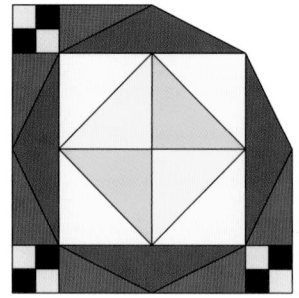

Patches of Sunshine
12" x 12" Block

PATCHES OF SUNSHINE

Bright yellow patches add a sunny look to this table topper.

PROJECT SPECIFICATIONS

Skill Lever: Beginner
Quilt Size: 24" x 24"
Block Size: 12" x 12"
Number of Blocks: 4

MATERIALS

- 1 each light, medium and dark yellow fat quarters
- 1 each black print and green print fat quarter
- 1 each black solid and yellow solid fat quarter
- Backing 30" x 30"
- Batting 30" x 30"
- All-purpose thread to match fabrics
- Quilting thread
- Basic tools and supplies

INSTRUCTIONS

Note: Block piecing instructions are given on page 113. Rotary-cutting sizes are given here for both block and setting pieces. If you prefer to cut the block pieces with templates, the letter/number label for each piece is given to identify the template that may be used. Block templates may be found by letter/number in the template section beginning on page 136.

CUTTING

Step 1. Cut one 4⅞" x 22" strip each medium and dark yellow; subcut each strip into four 4⅞" squares. Cut each square in half on one diagonal to make eight each medium and dark T19 triangles.

Step 2. Cut two 4⅞" x 22" strips light yellow; subcut strips into eight 4⅞" squares. Cut each square in half on one diagonal to make 16 light T19 triangles.

Step 3. Using T16 template, cut 12 dark T16 and 12 dark T16R black pieces.

Step 4. Using T35 template, cut 16 medium T35 green pieces.

Step 5. Cut two 1½" x 22" strips each black (dark) and yellow (light) solids; subcut strips into 24 each light and dark 1½" S3 squares.

COMPLETING THE PIECED TOP

Step 1. Piece four Patches of Sunshine blocks referring to the instructions given on page 113. **Note:** *Leave one black/yellow S3 unit and one each T16 and T16 reverse piece off the top right corner of each block as shown in the block drawing to make blocks for topper.*

Step 2. Join two blocks to make a row as shown in Figure 1; press seams in one direction. Repeat for two rows.

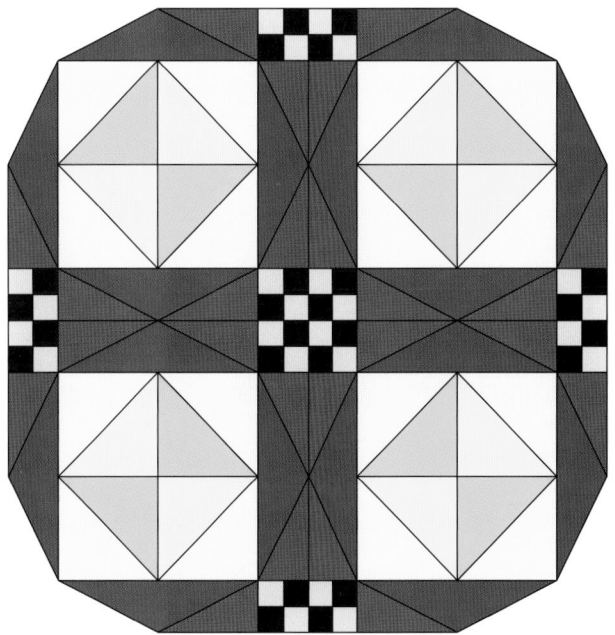

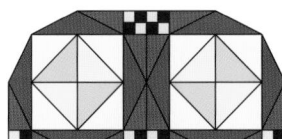

Figure 1

Step 3. Join the rows to complete the pieced top; press seam in one direction.

COMPLETING THE TOPPER

Step 1. Place the backing and pieced top right sides together; pin batting to the backing side of the layers.

Step 2. Stitch all around ¼" from edge of stitched top, leaving an 8" opening on one side.

Step 3. Trim backing and batting even with the edges of the stitched top.

Step 4. Turn right side out through opening; press edges flat.

Step 5. Turn edges of opening under ¼"; press. Hand-stitch opening closed.

Step 6. Quilt as desired by hand or machine to finish. ■

Patches of Sunshine
Placement Diagram
24" x 24"

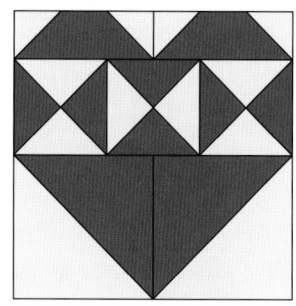

From the Heart
12" x 12" Block

FROM THE HEART

A pieced heart block is the perfect Valentine hello.

PROJECT SPECIFICATIONS

Skill Level: Beginner
Quilt Size: 18" x 14"
Block Size: 12" x 12"
Number of Blocks: 1

MATERIALS

- 2 red fat quarters
- 1 cream fat quarter
- 1 red/tan plaid fat quarter
- Backing 24" x 20"
- Batting 24" x 20"
- All-purpose thread to match fabrics
- Quilting thread
- Basic tools and supplies

INSTRUCTIONS

Note: *Block piecing instructions are given on page 95. Rotary-cutting sizes are given here for both block and setting pieces. If you prefer to cut the block pieces with templates, the letter/number label for each piece is given to identify the template that may be used. Block templates may be found by letter/number in the template section beginning on page 136.*

CUTTING

Step 1. Cut two 6⅞" x 6⅞" squares each cream and red; cut each square on one diagonal to make two each light and dark T39 triangles. Set aside one triangle of each fabric for another project.

Step 2. Cut two 5¼" x 5¼" squares each cream and red; cut each square on both diagonals to make eight each light and dark T18 triangles. Set aside two triangles of each fabric for another project.

Step 3. Cut two 2½" x 7¼" rectangles red. Trim both ends of each rectangle at a 45-degree angle to make two dark Z34 pieces as shown in Figure 1.

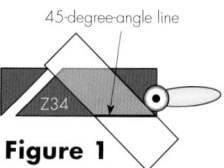

45-degree-angle line

Z34

Figure 1

Step 4. Cut two 2⅞" x 2⅞" squares cream; cut each square on one diagonal to make four light T11 triangles.

Step 5. Cut two 3½" x 12½" A strips red/tan plaid.

Step 6. Cut two 1½" x 18½" B strips red/tan plaid.

Step 7. Cut four 2¼" x 22" strips red for binding.

COMPLETING THE TOP

Step 1. Piece one From the Heart block referring to the instructions on page 95.

Step 2. Sew an A strip to opposite sides of the pieced block; press seams toward A.

Step 3. Sew a B strip to the top and bottom of the pieced block to complete the top; press seams toward B.

COMPLETING THE QUILT

Step 1. Sandwich batting between the completed top and prepared backing piece; pin or baste layers together to hold flat.

Step 2. Quilt as desired by hand or machine.

Step 3. When quilting is complete, remove pins or basting; trim batting and backing edges even with quilt top.

Step 4. Join binding strips on short ends to make one long strip; press seams open.

Step 5. Fold binding strip in half with wrong sides together along length; press.

Step 6. Sew binding strip to quilt top with raw edges even, mitering corners and overlapping ends. Turn binding to the back side; hand- or machine-stitch in place to finish. ■

From the Heart
Placement Diagram
18" x 14"

DESIGN BY **TOBY LISCHKO**

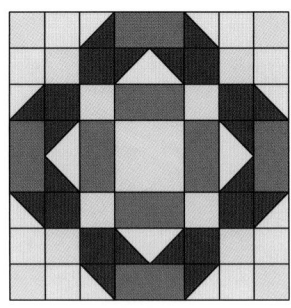

**Midnight in the
Garden**
12" x 12" Block

MIDNIGHT IN
THE GARDEN

The use of black fabrics provides the contrast needed for the
pastel colors used in this large runner.

PROJECT SPECIFICATIONS
Skill Level: Beginner
Quilt Size: 23" x 57"
Block Size: 12" x 12"
Number of Blocks: 3

MATERIALS
- 1 cream tonal fat quarter
- 1 each black, green and peach fat quarters
- 1 cream fat quarter
- ⅝ yard black floral
- 1 yard black tonal
- Backing 29" x 63"
- Batting 29" x 63"
- All-purpose thread to match fabrics
- Quilting thread
- Basic tools and supplies

INSTRUCTIONS
Note: Block piecing instructions are given on page
108. Rotary-cutting sizes are given here for both block
and setting pieces. If you prefer to cut the block pieces
with templates, the letter/number label for each piece

is given to identify the template that may be used.
Block templates may be found by letter/number in the
template section beginning on page 136.

CUTTING
Step 1. Cut three 2" x 22" strips each cream tonal
(light) and black (dark) fat quarter; subcut strips into 24
each light and dark 2" S30 squares.

Step 2. Cut four 2" x 22" strips peach; subcut strips
into (36) 2" medium S30 squares.

Step 3. Cut two 2⅜" x 22" strips cream tonal; subcut
strips into (12) 2⅜" squares. Cut each square in half on
one diagonal to make 24 light T1 triangles.

Step 4. Cut three 2⅜" x 22" strips black; subcut strips
into (24) 2⅜" squares. Cut each square in half on one
diagonal to make 48 dark T1 triangles.

Step 5. Cut three 3½" x 3½" S5 squares peach.

Step 6. Cut four 3½" x 22" strips green; subcut strips
into 24 medium 2" R44 rectangles.

Step 7. Cut three 4¼" x 4¼" squares cream; cut
each square on both diagonals to make 12 light
T33 triangles.

Step 8. Cut two 8⅜" x 8⅜" squares cream tonal;

cut each square in half on one diagonal to make four A triangles.

Step 9. Cut two 3¾" by fabric width strips black tonal; subcut strips into four 18¼" B strips. Cut the ends of each strip at a 45-degree angle as shown in Figure 1.

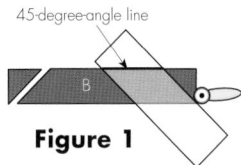

Figure 1

Step 10. Cut two 9⅜" x 9⅜" squares black tonal; cut each square in half on one diagonal to make four C triangles.

Step 11. Cut five 3½" by fabric width strips black floral; join strips on short ends to make one long strip. Subcut strip into two 26" D strips and two 60" E strips.

Step 12. Cut five 2¼" by fabric width strips black tonal for binding.

COMPLETING THE RUNNER TOP

Step 1. Piece three Midnight in the Garden blocks referring to the instructions on page 108.

Step 2. Sew A to B to make an A-B unit as shown in Figure 2; press seams toward B. Repeat for four A-B units.

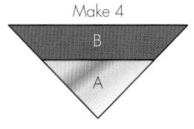

Figure 2

Step 3. Arrange the blocks with the A-B units and C triangles in diagonal rows as shown in Figure 3; join in rows. Press seams in one direction. Join all rows, adding C triangles at corners; press seams toward C.

Step 4. Center and sew D to each short end and E to

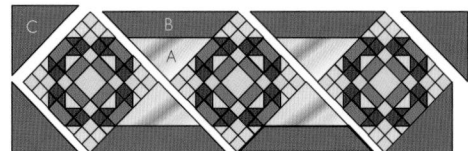

Figure 3

each long side of the pieced center, stopping stitching ¼" from each corner; miter corners. Trim mitered seams to ¼" and press seams open; press border seams toward D and E to complete the top.

COMPLETING THE RUNNER

Step 1. Sandwich batting between the completed top and prepared backing piece; pin or baste layers together to hold flat.

Step 2. Quilt as desired by hand or machine.

Step 3. When quilting is complete, remove pins or basting; trim batting and backing edges even with quilt top.

Step 4. Join binding strips on short ends to make one long strip; press seams open.

Step 5. Fold binding strip in half with wrong sides together along length; press.

Step 6. Sew binding strip to quilt top with raw edges even, mitering corners and overlapping ends. Turn binding to the back side; hand- or machine-stitch in place to finish. ■

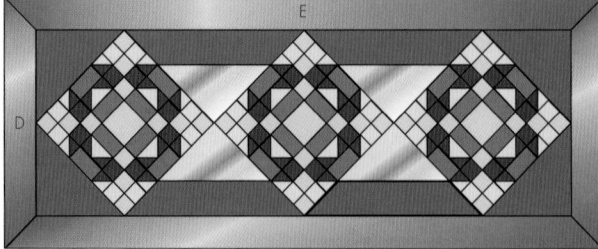

Midnight in the Garden
Placement Diagram
23" x 57"

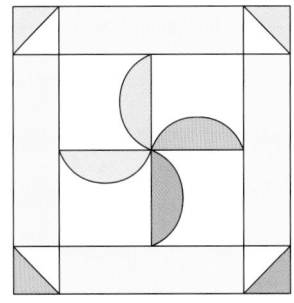

Pastel Pinwheel
12" x 12" Block

PASTEL PINWHEELS

Curved appliqué pieces create pretty pinwheel shapes
in this soft-color wall quilt.

PROJECT SPECIFICATIONS

Skill Level: Beginner
Quilt Size: 36" x 36"
Block Size: 12" x 12"
Number of Blocks: 9

MATERIALS

- 1 each pink, green, purple, blue and
  yellow fat quarters
- 3 different white fat quarters
- Backing 42" x 42"
- Batting 42" x 42"
- All-purpose thread to match fabrics
- Quilting thread
- Basic tools and supplies

INSTRUCTIONS

Note: *Block piecing instructions are given on page
113. Rotary-cutting sizes are given here for both block
and setting pieces. If you prefer to cut the block pieces
with templates, the letter/number label for each piece
is given to identify the template that may be used.*

Block templates may be found by letter/number in the template section beginning on page 136.

CUTTING

Step 1. Cut three 4½" x 22" strips from each white; subcut strips into 12 light 4½" S14 squares each fabric.

Step 2. Cut one 2⅞" x 22" strip from each white; subcut each strip into six 2⅞" squares. Cut each square in half on one diagonal to make 12 light T11 triangles each fabric.

Step 3. Cut one 8½" x 22" strip each pink, purple, green and blue; subcut each strip into eight 2½" medium R15 rectangles.

Step 4. Cut two 2⅞" x 2⅞" squares each pink, purple, green and blue; cut each square on one diagonal to make four medium T11 triangles each fabric.

Step 5. Cut two 2⅞" x 22" strips yellow; subcut strips into (10) 2⅞" squares. Cut each square in half on one diagonal to make 20 medium T11 triangles.

Step 6. Cut two 2½" x 22" strips yellow; subcut strips into four 8½" medium R15 medium rectangles.

Step 7. Using template Z20, cut nine Z20 pieces pieces each pink, purple, blue and green (mediums).

Step 8. Cut 1¼"-wide strips from remaining pink, green, purple and blue and join on short ends as shown in Figure 1 to make a 168" strip.

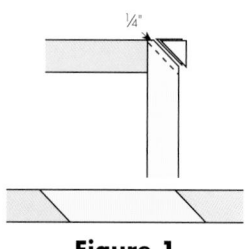

Figure 1

COMPLETING THE TOP

Step 1. Complete nine Pastel Pinwheel blocks referring to the instructions on page 113 and to the Placement Diagram for color combinations for each block. ***Note:*** *Refer to the Placement Diagram for color placement of the T11 block corners. Corners on the outside edges of the quilt are always the yellow/white combination.*

Step 2. Arrange the pieced blocks in three rows of three blocks each referring to the Placement Diagram for positioning of blocks. Join blocks in rows; press seams in one direction. Join rows to complete the pieced center.

COMPLETING THE QUILT

Step 1. Sandwich batting between the completed top and prepared backing piece; pin or baste layers together to hold flat.

Step 2. Quilt as desired by hand or machine.

Step 3. When quilting is complete, remove pins or basting; trim batting and backing edges even with quilt top.

Step 4. Fold under one long edge of the prepared binding strip ¼"; press.

Step 5. Stitch binding to the quilted top with right sides together, matching raw edge of binding with raw edge of quilted top and mitering corners and overlapping ends.

Step 6. Turn folded edge of binding to the back side; hand- or machine-stitch in place to finish. ∎

Pastel Pinwheels
Placement Diagram
36" x 36"

QUILT BLOCKS

1904 STAR PIECING INSTRUCTIONS

1. Referring to the Piecing Diagram to piece one block, sew T46 and T46R to the long sides of T48 and add T7 to complete a corner unit; repeat for four corner units
2. Join one dark and three light T33 triangles to complete a side unit; repeat for four side units.
3. Sew a corner unit to opposite sides of S22 to complete the center row.
4. Sew a side unit to each side of each of the remaining corner units to complete the block corners.
5. Sew a block corner to opposite sides of the center row to complete the block.

A DANDY PIECING INSTRUCTIONS

1. Referring to the Piecing Diagram to piece one block, sew a light T11 to each side of S29 to complete the center unit.
2. Sew a dark T11 to Z5 to make a side unit; repeat for four units.
3. Sew a light T19 to a dark T19 to make a corner unit; repeat for four units.
4. Arrange and join the pieced units in rows; join the rows to complete the block.

ADIRONDACK STAR PIECING INSTRUCTIONS

1. Referring to the Piecing Diagram to piece one block, sew T11 to each side of S29 to complete the block center.
2. Sew R7 to the top and bottom and a light R16 to opposite sides of the pieced center. Repeat with a dark R16 on the top and bottom and R8 on opposite sides.
3. Sew T37 to T25 and T37R to T25R; join the two pieced units. Repeat for four T units.
4. Sew a T unit to each side of the center unit and stitch corner seams to complete the block.

ALASKA PIECING INSTRUCTIONS

1. Referring to the Piecing Diagram to piece one block, sew T33 to Z63; repeat. Join the two units.
2. Sew T1 to each end of Z25; repeat. Sew one unit to each side of the stitched unit to complete the center unit.
3. Sew T33 to two adjacent sides of S2; add T7 to the pieced unit to make a side unit. Repeat for four side units.
4. Sew a side unit to opposite sides of the center unit.
5. Sew S5 to each end of the remaining side units; sew these units to the remaining sides of the center unit to complete the block.

1904 Star
12" x 12" Block

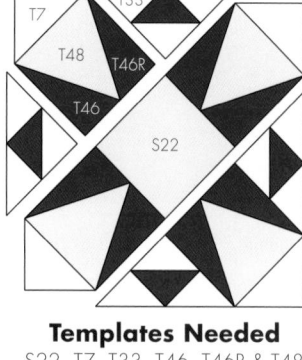

Templates Needed
S22, T7, T33, T46, T46R & T48

A Dandy
12" x 12" Block

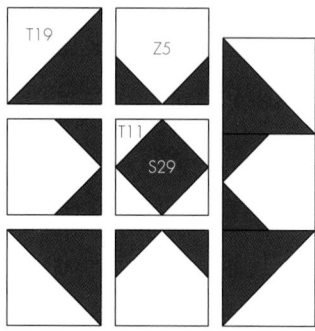

Templates Needed
S29, T11, T19 & Z5

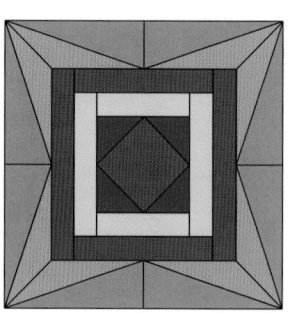

Adirondack Star
12" x 12" Block

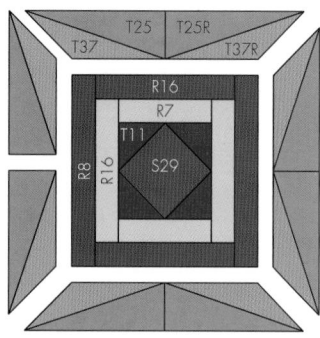

Templates Needed
R7, R8, R16, S29, T11,
T25, T25R, T37 & T37R

Alaska
12" x 12" Block

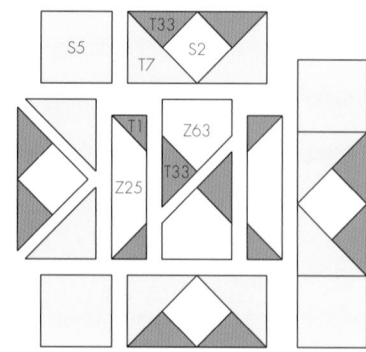

Templates Needed
S2, S5, T1, T7, T33, Z25 & Z63

ALL HALLOWS PIECING INSTRUCTIONS

1. Referring to the Piecing Diagram to piece one block, sew a medium Z26 to a dark Z26R; repeat for four units.

2. Set in a light T11 between points of each pieced unit; join two pieced units to make a half-star unit. Repeat for two half-star units.

3. Join the half-star units and set in S29 squares to complete the block center.

4. Sew a medium Z26 and Z26R to the short sides of a dark T11; repeat for four units.

5. Sew a light T18 to a dark T18 and sew to the Z-T unit to complete a corner unit; repeat for four corner units.

6. Sew a corner unit to each side of the block center to complete the block.

ARROW CROWN PIECING INSTRUCTIONS

1. Referring to the Piecing Diagram to piece one block, sew a lightest T1 to two adjacent sides of a medium T33; repeat for four medium units.

2. Repeat step 1 with the lightest T33 and dark T1; repeat for two lightest units.

3. Join one each medium and lightest units with R44; repeat and sew these units to opposite sides of S5 to complete the center row.

4. Sew a medium T1 to a dark T1; repeat for eight medium/dark T1 units.

5. Sew a medium T1 to a lightest T1 to make a medium/lightest T1 unit; repeat for eight units.

6. Sew a dark T1 to two adjacent sides of a lightest T33; repeat for four units.

7. Arrange the pieced units with the S30 squares to make rows referring to the Piecing Diagram; join in rows.

8. Join the rows with the center row to complete the block.

AUNT NANCY'S FAVORITE PIECING INSTRUCTIONS

1. Referring to the Piecing Diagram to piece one block, sew T33 to two adjacent sides of a medium T7; add a dark T7 and R43 to complete a corner unit.

2. Sew a corner unit to opposite sides of S22.

3. Sew a T32 to opposite sides of each remaining corner unit; sew these units to the remaining sides of S22 to complete the block.

BACHELOR'S PUZZLE PIECING INSTRUCTIONS

1. Referring to the Piecing Diagram to piece one block, sew a light Z58 to a dark Z58R; set in S5 between points and add T7 to complete one unit. Repeat for four units.

2. Sew a unit to each side of S22 and complete side seams to complete the block.

All Hallows
12" x 12" Block

Templates Needed
S29, T11, T18, Z26 & Z26R

Arrow Crown
12" x 12" Block

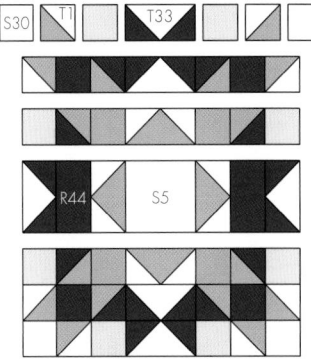

Templates Needed
R44, S5, S30, T1 & T33

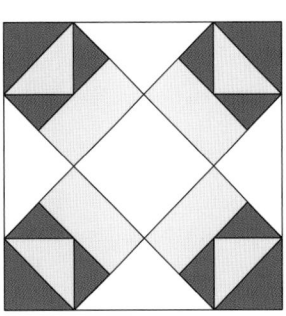

Aunt Nancy's Favorite
12" x 12" Block

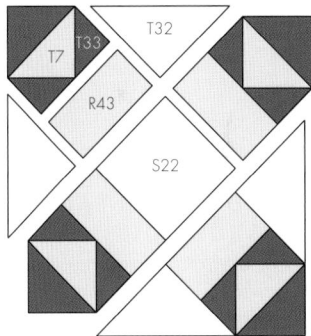

Templates Needed
R43, S22, T7, T32 & T33

Bachelor's Puzzle
12" x 12" Block

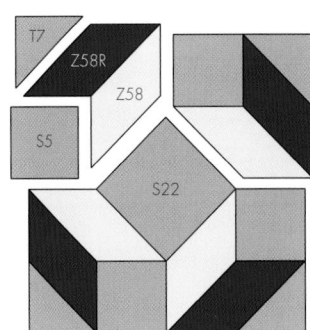

Templates Needed
S5, S22, T7, Z58 & Z58R

BATON ROUGE SQUARE PIECING INSTRUCTIONS

1. Referring to the Piecing Diagram to piece one block, sew a dark S8 to a medium S8; repeat for four S8 units.

2. Join two S8 units with a medium S8 to make the center strip.

3. Sew a light T42 to a dark T42; repeat for eight T42 units.

4. Join two T42 units with two light S8 squares to make a corner unit; repeat for four corner units.

5. Join two corner units with an S8 unit to make a side unit; repeat for two side units.

6. Sew a side unit to opposite sides of the center strip to complete the block.

BEACON LIGHTS PIECING INSTRUCTIONS

1. Referring to the Piecing Diagram to piece one block, sew R43 to opposite sides of S22.

2. Sew S2 to opposite ends of R43; repeat. Sew these units to the remaining sides of S22 to complete the center unit.

3. Sew a dark T33 to two adjacent sides of S5 and add a light T33 to each dark T33 side to complete a corner unit; repeat for four corner units.

4. Sew a corner unit to each side of the pieced center to complete the block.

BECKY'S NINE-PATCH PIECING INSTRUCTIONS

1. Referring to the Piecing Diagram to piece one block, sew S14 to a dark R9.

2. Sew a lightest S19 to a dark S19 and add R11. Sew this unit to a light R9.

3. Join the two pieced units and add R15 to the bottom referring to the Piecing Diagram.

4. Add R42 to the stitched unit to complete one block, again referring to the Piecing Diagram.

BLIND MAN'S FANCY PIECING INSTRUCTIONS

1. Referring to the Piecing Diagram to piece one block, sew T43 to two adjacent sides of T9; repeat for four units.

2. Sew a pieced unit to opposite sides of S34. Add S6 to each end of each remaining pieced unit; sew these units to the remaining sides of S34. Add T31 to each side of the pieced unit to complete the center unit.

3. Sew a dark T1 to two adjacent sides of T33; repeat for four units.

4. Sew a light T1 to a dark T1; repeat for 16 units.

5. Sew two T1 units to opposite sides of a T1/T33 unit to make a side unit; repeat for four side units. Sew a side unit to opposite sides of the center unit.

6. Sew an S30 square to each end of each remaining side unit and sew to the remaining sides of the center unit to complete the block.

Baton Rouge Square
12" x 12" Block

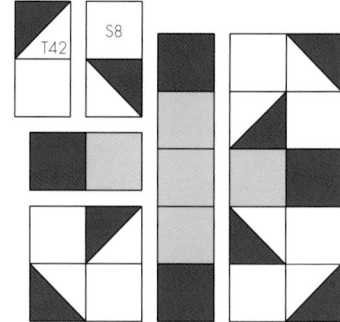

Templates Needed
S8 & T42

Beacon Lights
12" x 12" Block

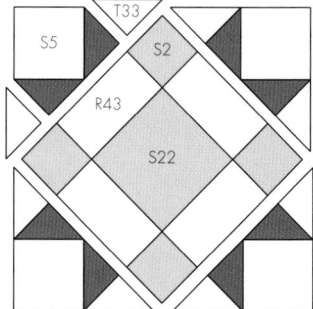

Templates Needed
R43, S2, S5, S22 & T33

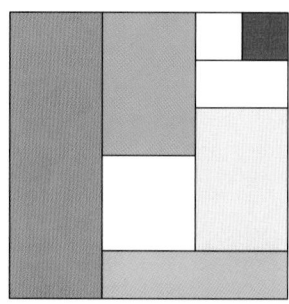

Becky's Nine-Patch
12" x 12" Block

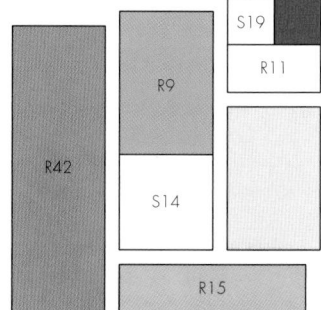

Templates Needed
R9, R11, R15, R42, S14 & S19

Blind Man's Fancy
12" x 12" Block

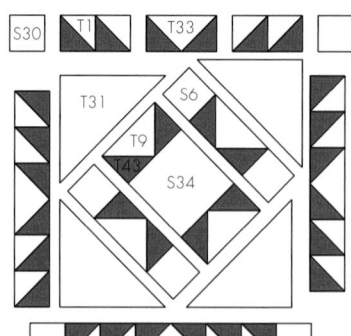

Templates Needed
S6, S30, S34, T1,
T9, T31, T33 & T43

BOXES PIECING INSTRUCTIONS

1. Referring to the Piecing Diagram to piece one block, sew Z23 to each side of S29; join Z23 pieces at angled seams.
2. Sew a medium T18 to two adjacent sides of T19; add T19 to the medium T18 side to make a corner unit. Repeat for four units.
3. Sew a corner unit to opposite sides of the pieced center unit.
4. Sew a dark T18 to each remaining corner unit and sew to the remaining sides of the pieced center unit to complete the block.

BRACED STAR I PIECING INSTRUCTIONS

1. Referring to the Piecing Diagram to piece one block, sew T11 to each side of S29 to make the center unit.
2. Sew a light T18 to a dark T18; repeat for eight T18 units.
3. Join two T18 units to make a side unit.
4. Arrange and join the pieced T18 units with S14 in rows; join the rows to complete the block.

BRACED STAR II PIECING INSTRUCTIONS

1. Referring to the Piecing Diagram to piece one block, sew R2 pieces to S29, leaving one end of the first R2 loose and completing that seam after all R2 pieces have been added to complete the center unit.
2. Sew a dark T18 to two adjacent sides of S14 to make a corner unit; repeat for four corner units.
3. Sew a corner unit to opposite sides of the center unit.
4. Sew a light T18 triangle to each dark T18 side of each of the remaining corner units; sew these units to the remaining sides of the center unit to complete the block.

BRICKWORK PIECING INSTRUCTIONS

1. Referring to the Piecing Diagram to piece one block, sew a light S2 square between two medium S2 squares; repeat for two units. Sew a unit to opposite sides of a light R19 to complete the center unit.
2. Sew T33 to opposite sides of a medium S2 and add T1; add a dark R19 to make a corner unit. Repeat for four corner units.
3. Sew a corner unit to opposite sides of the center unit.
4. Sew T33 to opposite ends of R19 on the remaining corner units; sew these units to the remaining sides of the center unit to complete the block.

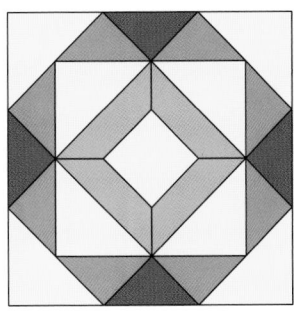

Boxes
12" x 12" Block

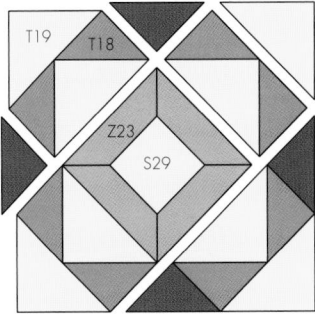

Templates Needed
S29, T18, T19 & Z23

Braced Star I
12" x 12" Block

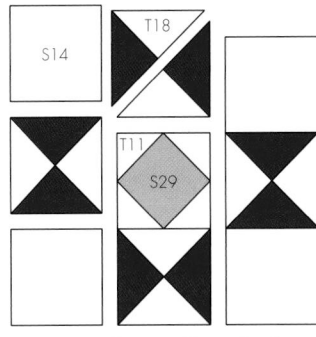

Templates Needed
S14, S29, T11 & T18

Braced Star II
12" x 12" Block

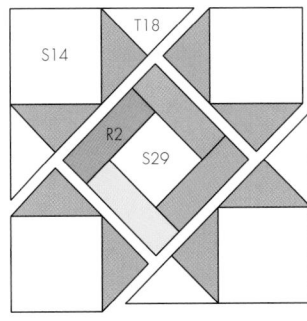

Templates Needed
R2, S14, S29 & T18

Brickwork
12" x 12" Block

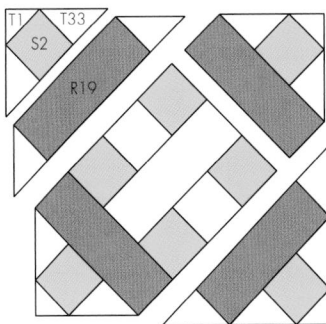

Templates Needed
R19, S2, T1 & T33

BRIDE'S BOUQUET PIECING INSTRUCTIONS

1. Referring to the Piecing Diagram to piece one block, join a medium Z49 with a dark Z49R; repeat with a dark Z49 and a medium Z49R and a dark Z49 and dark Z49R to make star points.

2. Sew Z1 and Z1R to S19 to make a corner unit; set a corner unit into each star point, referring to the Piecing Diagram.

3. Sew T15 to two adjacent long sides of S12 to make a side unit; repeat for two side units.

4. Join two star points and set in a side unit.

5. Sew T51 and T51R to opposite sides of Z38.

6. Join the pieced units referring to the Piecing Diagram to complete the block.

BROKEN ARROWS PIECING INSTRUCTIONS

1. Referring to the Piecing Diagram to piece one block, sew a light S8 to a dark S8 to make an S8 unit; repeat for four units.

2. Join two S8 units with a light S8 to make the center strip.

3. Sew a light T40 to a dark T40; repeat for four T40 units.

4. Join two T40 units with an S8 unit to make a side unit; repeat for two side units.

5. Sew a side unit to opposite sides of the center strip to complete the block.

BROKEN BAND PIECING INSTRUCTIONS

1. Referring to the Piecing Diagram to piece one block, sew T7 to each side of S22; add T32 to each side of this unit to complete the center unit.

2. Sew Z57R to one short side of T7 and Z57 to the remaining short side; add another T7 to the stitched unit to complete a corner unit. Repeat for four corner units.

3. Sew a corner unit to each side of the center unit to complete the block.

BROKEN CRYSTALS PIECING INSTRUCTIONS

1. Referring to the Piecing Diagram to piece one block, sew a dark T26 to T13 and a dark T26R to a light Z40; join the units to complete one side star point; repeat for four side star points.

2. Sew a light T26 to S18 and a light T26R to a dark Z40; join the units to complete one corner star point; repeat for four corner star points.

3. Join the side and corner star points in a clockwise direction to complete the block.

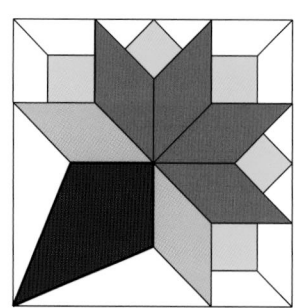

Bride's Bouquet
12" x 12" Block

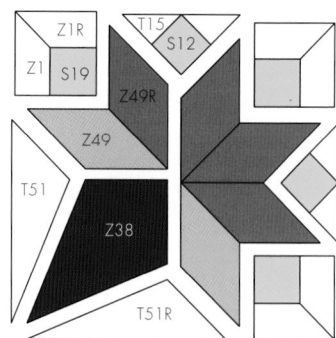

Templates Needed
S12, S19, T15, T51, T51R, Z1, Z1R, Z38, Z49 & Z49R

Broken Arrows
12" x 12" Block

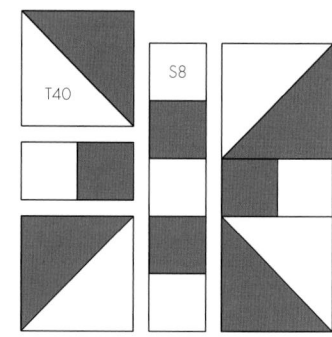

Templates Needed
S8 & T40

Broken Band
12" x 12" Block

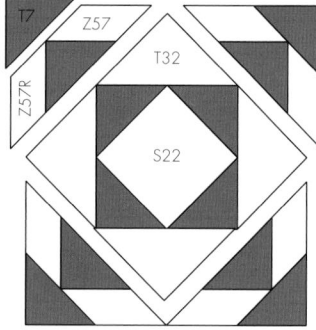

Templates Needed
S22, T7, T32, Z57 & Z57R

Broken Crystals
12" x 12" Block

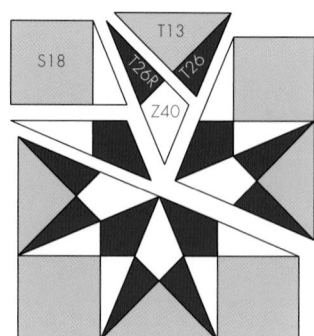

Templates Needed
S18, T13, T26, T26R & Z40

BROKEN DISHES PIECING INSTRUCTIONS

1. Referring to the Piecing Diagram to piece one block, sew T41 to each side of S17 to complete the center unit.
2. Sew a light T42 to a medium T42; repeat for eight units.
3. Sew a T42 unit to opposite sides of a light S8 to make a side unit; repeat for four side units.
4. Sew a side unit to opposite sides of the center unit.
5. Sew a dark S8 to each end of the remaining side units; repeat for two units.
6. Sew these side units to the remaining sides of the pieced center to complete the block.

BROKEN IRISH CHAIN PIECING INSTRUCTIONS

1. Referring to the Piecing Diagram to piece one block, sew a light S32 to a dark S32; repeat for six units. Sew a unit to opposite sides of S23.
2. Join two S32 units; repeat. Sew these units to the remaining sides of S23 to complete the center unit.
3. Sew T42 to one side of an S23 to make a corner unit; repeat for four corner units.
4. Referring to the Piecing Diagram, sew a light T29 to one side of a dark S32; repeat for two units. Sew a dark T29 to one side of a light S32. Sew one of each of these units to opposite sides of two corner units. Sew these units to opposite sides of the center unit.
5. Sew a light T29 to two adjacent sides of a dark S32; repeat for four side units. Repeat with two dark T29 triangles on two adjacent sides of a light S32; repeat for two units. Sew one of each of these units to opposite sides of each of the remaining two corner units.
6. Sew these larger corner units to the remaining sides of the center unit to complete the block.

BROKEN STAR PIECING INSTRUCTIONS

1. Referring to the Piecing Diagram to piece one block, sew a dark T33 to each side of S5 to make a center unit.
2. Sew a medium T33 to two adjacent sides of T7; repeat for four units.
3. Sew a medium T33 to adjacent sides of S5; repeat for four units.
4. Sew a T33-T7 unit to a T33-S5 unit to make a corner unit; repeat for four corner units. Sew a corner unit to opposite sides of the center unit.
5. Sew T32 to opposite sides of the remaining corner units; sew these units to the remaining sides of the center unit to complete the block.

BROKEN SUGAR BOWL PIECING INSTRUCTIONS

1. Referring to the Piecing Diagram to piece one block, sew a light S19 to a dark S19; repeat for four units. Join two units to make a center unit.
2. Sew a medium S19 to a dark S19; repeat for two units. Join one of these units with a light/dark S19 unit to complete a corner unit; repeat for two corner units.
3. Sew a light T19 to a dark T19 to make a side unit; repeat for four side units.
4. Arrange the pieced units with the S14 squares referring to the Piecing Diagram; join the units in rows and join the rows to complete the block.

Broken Dishes
12" x 12" Block

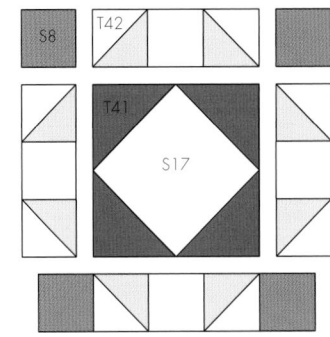

Templates Needed
S8, S17, T41 & T42

Broken Irish Chain
12" x 12" Block

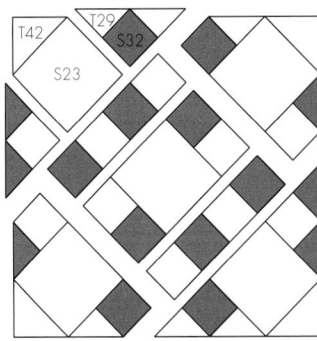

Templates Needed
S23, S32, T29 & T42

Broken Star
12" x 12" Block

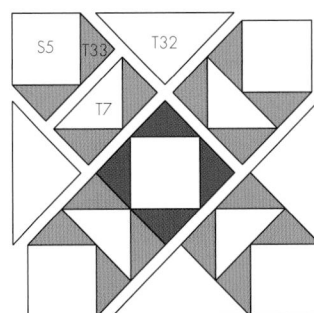

Templates Needed
S5, T7, T32 & T33

Broken Sugar Bowl
12" x 12" Block

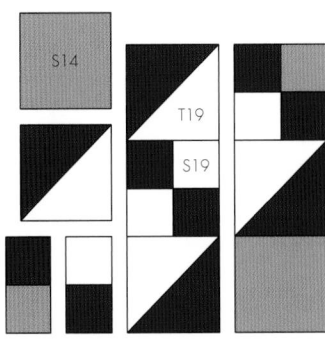

Templates Needed
S14, S19 & T19

BURNHAM SQUARE PIECING INSTRUCTIONS

1. Referring to the Piecing Diagram to piece one block, sew T1 to two adjacent sides of T33; repeat for four units. Sew a unit to opposite sides of S5. Sew an S30 square to opposite ends of the remaining two units; sew these units to the remaining sides of S5 to complete the center unit.

2. Sew a light R16 between two medium R16 strips to make a side unit; repeat for four side units. Sew a side unit to opposite sides of the center unit.

3. Sew a light T7 to a medium T7 to make a corner unit; repeat for four corner units.

4. Sew a corner unit to opposite ends of each remaining side unit; sew these units to the remaining sides of the pieced center to complete the block.

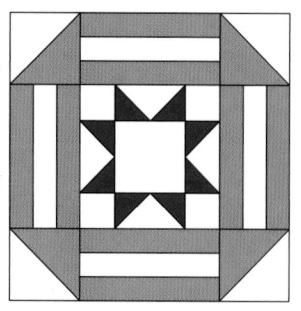

Burnham Square
12" x 12" Block

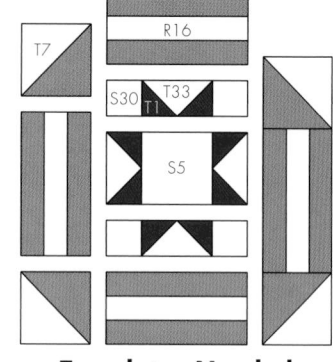

Templates Needed
R16, S5, S30, T1, T7 & T33

CALIFORNIA PIECING INSTRUCTIONS

1. Referring to the Piecing Diagram to piece one block, join two lightest, one light and one medium R31 pieces to make an R unit; repeat for four R units.

2. Sew S16 to one end of R52; repeat for four S-R units.

3. Sew an S-R unit to the lightest end of each R unit to complete four block quarters.

4. Join the block quarters to complete the block.

California
12" x 12" Block

Templates Needed
R31, R52 & S16

CALIFORNIA STARS PIECING INSTRUCTIONS

1. Referring to the Piecing Diagram to piece one block, sew a dark T1 to each side of a light T1 to make a dark T1 unit; repeat for four units.

2. Sew a light T1 to each side of a dark T1 to make a light T1 unit; repeat for four units.

3. Sew a light T1 unit to T7; repeat for four units. Join the units to complete the center unit.

4. Sew a dark T1 unit to one side of T32 and T7 to the adjacent side to complete a side unit; repeat for four side units.

5. Sew a side unit to opposite sides of the center unit.

6. Sew S5 to each end of the remaining side units; sew these units to the remaining sides of the center unit to complete the block.

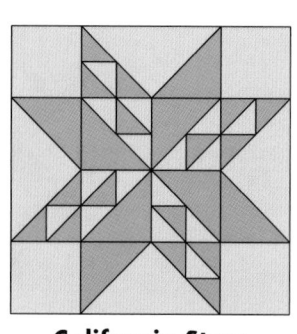

California Stars
12" x 12" Block

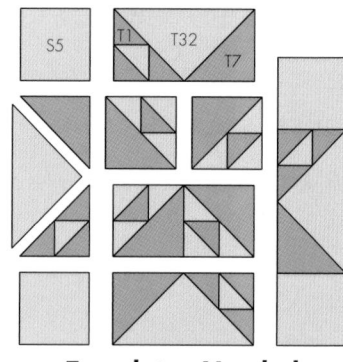

Templates Needed
S5, T1, T7 & T32

CARPENTER'S SQUARE PIECING INSTRUCTIONS

1. Referring to the Piecing Diagram to piece one block, sew a dark S13 to each side of a medium S13; add R23 to opposite sides.

2. Sew a dark S13 to one end of R12; repeat for two units. Sew these units to the R23 sides of the previously pieced unit.

3. Sew one medium and one dark S13 to R36; repeat and sew these units to the long sides of the previously pieced unit.

4. Sew a dark R27 to the R12 sides and R25 to the R36 sides of the pieced unit.

5. Sew one medium and two dark S13 squares to one end of a light R27; repeat for two units. Sew these units to the dark R27 side of the pieced unit.

6. Join two medium and two dark S13 squares with a light R27; repeat for two units. Sew these units to the dark R25 sides of the pieced unit.

7. Sew R26 to opposite sides and R35 to the top and bottom of the pieced unit to complete the block.

Carpenter's Square
12" x 12" Block

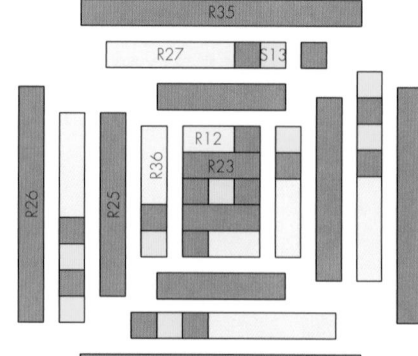

Templates Needed
R12, R23, R25, R26, R27, R35, R36 & S13

CARSON CITY PIECING INSTRUCTIONS

1. Referring to the Piecing Diagram to piece one block, sew Z23 to each side of S29, joining angled ends to complete the center unit.

2. Sew a light T3 to a dark T3 to make a T unit; repeat for four T units.

3. Sew T18 to adjacent dark sides of a T unit to complete a corner unit; repeat for four corner units.

4. Sew a corner unit to opposite sides of the center unit.

5. Sew T18 to each T18 side of the remaining corner units; sew these units to the remaining sides of the center unit to complete the block.

CAT TRAILS PIECING INSTRUCTIONS

1. Referring to the Piecing Diagram to piece one block, sew a lightest T7 to each side of S22 to complete the center unit.

2. Sew a dark T33 to each side of a lightest T33 to make a side unit; repeat for four side units.

3. Sew a side unit to each side of the center unit.

4. Sew a light T7 to Z30 to complete a corner unit; repeat for four corner units.

5. Sew a corner unit to each side of the pieced center unit to complete the block.

CHAIN LINKS PIECING INSTRUCTIONS

1. Referring to the Piecing Diagram to piece one block, sew a light S30 square between two lightest S30 squares to make a lightest S unit; repeat for four lightest S units.

2. Sew a lightest T1 to a light T1 and a lightest T1 to a medium T1; join these two units with a lightest S30 to complete an S-T unit. Repeat for four S-T units.

3. Sew a lightest S30 to a medium S30 to a light S30 to make a medium S unit; repeat for four medium S units.

4. Join one lightest S unit with one S-T unit and one medium S unit to make a corner unit; repeat for four corner units.

5. Sew a lightest T1 to two adjacent short sides of a dark T33; add a lightest R44 and a medium R44 to make a side unit; repeat for two side units.

6. Sew a side unit between two corner units to make the bottom row; repeat for the top row.

7. Sew a lightest T1 to two adjacent short sides of a dark T33; repeat for two units. Sew a lightest T1 to two adjacent short sides of a light T33; repeat for two units. Join one of each of these units with a medium R44 to make a side center unit; repeat for two units.

8. Sew a side center unit to opposite sides of S5 to complete the center row. Join the rows to complete the block.

CHEYENNE PIECING INSTRUCTIONS

1. Referring to the Piecing Diagram to piece one block, sew a medium T7 to opposite sides of S22; repeat with a dark T7 on the remaining sides to complete the center unit.

2. Sew a medium S5 to a dark S5 to complete a side unit; repeat for four side units. Sew a side unit to opposite sides of the center unit.

3. Sew a light T7 to a dark T7 to make a corner unit; repeat for four corner units.

4. Sew a corner unit to each end of each of the remaining side units. Sew these units to the remaining sides of the center unit to complete the block.

Carson City
12" x 12" Block

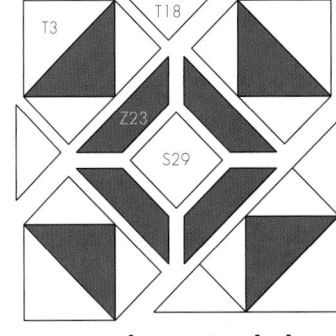

Templates Needed
S29, T3, T18 & Z23

Cat Trails
12" x 12" Block

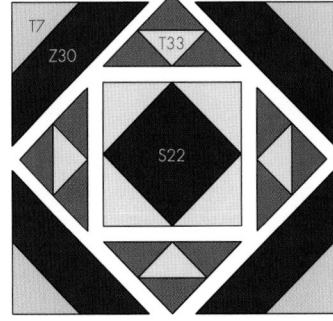

Templates Needed
S22, T7, T33 & Z30

Chain Links
12" x 12" Block

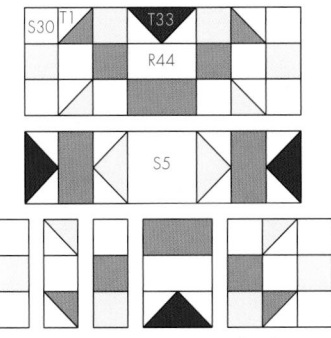

Templates Needed
R44, S5, S30, T1 & T33

Cheyenne
12" x 12" Block

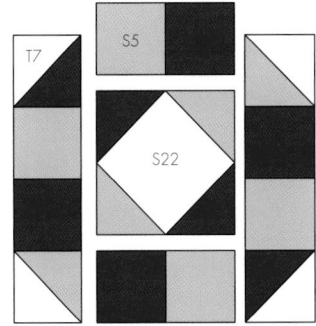

Templates Needed
S5, S22 & T7

CHILDREN OF ISRAEL PIECING INSTRUCTIONS

1. Referring to the Piecing Diagram to piece one block, sew a dark R32 to opposite sides of a light R32 to make an R unit; repeat for four R units.

2. Sew an R4 to one side of each R unit and add T13 to complete a corner unit; repeat for four corner units.

3. Sew a corner unit to opposite sides of S4 to complete a center unit.

4. Sew T15 to two adjacent sides of S12 to complete a side unit; repeat for four side units.

5. Sew a side unit to opposite sides of each of the remaining corner units; sew these units to opposite sides of the center unit to complete the block.

CHINESE PUZZLE PIECING INSTRUCTIONS

1. Referring to the Piecing Diagram to piece one block, sew T33 to two adjacent sides of S2; add T7 to the remaining sides of the pieced unit to make a T-S unit; repeat for two T-S units.

2. Add S5 to one end of each T-S unit.

3. Join a light and dark T32 with two T7 triangles to make a side unit; repeat for two side units.

4. Sew T7 to two adjacent sides of a light T32 to make an end unit; repeat for two end units.

5. Arrange the pieced units referring to the Piecing Diagram; join the units to complete the block.

CHISHOLM TRAIL PIECING INSTRUCTIONS

1. Referring to the Piecing Diagram to piece one block, sew a light T7 to a medium T7 to make a T7 unit; repeat for six units.

2. Join two T7 units with two S5 squares to complete the center unit.

3. Sew a medium T7 to two adjacent short sides of T32 to make a side unit; repeat for four side units.

4. Sew a side unit to opposite sides of the center unit.

5. Sew a T7 unit to each end of each remaining side unit; sew these units to the remaining sides of the center unit to complete the block.

CHRISTMAS STAR PIECING INSTRUCTIONS

1. Referring to the Piecing Diagram to piece one block, sew T17 to two adjacent sides of S25; add T11 to the two short sides of the pieced unit to complete a side unit; repeat for four side unit.

2. Sew a side unit to opposite sides of S14. Sew S19 to each end of the remaining side units; sew these units to the remaining sides of the S14 unit to complete the center unit.

3. Sew a light T18 to opposite short sides of a medium T18; add T11 to each end to complete a T unit. Repeat for four T units.

4. Sew a T unit to opposite sides of the center unit.

5. Sew S19 to each end of the remaining T units; sew these units to the remaining sides of the center unit to complete the block.

Children of Israel
12" x 12" Block

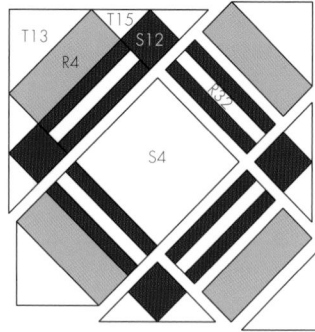

Templates Needed
R4, R32, S4, S12, T13 & T15

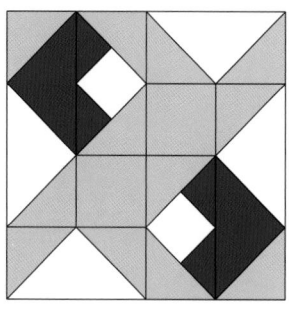

Chinese Puzzle
12" x 12" Block

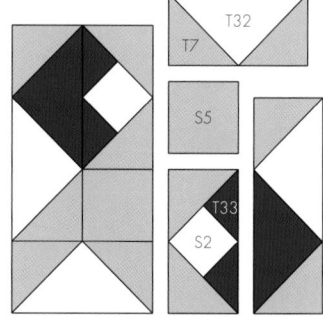

Templates Needed
S2, S5, T7, T32 & T33

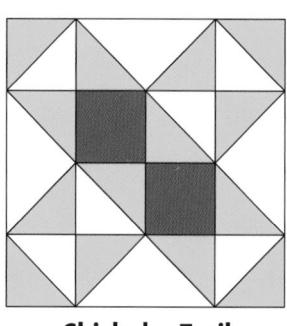

Chisholm Trail
12" x 12" Block

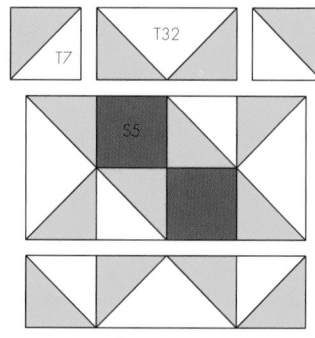

Templates Needed
S5, T7 & T32

Christmas Star
12" x 12" Block

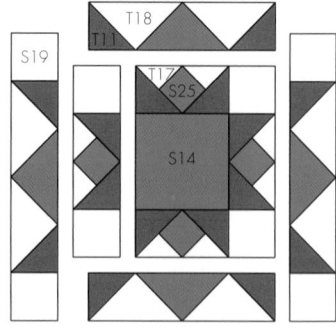

Templates Needed
S14, S19, S25,
T11, T17 & T18

COLONIAL GARDEN PIECING INSTRUCTIONS

1. Referring to the Piecing Diagram to piece one block, sew a darkest T33 to each side of S5 to make a center unit.
2. Sew a medium T33 to two adjacent short sides of a dark T7 to make a dark unit; repeat for four dark units.
3. Sew a medium T33 to two adjacent short sides of a light T7 to make a light unit; repeat for four light units.
4. Join a light unit with a dark unit and add a light T7 to make a corner unit; repeat for four corner units. Sew a corner unit to opposite sides of the center unit.
5. Sew a light T33 to two adjacent sides of S2 to make a side unit; repeat for four side units.
6. Sew a side unit to opposite sides of each of the remaining corner units; sew these units to the remaining sides of the center unit to complete the block.

COMBINATION STAR PIECING INSTRUCTIONS

1. Referring to the Piecing Diagram to piece one block, sew a light T18 to a dark T18 to make a T unit; repeat for eight T units. Join two T units to complete a side unit; repeat for four side units.
2. Sew T11 to each side of S29 to make a corner unit; repeat for four corner units.
3. Arrange the side and corner units in rows with S14; join to make rows. Join the rows to complete the block.

CONNECTION PIECING INSTRUCTIONS

1. Referring to the Piecing Diagram to piece one block, sew a light T7 to a dark T7 to make a T7 unit; repeat for four units.
2. Sew S5 to the dark side of each T7 unit to complete end units.
3. Sew a light T7 to each long side of each Z58 and Z58R piece to make two each Z and ZR units.
4. Sew a Z unit to a ZR unit to make a side unit; repeat for two side units.
5. Sew an end unit to each end of each side unit referring to the Piecing Diagram; join the pieced units to complete the block.

COOL CATS PIECING INSTRUCTIONS

1. Referring to the Piecing Diagram to piece one block, sew a light T18 to a medium T18 on the short sides; repeat for two units. Join the units to complete the center unit.
2. Sew a dark R11 to a darkest R11 to complete a side unit; repeat for four side units.
3. Sew T11 to two adjacent sides of S19 and add T19 to complete a corner unit; repeat for four corner units.
4. Sew a side unit to opposite sides of the center unit to make the center row.
5. Sew a corner unit to opposite sides of a side unit to complete a side row; repeat for two side rows.
6. Sew a side row to opposite sides of the center row to complete the block.

Colonial Garden
12" x 12" Block

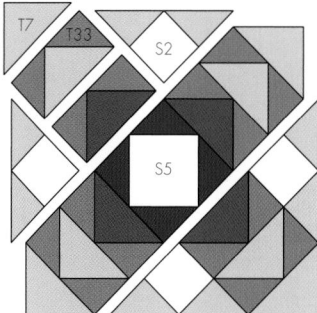

Templates Needed
S2, S5, T7 & T33

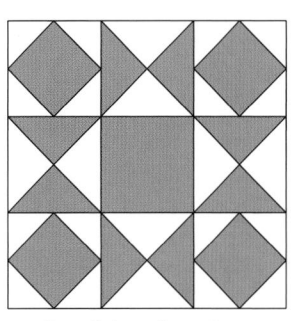

Combination Star
12" x 12" Block

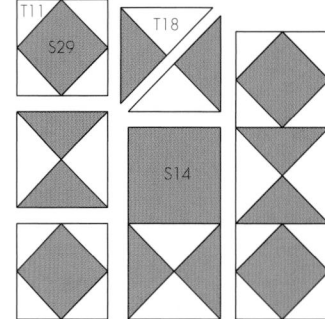

Templates Needed
S14, S29, T11 & T18

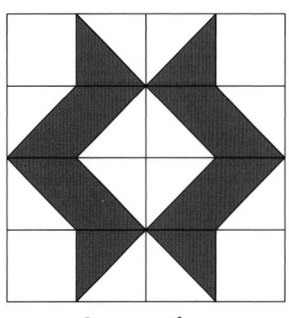

Connection
12" x 12" Block

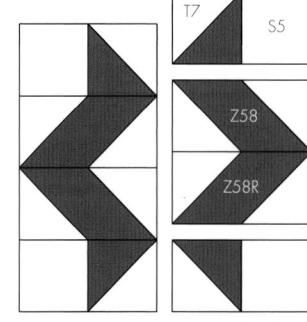

Templates Needed
S5, T7, Z58 & Z58R

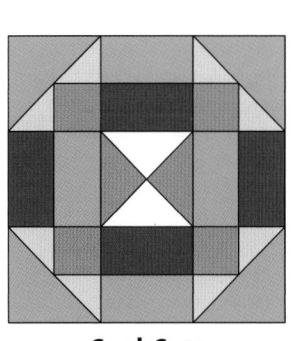

Cool Cats
12" x 12" Block

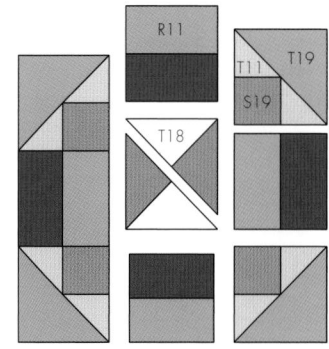

Templates Needed
R11, S19, T11, T18 & T19

CORN & BEANS PIECING INSTRUCTIONS

1. Referring to the Piecing Diagram to piece one block, join two light, two dark and one medium T11 triangles to make a dark T11 row; repeat for four rows.

2. Join two medium and three light T11 triangles to make a light T11 row; repeat for four rows.

3. Join one each light and dark T11 rows and add a light T19 to each long side to complete a light quarter unit; repeat for two light quarter units.

4. Join one each light and dark T11 rows and add a dark T19 to one long side and a light T19 to the opposite long side to complete a dark quarter unit; repeat for two dark quarter units. Join the quarter units to complete the block.

COUNTY FAIR PIECING INSTRUCTIONS

1. Referring to the Piecing Diagram to piece one block, sew T4 to two adjacent sides of S16; repeat for four units. Sew a unit to each side of S23 to complete the center unit.

2. Sew T4 to the short sides of a light T29 to make a T unit; repeat for 12 T units.

3. Sew a light T29 to a dark T29 on the short sides; repeat for two units. Join the two units to complete a T29 unit; repeat for four T29 units.

4. Sew a T unit to opposite sides of a T29 unit; add an S16 square to each end of a T unit and sew this unit to one long side of the pieced unit to complete a side unit; repeat for four side units.

5. Sew a side unit to opposite sides of the center unit. Sew S11 to opposite sides of the remaining side units; sew these units to the remaining sides of the center unit to complete the block.

COURTHOUSE STEPS STAR PIECING INSTRUCTIONS

1. Referring to the Piecing Diagram to piece one block, sew a light R41 to opposite sides of S19.

2. Sew an S3 square to each end of the remaining R41 pieces; repeat for two units. Sew these units to the remaining sides of the stitched unit.

3. Repeat steps 1 and 2 with the R7 and S3 pieces; sew to the center unit.

4. Repeat steps 1 and 2 with the R16 and S3 pieces; sew to the center unit.

5. Sew a dark T11 to a light T11 on the diagonal; repeat for eight T11 units. Sew a medium T11 to the short sides of T18 to make a side unit; repeat for four side units.

6. Sew a T11 unit to each short end of a side unit. Sew a T11 side unit to opposite sides of the pieced center.

7. Sew S19 to opposite ends of the remaining T11 side units; sew these units to the remaining sides of the pieced unit to complete the block.

CROSS PIECING INSTRUCTIONS

1. Referring to the Piecing Diagram to piece one block, sew R57 to opposite sides of S29. Sew S25 to each end of the remaining R57 pieces. Sew these units to the remaining sides of S29 to complete the center unit.

2. Sew T17 to opposite short sides of Z61 and add R17 to complete a corner unit; repeat for four corner units.

3. Sew a corner unit to opposite sides of the center unit.

4. Sew T18 to the R17 ends of the remaining corner units and add these units to the remaining sides of the center unit to complete the block.

Corn & Beans
12" x 12" Block

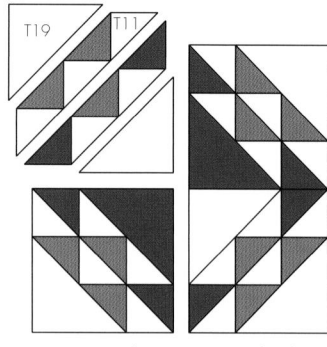

Templates Needed
T11 & T19

County Fair
12" x 12" Block

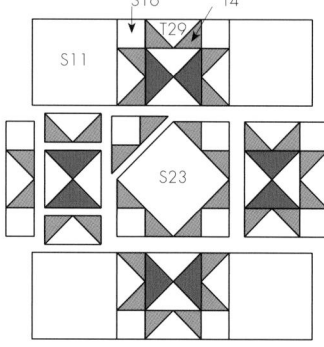

Templates Needed
S11, S16, S23, T4 & T29

Courthouse Steps Star
12" x 12" Block

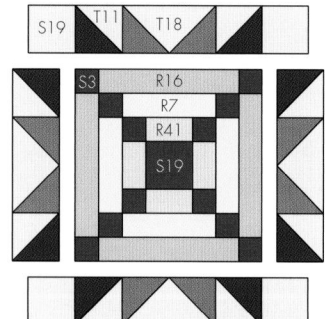

Templates Needed
R7, R16, R41, S3,
S19, T11 & T18

Cross
12" x 12" Block

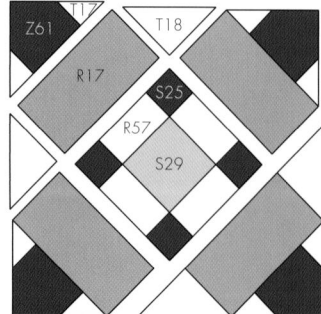

Templates Needed
R17, R57, S25,
S29, T17, T18 & Z61

CROSSED SQUARES PIECING INSTRUCTIONS

1. Referring to the Piecing Diagram to piece one block, join two light T42 triangles on the short ends to make a light T42 unit; repeat for four light T42 units. Repeat with one light and one dark T42 to make a dark T42 unit; repeat for four dark T42 units.

2. Join one light and one dark T42 unit with one dark T42 and one R18 to complete a corner unit; repeat for four corner units.

3. Sew T29 to two adjacent sides of a light S32 to complete an S-T unit; repeat for four S-T units.

4. Sew a dark S32 to a light S32 and add T29 to complete an S unit; repeat for four S units.

5. Sew an S unit to an S-T unit to complete a side unit referring to the Piecing Diagram; repeat for four side units.

6. Sew a corner unit to opposite sides of S23 to complete the center row.

7. Sew a side unit to opposite sides of the remaining corner units; sew these units to opposite sides of the center row to complete the block.

CROSSROADS PIECING INSTRUCTIONS

1. Referring to the Piecing Diagram to piece one block, sew a dark T7 to each side of S22 to make the center unit.

2. Join two light and two medium R44 pieces to make a side unit; repeat for four side units.

3. Sew a side unit to opposite sides of the center unit.

4. Sew a light T7 to a dark T7 to make a corner unit; repeat for four corner units.

5. Sew a corner unit to each end of the remaining side units; sew these units to the remaining sides of the center unit to complete the block.

CUBE LATTICE PIECING INSTRUCTIONS

1. Referring to the Piecing Diagram to piece one block, sew a light Z56R to a medium Z56 and a light S30; repeat for eight medium Z units.

2. Sew a light Z56 to a medium Z56R and set in a light S30; repeat for eight light Z units.

3. Join two light Z units and two medium Z units with two T33 triangles to make a quarter unit; repeat for four quarter units.

4. Join the quarter units with the dark S2 squares to complete the block.

CUBES & TILES PIECING INSTRUCTIONS

1. Referring to the Piecing Diagram to piece one block, sew a light S30 to a dark S30 to make an S unit; repeat for 14 S units.

2. Join two S units to make a Four-Patch unit; repeat for five Four-Patch units.

3. Sew a dark T1 to each side of S2 to make an S-T unit; repeat for four S-T units.

4. Sew an S unit to one side of an S-T unit; repeat for two units. Sew these units to opposite sides of one Four-Patch unit to complete the center row.

5. Sew T1 to two adjacent short sides of T33 to make a T unit; repeat for eight T units. Sew a T unit to one side of a Four-Patch unit. Sew a dark S30 square to a T unit and add to the pieced unit to complete a corner unit; repeat for four corner units.

6. Sew an S unit to an S-T unit to make a side unit; repeat for two side units.

7. Sew a side unit between two corner units to make a side row; repeat for two side rows. Sew a side row to opposite sides of the center row to complete one block.

Crossed Squares
12" x 12" Block

Templates Needed
R18, S23, S32, T29 & T42

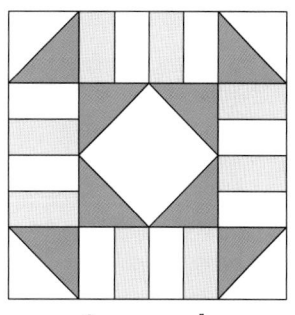

Crossroads
12" x 12" Block

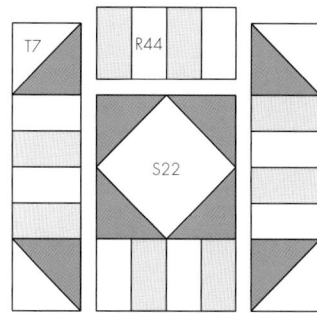

Templates Needed
R44, S22 & T7

Cube Lattice
12" x 12" Block

Templates Needed
S2, S30, T33, Z56 & Z56R

Cubes & Tiles
12" x 12" Block

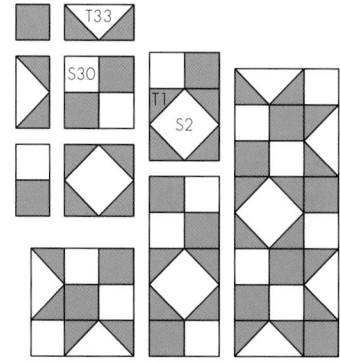

Templates Needed
S2, S30, T1 & T33

CUT GLASS DISH PIECING INSTRUCTIONS

1. Referring to the Piecing Diagram to piece one block, sew a light T11 to a medium T11 to make a T unit; repeat for 24 T units.

2. Join four T units to complete a pieced unit; repeat for six pieced units.

3. Arrange the pieced units with S14 in rows referring to the Piecing Diagram; join to make rows. Join the rows to complete the block.

DANCING DIAMONDS PIECING INSTRUCTIONS

1. Referring to the Piecing Diagram to piece one block, sew a light T7 to a medium T7 to make a T7 unit; repeat for four T7 units.

2. Sew a T7 unit to each end of R21 to make a side row; repeat for two side rows.

3. Sew a light T7 to two adjacent sides of S22; sew T32 to one remaining side; repeat for two units. Join these units to complete the center row.

4. Sew a side row to opposite sides of the center row to complete the block.

DEPRESSION PIECING INSTRUCTIONS

1. Referring to the Piecing Diagram to piece one block, sew a light T7 to a dark Z30 to a medium Z30 to a dark T7 to make a corner unit; repeat for four corner units.

2. Join the corner units with light T7 toward the center to complete the block.

DIAMONDS GALORE PIECING INSTRUCTIONS

1. Referring to the Piecing Diagram to piece one block, sew a light T7 to a dark T7 to make a corner unit; repeat for four corner units.

2. Sew a light T33 to two adjacent sides of a dark S2; repeat for four units.

3. Join a dark T33 to a dark T33 on the short sides; repeat for four and four reversed units.

4. Sew a T33 unit and a T33R unit to two adjacent sides of a T33-S2 unit to make a side unit; repeat for four side units.

5. Sew a dark T7 to each side of S22 to complete the center unit.

6. Sew a side unit to opposite sides of the center unit.

7. Sew a corner unit to opposite ends of a side unit; repeat for two units. Sew these units to opposite sides of the center unit to complete the block.

Cut Glass Dish
12" x 12" Block

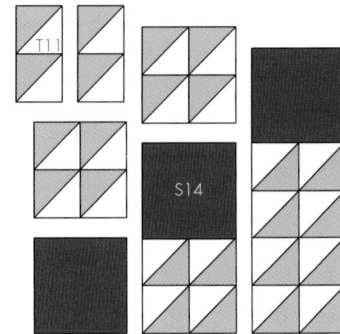

Templates Needed
S14 & T11

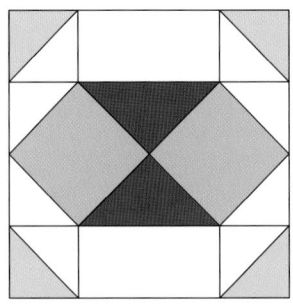

Dancing Diamonds
12" x 12" Block

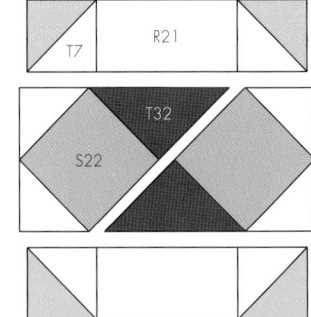

Templates Needed
R21, S22, T7 & T32

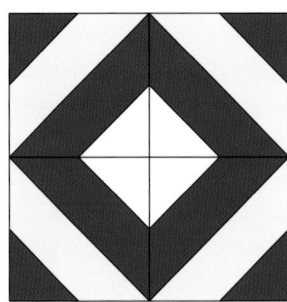

Depression
12" x 12" Block

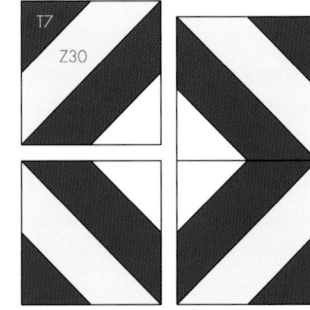

Templates Needed
T7 & Z30

Diamonds Galore
12" x 12" Block

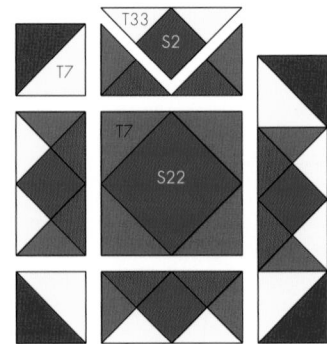

Templates Needed
S2, S22, T7 & T33

DOGTOOTH VIOLET PIECING INSTRUCTIONS

1. Referring to the Piecing Diagram to piece one block, sew T33 to each short side of Z41 to make a corner unit; repeat for four corner units.

2. Sew a corner unit to opposite sides of S22 to make the center row.

3. Sew S2 on the T33 sides of the remaining corner units.

4. Sew the corner units to the center row.

5. Set in T24 and T24R between Z41 and S2 pieces to complete the block.

DOMINO PIECING INSTRUCTIONS

1. Referring to the Piecing Diagram to piece one block, sew a dark S19 between two light S19 squares to make row 1; repeat for two rows.

2. Sew a light S19 between two dark S19 squares to make row 2; repeat for two rows.

3. Sew a light S19 to one end of R11 to make an R11 unit; repeat for four R11 units.

4. Join one row 1, one row 2 and one R11 unit to make one S19 quarter unit; repeat for two S19 quarter units.

5. Sew R11 to one side of S14; sew an R11 unit to two adjacent sides of S14 to complete an S14 quarter unit; repeat for two S14 quarter units.

6. Join the quarter units to complete one block referring to the Piecing Diagram.

DOMINO & SQUARE PIECING INSTRUCTIONS

1. Referring to the Piecing Diagram to piece one block, sew R18 to a medium S23 and add T42 to make a corner unit; repeat for four corner units.

2. Sew a corner unit to opposite sides of the dark S23 to make the center row.

3. Sew a dark S32 to a light S32 and add T29; repeat for four S-T units.

4. Sew a dark T29 to two adjacent short sides of a light S32 to make a T-T-S unit; repeat for four T-T-S units.

5. Sew a T-T-S unit to an S-T unit to complete a side unit; repeat for four side units.

6. Sew a side unit to opposite sides of each remaining corner unit. Sew these units to opposite sides of the center row to complete the block.

DORIS' DELIGHT PIECING INSTRUCTIONS

1. Referring to the Piecing Diagram to piece one block, sew T16 and T16R to the long sides of T56 to complete a side unit; repeat for four side units.

2. Sew a light T19 to a dark T19 to complete a corner unit; repeat for four corner units.

3. Sew a side unit to opposite sides of S14 to complete the center row.

4. Sew a corner unit to opposite sides of each of the remaining side units to complete two side rows.

5. Sew a side row to opposite sides of the center row to complete the block.

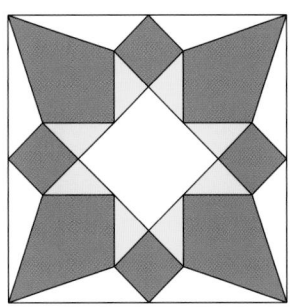

Dogtooth Violet
12" x 12" Block

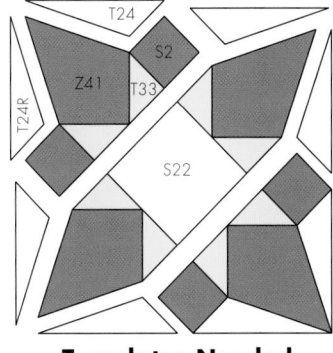

Templates Needed
S2, S22, T24,
T24R, T33 & Z41

Domino
12" x 12" Block

Templates Needed
R11, S14 & S19

Domino & Square
12" x 12" Block

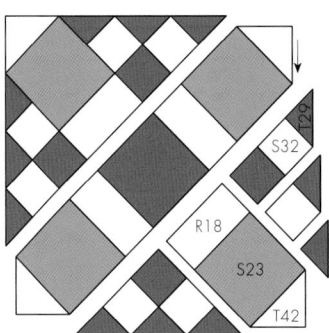

Templates Needed
R18, S23, S32, T29 & T42

Doris' Delight
12" x 12" Block

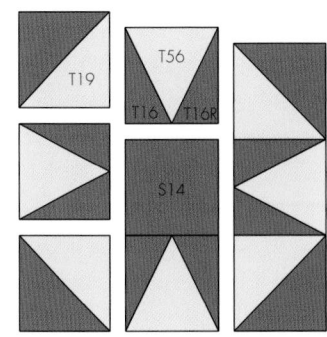

Templates Needed
S14, T16, T16R, T19 & T56

DOUBLE SAWTOOTH PIECING INSTRUCTIONS

1. Referring to the Piecing Diagram to piece one block, sew a light T42 to a dark T42 to make a T42 unit; repeat for 12 units.

2. Join three T42 units to make a side unit; repeat for four side units.

3. Sew a side unit to opposite sides of S26 to complete the center row.

4. Sew a light S8 to the dark end and a dark S8 to the light end of each remaining side unit to make a side row.

5. Sew the center row between the two side rows to complete the block.

DOUBLE T PIECING INSTRUCTIONS

1. Referring to the Piecing Diagram to piece one block, sew T33 to two adjacent sides of S5; repeat for four S5 units.

2. Sew T33 to two adjacent short sides of T7; repeat for four T7 units. Sew the T7 side of a T7 unit to the T33 side of an S5 unit to complete a corner unit; repeat for four corner units.

3. Sew a corner unit to opposite sides of S22 to complete the center row.

4. Sew T32 to opposite sides of the remaining corner units; sew these units to opposite sides of the center row to complete the block.

DOUBLE Z PIECING INSTRUCTIONS

1. Referring to the Piecing Diagram to piece one block, join two dark and one light T32 and add T7 to each end to make a side row; repeat for two side rows.

2. Sew Z58 and Z58R to the short sides of T32 to complete a Z unit; repeat for two Z units. Join the two Z units and set T32 in at the ends to complete the center row.

3. Sew a side row to opposite sides of the center row to complete the block.

DOVE IN THE WINDOW PIECING INSTRUCTIONS

1. Referring to the Piecing Diagram to piece one block, sew a light T29 to a dark T29 to make a T unit; repeat for 16 units. Sew the two units together to make eight T units.

2. Sew a T unit to one side of S23 to make an S-T unit; sew S32 to the light end of one T unit and sew this unit to the S-T unit to complete a corner unit. Repeat for four corner units.

3. Join two corner units with R22 to make a side row; repeat for two side rows.

4. Join two R22 pieces with S32 to make the center row. Join the two side rows with the center row to complete the block.

Double Sawtooth
12" x 12" Block

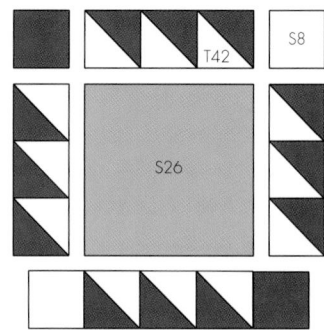

Templates Needed
S8, S26 & T42

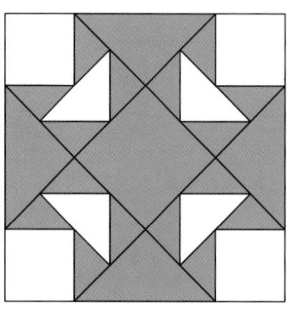

Double T
12" x 12" Block

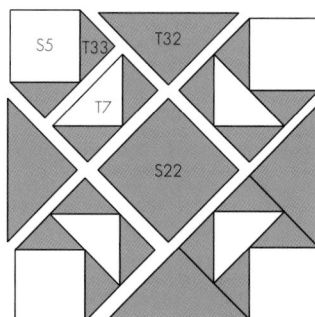

Templates Needed
S5, S22, T7, T32 & T33

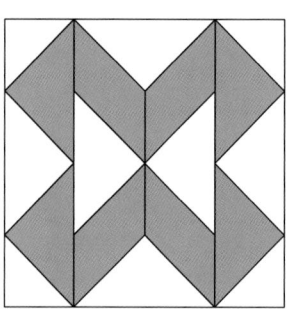

Double Z
12" x 12" Block

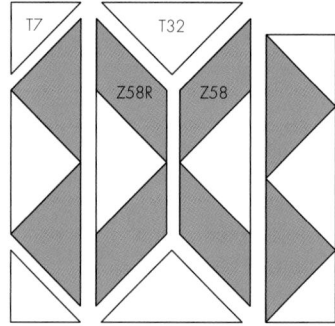

Templates Needed
T7, T32, Z58 & Z58R

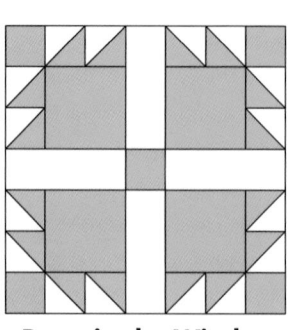

Dove in the Window
12" x 12" Block

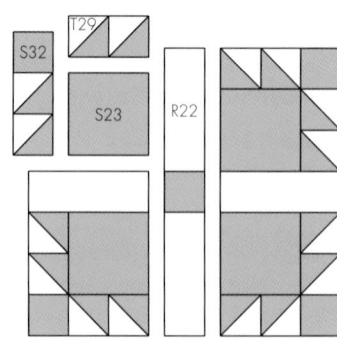

Templates Needed
R22, S23, S32 & T29

DUCK & DUCKLING PIECING INSTRUCTIONS

1. Referring to the Piecing Diagram to piece one block, alternate and join three dark and two light S8 squares to make the center strip.

2. Sew a light S8 to a dark S8 to make a side unit; repeat for four side units.

3. Sew a light T42 to each side of a dark T42 and add T40 to complete a corner unit; repeat for four corner units.

4. Sew a side unit between two corner units to make a side strip; repeat for two side strips.

5. Sew the center strip between two side strips to complete the block.

EASY DO PIECING INSTRUCTIONS

1. Referring to the Piecing Diagram to piece one block, sew a lightest S16 to a dark S16; repeat for eight units. Join two units to make a Four-Patch unit. Repeat for four lightest units. Repeat with light S16 and dark S16 to make four light units.

2. Sew a T4 to the short side of Z3 and Z3R. Sew these units to two adjacent sides of a light Four-Patch unit to make a triangle unit; repeat for four units.

3. Sew T42 to two adjacent sides of each of the lightest Four-Patch units. Sew one of these units to a triangle unit to complete a corner unit; repeat for four corner units.

4. Join two R13 pieces with S8 to make the center row.

5. Join two corner units with R13 to make a side row; repeat for two side rows.

6. Sew the center row between two side rows to complete the block.

EDDYSTONE LIGHT PIECING INSTRUCTIONS

1. Referring to the Piecing Diagram to piece one block, sew a light T11 to two adjacent sides of a medium T18 to complete a T unit; repeat for four T units.

2. Sew a T unit to opposite sides of S14. Sew S19 to each end of the remaining T units; sew these units to the remaining sides of S14 to complete the center unit.

3. Join two light and one dark T18 triangles; add a dark T11 to each light end to make a side unit. Repeat for four side units.

4. Sew a side unit to opposite sides of the center unit.

5. Sew S19 to each end of each remaining side unit; sew these units to the remaining sides of the center unit to complete the block.

EIGHT HANDS AROUND PIECING INSTRUCTIONS

1. Referring to the Piecing Diagram to piece one block, sew T1 to two adjacent short sides of T33 to make a T unit; repeat for four T units. Sew a T unit to opposite sides of S5.

2. Sew S30 to each end of the remaining T units; sew these units to the remaining sides of S5 to complete the center unit.

3. Sew a dark T7 to two adjacent short sides of T32 to make a side unit; repeat for four side units. Sew a side unit to opposite sides of the center unit to make the center row.

4. Sew a light T7 to a dark T7 to make a corner unit; repeat for four corner units.

5. Sew a corner unit to each end of the remaining side units to make side rows.

6. Sew the center row between two side rows to complete one block.

Duck & Duckling
12" x 12" Block

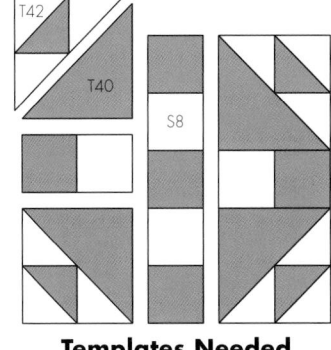

Templates Needed
S8, T40 & T42

Easy Do
12" x 12" Block

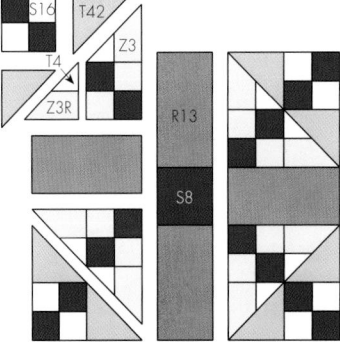

Templates Needed
R13, S8, S16, T4,
T42, Z3 & Z3R

Eddystone Light
12" x 12" Block

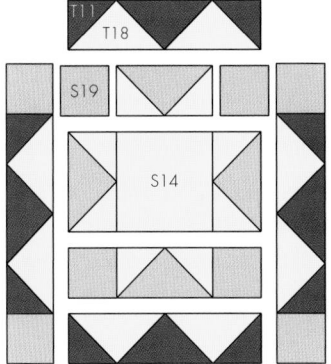

Templates Needed
S14, S19, T11 & T18

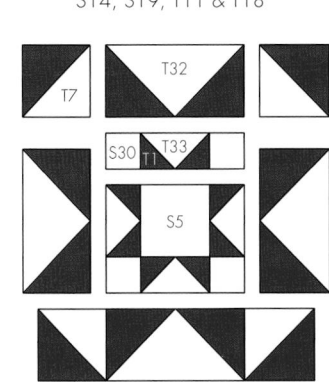

Eight Hands Around
12" x 12" Block

Templates Needed
S5, S30, T1, T7, T32 & T33

EIGHT-POINTED STAR PIECING INSTRUCTIONS

1. Referring to the Piecing Diagram to piece one block, sew T33 to two adjacent sides of S5; repeat for four S5 units.

2. Sew T33 to two adjacent short sides of T7; repeat for four T7 units.

3. Sew a T7 unit to the T33 side of an S5 unit to complete a corner unit; repeat for four corner units.

4. Sew a corner unit to opposite sides of S22 to make the center row.

5. Sew T32 to the sides of each remaining corner unit; sew these units to opposite sides of the center row to complete the block.

ELECTRIC FAN PIECING INSTRUCTIONS

1. Referring to the Piecing Diagram to piece one block, sew a light T32 to a medium T32 on the short sides to make a light T32 unit; repeat for four units.

2. Sew a dark T32 to a light T32 on the short sides to make a dark T32 unit; repeat for four units.

3. Sew a light T32 unit to a dark T32 unit to complete a block quarter; repeat for four quarters.

4. Join the quarter sections to complete the block.

EMPIRE STAR PIECING INSTRUCTIONS

1. Referring to the Piecing Diagram to piece one block, sew Z58 and Z58R to the short sides of a light T32 and add T7 to each end to make a side row; repeat for two side rows.

2. Sew a light T32 to opposite sides of S22.

3. Sew a light T32 to a dark T32 on the short sides; repeat for two T32 units.

4. Sew a T32 unit to opposite sides of the S22 unit to complete the center row.

5. Sew the center row between the two side rows to complete the block.

EVENING STAR PIECING INSTRUCTIONS

1. Referring to the Piecing Diagram to piece one block, sew a dark T49 to a medium T49 on the short sides; add a light T49 to each medium side to complete a side unit; repeat for four side units.

2. Sew a dark T49 to a medium T49 on the short sides; add a lightest T49 to each dark T49 side and add T13 to the lightest end to complete a corner unit; repeat for four corner units.

3. Join the corner and side units referring to the Piecing Diagram to complete the block.

Eight-Pointed Star
12" x 12" Block

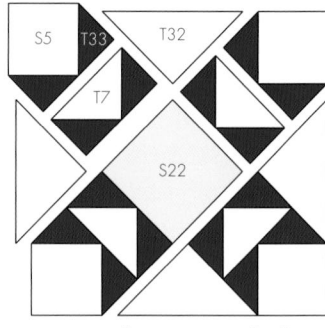

Templates Needed
S5, S22, T7, T32 & T33

Electric Fan
12" x 12" Block

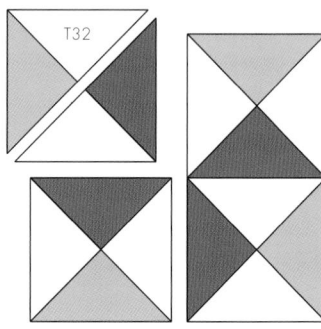

Template Needed
T32

Empire Star
12" x 12" Block

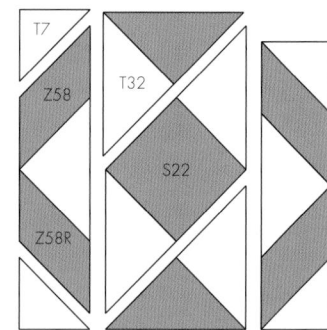

Templates Needed
S22, T7, T32, Z58 & Z58R

Evening Star
12" x 12" Block

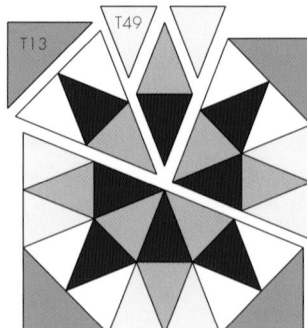

Templates Needed
T13 & T49

EVERYBODY'S FAVORITE PIECING INSTRUCTIONS

1. Referring to the Piecing Diagram to piece one block, sew Z61 to opposite sides of S12.

2. Sew T17 to opposite short sides of Z61; repeat for two units. Sew these units to the remaining sides of S12 to complete the center unit.

3. Sew a dark R56 between two light R56 pieces to complete a side unit; repeat for four side units.

4. Sew a medium T7 to a dark T7 to make a corner unit; repeat for four corner units.

5. Sew a side unit to opposite sides of the center unit.

6. Sew a corner unit to each end of each remaining side unit; sew these pieced units to the remaining sides of the pieced center to complete the block.

FALL FANTASY PIECING INSTRUCTIONS

1. Referring to the Piecing Diagram to piece one block, sew a light S5 to a medium S5; repeat for four S5 units.

2. Sew a light R44 to a medium R44 and add a dark S5; repeat for four R44 units.

3. Sew an R44 unit to an S5 unit to complete a block quarter; repeat for four quarters.

4. Join the quarter sections to complete the block.

FANCY FLOWERS PIECING INSTRUCTIONS

1. Referring to the Piecing Diagram to piece one block, sew a medium Z48 to a dark Z48R and set in T42 to make a medium T-Z unit. Repeat for four medium T-Z units.

2. Sew a dark Z48 to a medium Z48R and set in T42 to make a dark T-Z unit; repeat for four dark T-Z units.

3. Join a medium and dark T-Z unit and set in a light S32; add T12 to make a corner unit. Repeat for four corner units.

4. Join two corner units with R22 to make a side row; repeat for two side rows.

5. Join two R22 pieces with the medium S32 to make a center row.

6. Join two side rows with the center row to complete the block.

FANNY'S FAVORITE PIECING INSTRUCTIONS

1. Referring to the Piecing Diagram to piece one block, sew T5 to each short side of T17 to make a T unit; repeat for four T units.

2. Sew R11 to opposite sides of S19 and add a T unit to each end to make the center row.

3. Sew a T unit to one end of the remaining R11 pieces to complete two side units.

4. Sew T11 to two adjacent sides of S19 to make an S-T unit; repeat for four S-T units.

5. Sew R7 to one short side of T19; sew S3 to one end of R7. Join these two units to complete an R-T unit; Repeat for four R-T units.

6. Sew an R-T unit to an S-T unit to complete a corner unit; repeat for four corner units.

7. Join two corner units with a side unit to complete a side row; repeat for two side rows.

8. Sew the center row between two side rows to complete the block.

Everybody's Favorite
12" x 12" Block

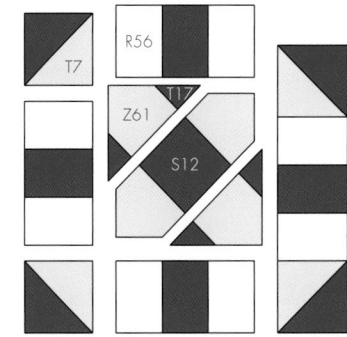

Templates Needed
R56, S12, T7, T17 & Z61

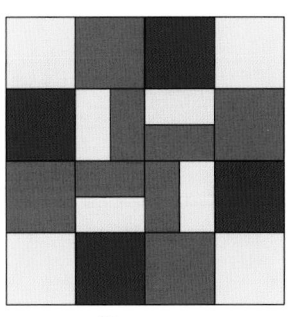

Fall Fantasy
12" x 12" Block

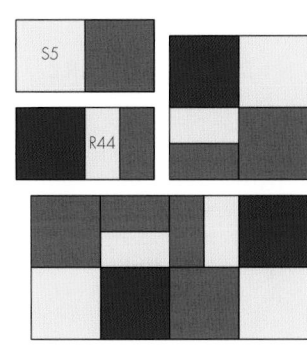

Templates Needed
R44 & S5

Fancy Flowers
12" x 12" Block

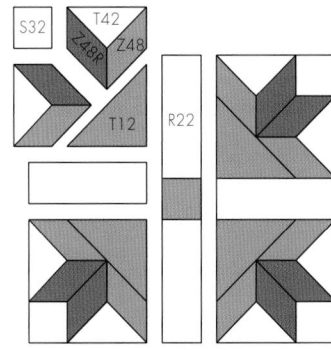

Templates Needed
R22, S32, T12,
T42, Z48 & Z48R

Fanny's Favorite
12" x 12" Block

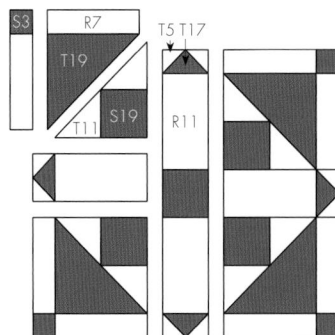

Templates Needed
R7, R11, S3, S19,
T5, T11, T17 & T19

FATHER'S CHOICE PIECING INSTRUCTIONS

1. Referring to the Piecing Diagram to piece one block, join two light and three dark S8 squares to make the center row.

2. Sew a light S8 to a dark S8 to make a side row; repeat for two side rows.

3. Sew a light T42 to a medium T42 to make a T42 unit; repeat for eight T42 units.

4. Sew a T42 unit to a medium S8 and a T42 unit to a light S8; join these two units to complete a corner unit. Repeat for four corner units.

5. Sew a side unit between two corner units to make a side row; repeat for two side rows.

6. Sew the center row between the side rows to complete the block.

FEDERAL SQUARE PIECING INSTRUCTIONS

1. Referring to the Piecing Diagram to piece one block, sew a medium T33 to each side of S5 to complete the center unit.

2. Sew a medium T33 to two adjacent sides and a dark T33 to the remaining adjacent sides of S5; add T7 to make a corner unit. Repeat for four corner units.

3. Sew a lightest T33 to two adjacent sides of S2 to make a side unit; repeat for four side units.

4. Sew a corner unit to opposite sides of the center unit to make the center row.

5. Sew a side unit to opposite sides of the remaining corner units; sew these units to opposite sides of the center row to complete the block.

FIREFLIES PIECING INSTRUCTIONS

1. Referring to the Piecing Diagram to piece one block, sew a light T7 to each side of a darkest T7; add T39 to complete a T corner unit. Repeat for two T corner units.

2. Sew a dark T7 to a light T7 to complete one T7 unit; repeat for four T7 units.

3. Sew one T7 unit to a dark S5 and one to a darkest S5; join these two units to complete an S corner unit. Repeat for two S corner units.

4. Join the S and T corner units to complete the block.

FIVE SPOT PIECING INSTRUCTIONS

1. Referring to the Piecing Diagram to piece one block, sew T11 to each side of S29 to complete an S-T unit; repeat for five S-T units.

2. Sew T11 to two adjacent sides of S19 and add T19 to the T11 sides to complete a corner unit; repeat for four corner units.

3. Join three S-T units to make the center row.

4. Sew an S-T unit between two corner units to complete a side row; repeat for two side rows.

5. Sew the center row between the two side rows to complete the block.

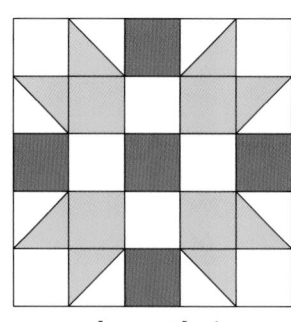

Father's Choice
12" x 12" Block

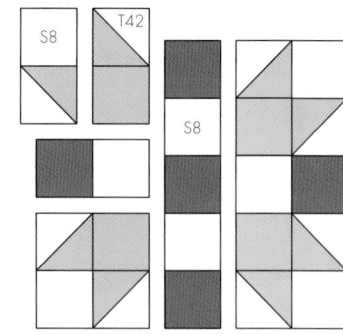

Templates Needed
S8 & T42

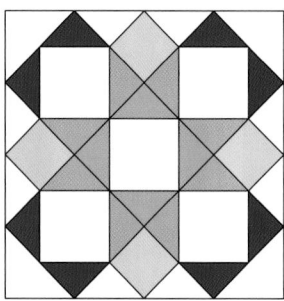

Federal Square
12" x 12" Block

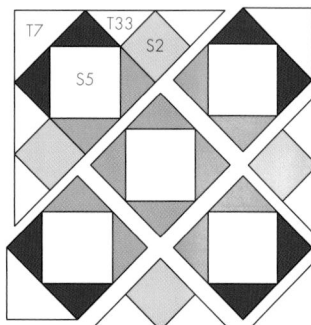

Templates Needed
S2, S5, T7 & T33

Fireflies
12" x 12" Block

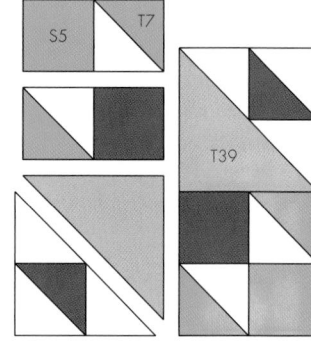

Templates Needed
S5, T7, T39

Five Spot
12" x 12" Block

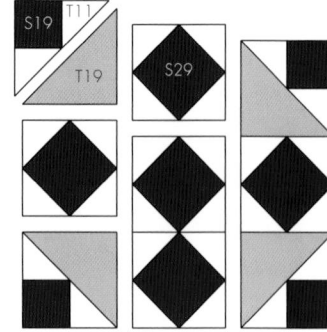

Templates Needed
S19, S29, T11 & T19

FLATIRON PATCHWORK PIECING INSTRUCTIONS

1. Referring to the Piecing Diagram to piece one block, join two dark and three light S19 squares and one T11 to make row 1.

2. Join two dark and two light S19 squares and one T11 to make row 2.

3. Join one dark and two light S19 squares and one T11 to make row 3.

4. Join one light and one dark S19 squares and one T11 to make row 4.

5. Sew T11 to a light S19 to make row 5.

6. Join the rows with one T11 to complete half the block.

7. Sew a light T19 to a dark T19 to make a corner unit; sew the corner unit to Z13.

8. Sew a dark T19 to Z13R and join with the previously pieced unit to complete the second half of the block.

9. Join the two pieced halves to complete the block.

FLOWERPOT PIECING INSTRUCTIONS

1. Referring to the Piecing Diagram to piece one block, sew a dark T33 to each side of a light T33 and add a light T7 to two sides to complete a side unit; repeat for four side units.

2. Sew a light T7 to a medium T7 to complete a corner unit; repeat for four corner units.

3. Sew a side unit to opposite sides of S21.

4. Sew a corner unit to each end of each of the remaining side units; sew these units to the remaining sides of S21 to complete the block.

FLYING GEESE STAR PIECING INSTRUCTIONS

1. Referring to the Piecing Diagram to piece one block, sew T11 to each short side of T18; repeat for eight units.

2. Join two same-fabric T11-T18 units; repeat for four units.

3. Join the four pieced units to complete the block center.

4. Sew a dark T11 to a light T11 on the diagonal; repeat for eight T11 units.

5. Sew a medium T11 to the short sides of T18 to make a side unit; repeat for four side units.

6. Sew a T11 unit to each short end of a side unit. Sew a T11 side unit to opposite sides of the pieced center.

7. Sew S19 to opposite ends of the remaining T11 side units; sew these units to the remaining sides of the pieced unit to complete the block.

FLYING SHUTTLES PIECING INSTRUCTIONS

1. Referring to the Piecing Diagram to piece one block, sew a light T11 to each side of S12 to complete an S unit; repeat for three S units.

2. Sew a light T11 to a dark T11 to complete one T unit; repeat for 12 T units.

3. Sew S19 to the dark side of a T unit; repeat with S19 on the light side of a T unit referring to the Piecing Diagram. Join the pieced units to complete an S-T unit; repeat for six S-T units.

4. Arrange the S-T units with the S units in rows referring to the Piecing Diagram; join in rows. Join the rows to complete the block.

Flatiron Patchwork
12" x 12" Block

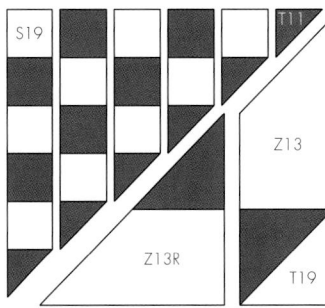

Templates Needed
S19, T11, T19, Z13 & Z13R

Flowerpot
12" x 12" Block

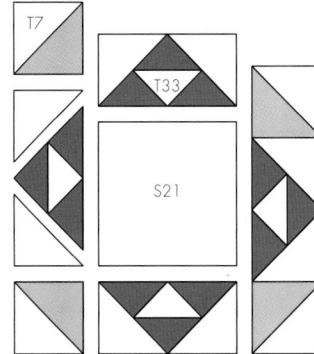

Templates Needed
S21, T7 & T33

Flying Geese Star
12" x 12" Block

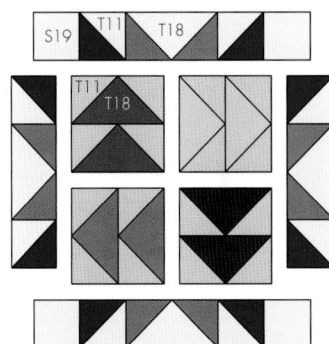

Templates Needed
S19, T11 & T18

Flying Shuttles
12" x 12" Block

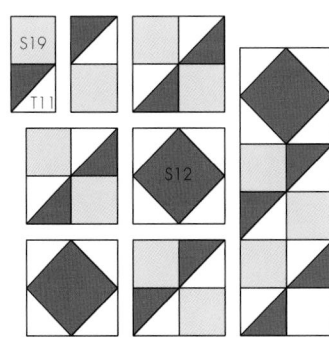

Templates Needed
S12, S19 & T11

FOOL'S PUZZLE PIECING INSTRUCTIONS

1. Referring to the Piecing Diagram to piece one block, join two dark and one light T32 and add T7 to make a side row; repeat for two side rows.

2. Sew a light T32 to a dark T32 on the short ends; repeat for two T32 units. Join the two units to complete the center unit.

3. Sew T7 to two short sides of a dark T32 to make a side unit; repeat for two side units.

4. Sew a side unit to opposite sides of the center unit; add a side row to opposite sides to complete the block.

FOOL'S SQUARE PIECING INSTRUCTIONS

1. Referring to the Piecing Diagram to piece one block, sew a dark S8 between two light S8 squares to make the center row.

2. Sew a light S8 between two medium S8 squares to make a side row; repeat for two side rows. Sew a side row to opposite sides of the center row to complete the center unit.

3. Sew a medium T42 to each end of Z21 to complete a side unit; repeat for four side units. Sew a side unit to opposite sides of the center unit.

4. Sew a dark T42 to a light T42 to make a T unit; repeat for four T units. Sew a T unit to each end of the remaining side units; sew these units to the center unit to complete the block.

FOOTSTOOL PIECING INSTRUCTIONS

1. Referring to the Piecing Diagram to piece one block, join two light and two dark T29 triangles to make a T29 unit; repeat for four T29 units.

2. Join two T29 units with three S8 squares to make the center row.

3. Sew a T29 unit to an S8 square to make a side unit; repeat for two side units.

4. Sew a light T42 to a dark T42 to make a T42 unit; repeat for 12 T42 units.

5. Join three T42 units with an S8 square to make a corner unit; repeat for four corner units.

6. Join two corner units with a side unit to make a side row; repeat for two side rows.

7. Sew the center row between two side rows to complete the block.

FOUR BIRDS PIECING INSTRUCTIONS

1. Referring to the Piecing Diagram to piece one block, sew a lightest T29 to a medium T29 to make a T29 unit; repeat for 16 T29 units.

2. Join two T29 units; repeat for two units. Sew the medium side of a T29 unit to S23. Sew S32 to the light end of a second T29 unit; sew this unit to the adjacent side of S23 to complete a corner unit. Repeat for four corner units.

3. Join two corner units with R22 to complete a side row; repeat for two side rows.

4. Join the remaining two R22 pieces to opposite sides of S32 to complete the center row.

5. Sew the center row between the two side rows to complete the block.

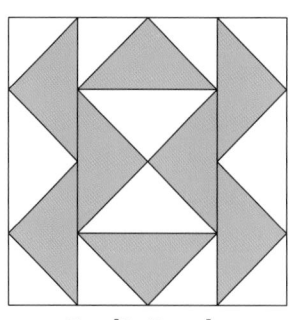

Fool's Puzzle
12" x 12" Block

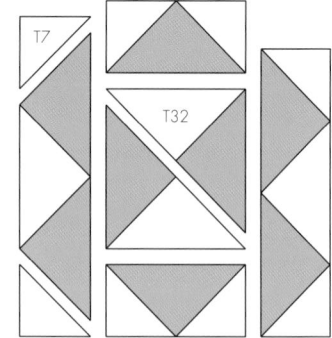

Templates Needed
T7 & T32

Fool's Square
12" x 12" Block

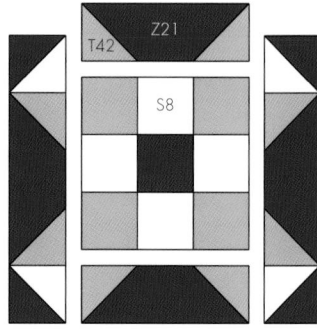

Templates Needed
S8, T42 & Z21

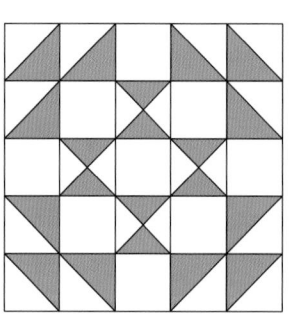

Footstool
12" x 12" Block

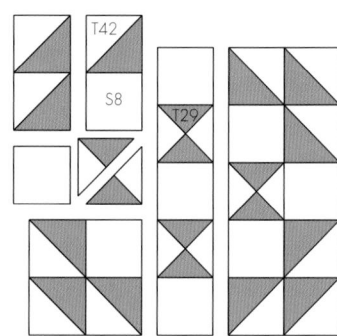

Templates Needed
S8, T29 & T42

Four Birds
12" x 12" Block

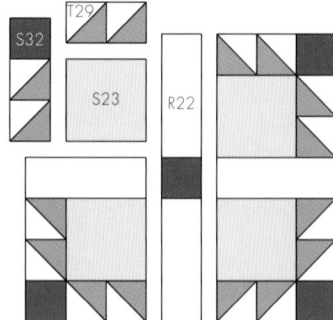

Templates Needed
R22, S23, S32 & T29

FOUR-PATCH STAR PIECING INSTRUCTIONS

1. Referring to the Piecing Diagram to piece one block, sew a dark S19 to a light S19; repeat for eight units.

2. Join two S19 units; press; repeat for four joined units. Join the four units to complete the block center.

3. Sew a dark T11 to a light T11 on the diagonal; repeat for eight T11 units.

4. Sew a medium T11 to the short sides of T18 to make a side unit; repeat for four side units.

5. Sew a T11 unit to each short end of a side unit. Sew a T11 side unit to opposite sides of the pieced center.

6. Sew S19 to opposite ends of the remaining T11 side units; sew these units to the remaining sides of the pieced unit to complete the block.

Four-Patch Star
12" x 12" Block

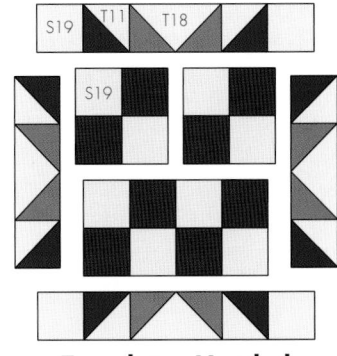

Templates Needed
S19, T11 & T18

FOUR QUEENS PIECING INSTRUCTIONS

1. Referring to the Piecing Diagram to piece one block, sew R14 to opposite sides of S24. Sew S16 to each end of the remaining R14 pieces; sew these units to the remaining sides of S24.

2. Sew T4 to each angled end of Z24; repeat for two units. Add T12 to the Z24 edge of each unit. Sew these units to the R14-S16 sides of the pieced S24 unit to complete the center unit.

3. Sew a lightest T29 to each end of the remaining Z24 pieces; add T12 to the Z24 edges. Sew these units to opposite sides of the center unit.

4. Sew a medium T29 to two adjacent short sides of T42 to make a T42 unit; repeat for eight T42 units.

5. Sew S32 between two T42 units to make a row; repeat for two rows. Sew a row to opposite sides of the center unit.

6. Sew S32 between two T42 units and add S32 at each end to make a row; repeat for two rows. Sew a row to the remaining sides of the center unit to complete the block.

Four Queens
12" x 12" Block

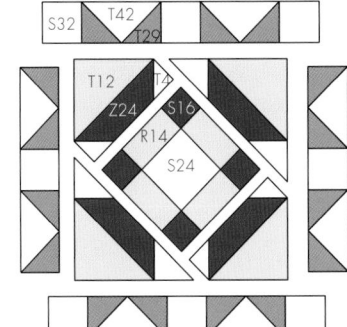

Templates Needed
R14, S16, S24, S32,
T4, T12, T29, T42 & Z24

FOUR SQUARES PIECING INSTRUCTIONS

1. Referring to the Piecing Diagram to piece one block, sew a medium T17 to each side of S19 to complete the center unit.

2. Sew a light R57 to a medium R57 to make a side unit; repeat for four side units.

3. Sew a dark T17 to each side of S19 to make a corner unit; repeat for four corner units.

4. Sew a side unit to opposite sides of the center unit.

5. Sew a corner unit to opposite sides of the remaining side units; sew these units to opposite sides of the center unit.

6. Add T39 to each corner of the pieced center unit to complete the block.

Four Squares
12" x 12" Block

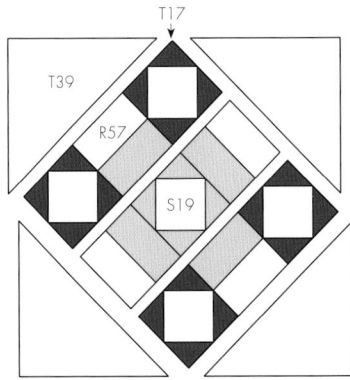

Templates Needed
R57, S19, T17 & T39

FOUR WINDS PIECING INSTRUCTIONS

1. Referring to the Piecing Diagram to piece one block, sew a lightest T11 to a medium T11 to make a lightest T unit; repeat for 12 lightest T units.

2. Sew a dark T11 to a lightest T11 to make a dark T unit; repeat for two dark T units.

3. Sew a medium T11 to a light T11 to make a medium T unit; repeat for eight medium T units.

4. Sew a medium T11 to a dark T11 to make a medium/dark T unit; repeat for six medium/dark T units.

5. Arrange the T units in rows with the lightest and dark S19 squares referring to the Piecing Diagram. Join the squares and units in rows; join the rows to complete the block.

Four Winds
12" x 12" Block

Templates Needed
S19 & T11

FOX & GEESE PIECING INSTRUCTIONS

1. Referring to the Piecing Diagram to piece one block, sew T1 to two adjacent short sides of T33 to make a T unit; repeat for 16 T units.

2. Join four T units to make a side strip; sew a strip to opposite sides of S21 to make the center row.

3. Sew a light T7 to a dark T7 to make a corner unit; repeat for four corner units.

4. Sew a corner unit to each end of each remaining side unit; sew these pieced units to opposite sides of the center row to complete the block.

FREE TRADE PIECING INSTRUCTIONS

1. Referring to the Piecing Diagram to piece one block, sew a light T1 to a dark T1 to make a T1 unit; repeat for 10 T1 units.

2. Sew a dark T1 to the two short sides of T33 to make a T33 unit; repeat for four T33 units.

3. Sew a T1 unit to S30; repeat for 10 units. Join two units to complete an S-T unit; repeat for five S-T units.

4. Sew a T33 unit to two adjacent sides of an S-T unit; sew S30 to each end of two T33 units and sew these units to the pieced unit to complete the center unit.

5. Sew a T7 triangle to the short sides of T32 to make a side unit; repeat for four side units.

6. Sew a side unit to opposite sides of the center unit.

7. Sew an S-T unit to each end of the remaining side units; sew these pieced units to the remaining sides of the center unit to complete the block.

FRIENDSHIP STAR I PIECING INSTRUCTIONS

1. Referring to the Piecing Diagram to piece one block, sew R2 to S29, matching one end and leaving the other end loose. Add remaining R2 pieces around S29; finish the beginning seam to complete the center unit.

2. Sew a dark T18 and a darkest T18 to adjacent sides of S14 to make a corner unit; repeat for four corner units.

3. Sew a corner unit to opposite sides of the center unit.

4. Sew a light T18 to the T18 sides of the remaining corner units; sew these pieced units to the remaining sides of the center unit to complete the block.

FRIENDSHIP STAR II PIECING INSTRUCTIONS

1. Referring to the Piecing Diagram to piece one block, sew a medium Z56 to a light Z56R; set in a lightest S30 to make a light Z unit; repeat for four light Z units.

2. Sew a light Z56 to a medium Z56R; set in a lightest S30 to make a medium Z unit; repeat for four medium Z units.

3. Sew a light Z56 and a light Z56R to the short sides of a dark T33 to make a Z-T unit; repeat for four Z-T units.

4. Sew a light Z unit to one end and a medium Z unit to the opposite end of a Z-T unit; set light T33 triangles between the points to complete a side unit; repeat for four side units.

5. Sew R44 to opposite sides of S5; sew a medium S30 to each end of the remaining R44 pieces. Sew these units to the remaining sides of S5 to complete the center unit.

6. Sew a side unit to each side of the center unit and set in a medium S30 at each corner to complete the block.

Fox & Geese
12" x 12" Block

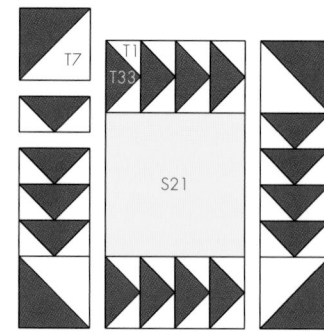

Templates Needed
S21, T1, T7 & T33

Free Trade
12" x 12" Block

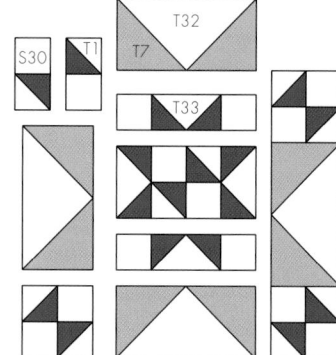

Templates Needed
S30, T1, T7, T32 & T33

Friendship Star I
12" x 12" Block

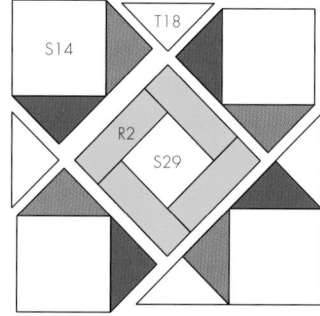

Templates Needed
R2, S14, S29 & T18

Friendship Star II
12" x 12" Block

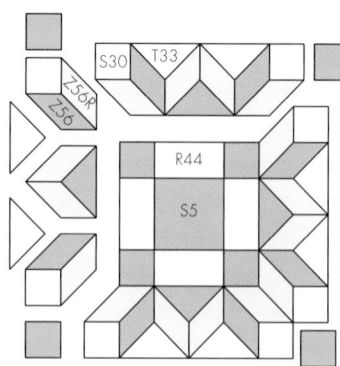

Templates Needed
R44, S5, S30,
T33, Z56 & Z56R

FROM THE HEART PIECING INSTRUCTIONS

1. Referring to the Piecing Diagram to piece one block, sew T11 to each angled side of Z34 to make a top unit; repeat for two units. Join the two units to make the top row.
2. Join a light T18 and a dark T18 on the short sides; repeat for six units. Join two units to make a square; repeat for three squares. Join the three squares to make the center row.
3. Sew a light T39 to a dark T39 on the diagonal to make a square; repeat for two squares. Join the two squares to make the bottom row.
4. Join the rows to complete the block.

GAMECOCKS PIECING INSTRUCTIONS

1. Referring to the Piecing Diagram to piece one block, join two light and two medium R14 pieces with two light and one medium S8 squares to complete the center row.
2. Sew a medium and light R14 piece with a light S8 to make a side unit; repeat for two side units.
3. Sew a light S16 to a dark S16; repeat and join the two units to make a Four-Patch unit. Repeat for four Four-Patch units.
4. Sew a light T42 to a dark T42 to make a T42 unit; repeat for eight T42 units.
5. Sew a light S16 to a dark S16 and add R14 to make an R-S unit; repeat for four R-S units.
6. Join one each R-S and Four-Patch units with two T42 units to complete a corner unit; repeat for four corner units.
7. Join two corner units with a side unit to make a side row; repeat for two side rows.
8. Sew the center row between the two side rows to complete the block.

GAY TWO-PATCH PIECING INSTRUCTIONS

1. Referring to the Piecing Diagram to piece one block, sew a lightest T42 to a dark T42 to make a T42 unit; repeat for 16 T42 units.
2. Sew a light S11 to a medium S11; repeat for two units. Join the two units to complete the center unit.
3. Join three T42 units to make a side unit referring to the Piecing Diagram; repeat for four side units.
4. Sew a side unit to opposite sides of the center unit.
5. Sew a T42 unit to each end of the remaining side units and sew to the remaining sides of the center unit to complete the block.

GENTLEMAN'S FANCY PIECING INSTRUCTIONS

1. Referring to the Piecing Diagram to piece one block, sew a light T18 to each side of S14 to complete the center unit.
2. Sew a light T18 to two adjacent short sides of T19 and add a second T19 to the T18 sides to complete a corner unit; repeat for four corner units.
3. Sew a corner unit to opposite sides of the center unit.
4. Sew a dark T18 to opposite light T18 sides of each of the remaining corner units; sew these units to the remaining sides of the center unit to complete the block.

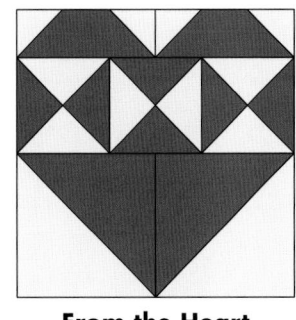

From the Heart
12" x 12" Block

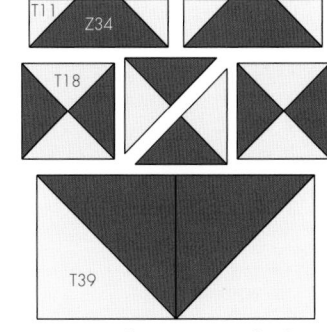

Templates Needed
T11, T18, T39 & Z34

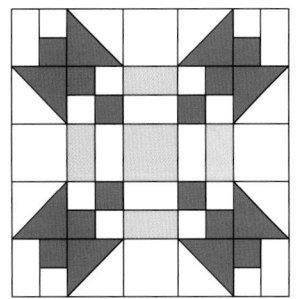

Gamecocks
12" x 12" Block

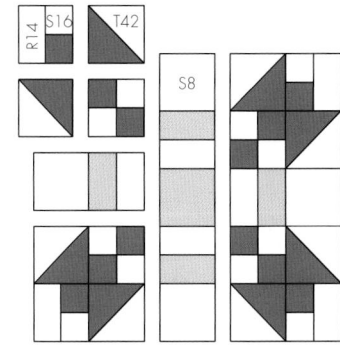

Templates Needed
R14, S8, S16 & T42

Gay Two-Patch
12" x 12" Block

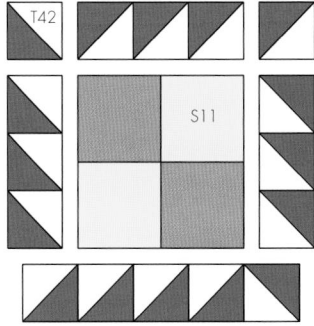

Templates Needed
S11 & T42

Gentleman's Fancy
12" x 12" Block

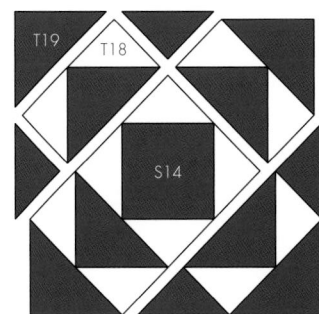

Templates Needed
S14, T18 & T19

GEORGETOWN CIRCLES PIECING INSTRUCTIONS

1. Referring to the Piecing Diagram to piece one block, sew T7 to each side of S22 to complete the center unit.
2. Sew a lightest T33 to a dark T33 to make a T unit; repeat for four T units. Sew a medium T33 to the two dark sides of the T units.
3. Sew a light T33 to a lightest T33 on the short ends; repeat for four T33 units and four reversed T33 units. Sew one of each of these units to two sides of each pieced T unit to complete four side units.
4. Sew a side unit to opposite sides of the center unit.
5. Sew S5 to each end of the remaining side units; sew these pieced units to the remaining sides of the center unit to complete the block.

GLITTER, GLITTER PIECING INSTRUCTIONS

1. Referring to the Piecing Diagram to piece one block, sew a light T1 to each side of S2; repeat for four T1-S2 units.
2. Sew a T-S2 unit to opposite sides of S5 and add R44 to each end to complete the center row.
3. Sew T1 to each short side of T33 to complete a T1-T33 unit; repeat for eight T1-T33 units.
4. Sew a T1-T33 unit to one side of S5; sew S30 to one end of a T1-T33 unit and sew this unit to the adjacent side of S5 to complete a corner unit. Repeat for four corner units.
5. Sew R44 to one side of a T1-S2 unit to complete a side unit; repeat for two side units.
6. Join two corner units with a side unit to make a side row; repeat for two side rows. Sew the center row between the two side rows to complete the block.

GOLDEN HOLIDAY PIECING INSTRUCTIONS

1. Referring to the Piecing Diagram to piece one block, cut one 12⅞" x 12⅞" dark square. Cut the square in half on one diagonal to make two A triangles. Set aside one triangle for another project or block.
2. Turn under the curved edge seam allowances on Z54, Z62 and Z62R pieces; baste to hold. Align straight edges of pieces with edges of A; baste in place. Hand-stitch curved edges of Z54, Z62 and Z62R pieces in place.
3. Trim off corner of A even with ends of Z62 and Z62R.
4. Sew T7 to the corner of the A-Z unit.
5. Sew a light T39 to a medium T39 on the diagonal to make a square.
6. Sew a dark T39 to the medium sides of the square to make a corner unit.
7. Sew the corner unit to the A-Z-T7 unit to complete the block.

GOLDEN STAR PIECING INSTRUCTIONS

1. Referring to the Piecing Diagram to piece one block, sew T2 to Z22; repeat for four units. Sew a pieced unit to each side of S21.
2. Sew T6 to Z33; repeat for eight units. Join two units; repeat four times.
3. Sew a T6-Z33 unit to each side of the pieced unit to complete the block.

Georgetown Circles
12" x 12" Block

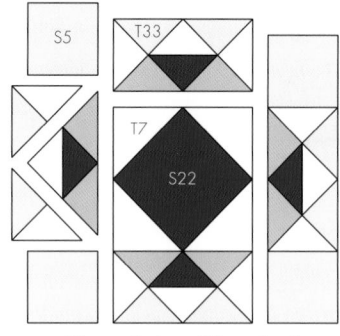

Templates Needed
S5, S22, T7 & T33

Glitter, Glitter
12" x 12" Block

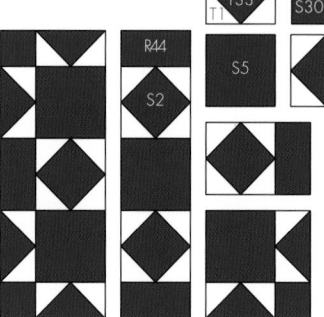

Templates Needed
R44, S2, S5, S30, T1 & T33

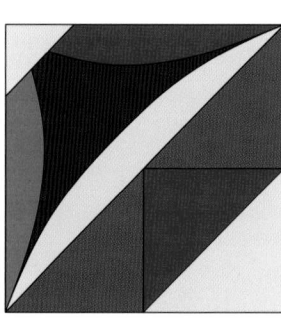

Golden Holiday
12" x 12" Block

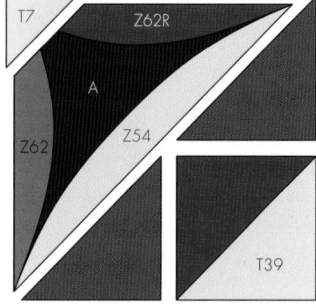

Templates Needed
T7, T39, Z54, Z62 & Z62R

Golden Star
12" x 12" Block

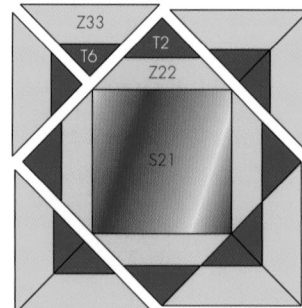

Templates Needed
S21, T2, T6, Z22 & Z33

GRANDMA'S HOPSCOTCH PIECING INSTRUCTIONS

1. Referring to the Piecing Diagram to piece one block, sew a light T18 to a dark T18 along the short sides to make a T18 unit; repeat for four T18 units and two reversed T18 units.

2. Sew a reversed T18 unit to a medium T19 to make a triangle unit; repeat for two triangle units.

3. Sew a light T19 to a dark T19 to make a T19 unit; repeat for two T19 units.

4. Sew a triangle unit to a T19 unit; repeat. Join these two units to complete the center square unit.

5. Sew a medium T18 to each short side of a light T18 to make a side unit; repeat for four side units.

6. Sew a side unit to each side of the center square unit; add a T18 unit to each corner to complete the block.

GRANDMOTHER'S CHOICE PIECING INSTRUCTIONS

1. Referring to the Piecing Diagram to piece one block, sew T42 to two adjacent sides of S8 and add T40 to complete a corner unit; repeat for four corner units.

2. Join two corner units with R13 to make a side row; repeat for two side rows.

3. Sew S8 between two R13 pieces to make the center row; sew between the two side rows to complete the block.

GRANDMOTHER'S PUZZLE PIECING INSTRUCTIONS

1. Referring to the Piecing Diagram to piece one block, sew T42 to two adjacent sides of S8 and add T40 to make an S-T unit; repeat for three units.

2. Sew S8 to the end of R13; repeat for two S-R units.

3. Sew R13 to the T40 side of one S-T unit; add an S-R unit to the remaining T40 side to complete one block corner.

4. Sew R13 to one short side of T40; add the remaining S-R unit to the remaining short side.

5. Arrange the pieced units with the remaining T42 triangles and join referring to the Piecing Diagram to complete the block.

GREEN MOUNTAIN STAR PIECING INSTRUCTIONS

1. Referring to the Piecing Diagram to piece one block, sew a medium T1 to two adjacent sides of S2; add a dark T33 to one side. Sew a light T33 to a dark T33 on the short sides; sew this unit to the stitched S2 unit to complete a side unit; repeat for four side units.

2. Sew a dark T1 to Z18 and Z18R; sew one of these units to one side of a light S5. Sew S30 to the remaining unit and sew to the S5 unit to complete a corner unit; repeat for four corner units.

3. Sew a side unit to opposite sides of the medium S5 to complete the center row.

4. Sew a side unit between two corner units to make a side row; repeat for two side rows.

5. Sew the center row between two side rows to complete the block.

Grandma's Hopscotch
12" x 12" Block

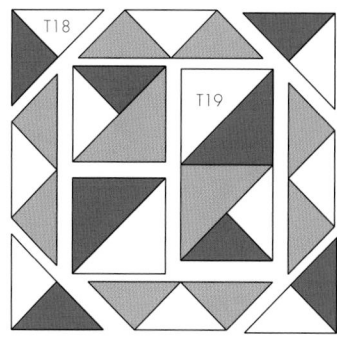

Templates Needed
T18 & T19

Grandmother's Choice
12" x 12" Block

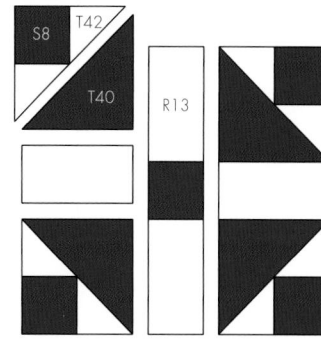

Templates Needed
R13, S8, T40 & T42

Grandmother's Puzzle
12" x 12" Block

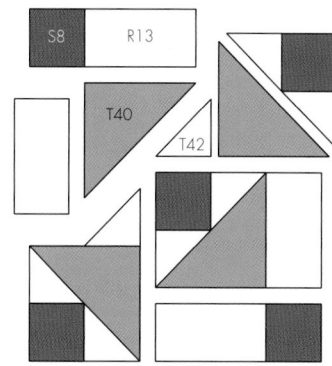

Templates Needed
R13, S8, T40 & T42

Green Mountain Star
12" x 12" Block

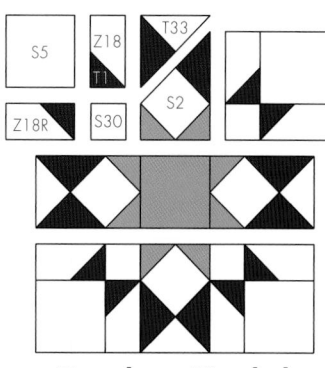

Templates Needed
S2, S5, S30, T1,
T33, Z18 & Z18R

GRETCHEN PIECING INSTRUCTIONS

1. Referring to the Piecing Diagram to piece one block, sew a dark T11 to each angled end of a light Z23. Sew a dark T19 to the Z23 side.

2. Sew a light T11 to each angled end of a dark Z23. Sew a light T19 to the Z23 side.

3. Join the two pieced units to complete one block quarter; repeat for four block quarters.

4. Join the block quarters referring to the Piecing Diagram to complete the block.

HALF-SQUARE TRIANGLE STAR
PIECING INSTRUCTIONS

1. Referring to the Piecing Diagram to piece one block, sew a dark T19 to a medium T19 along the diagonal; repeat for two units.

2. Sew a medium T19 to a light T19 along the diagonal; repeat for two units.

3. Join a light/medium unit with a dark/medium unit; repeat. Join the two units to complete the block center.

4. Sew a dark T11 to a light T11 on the diagonal; repeat for eight T11 units.

5. Sew a medium T11 to the short sides of T18 to make a side unit; repeat for four side units.

6. Sew a T11 unit to each short end of a side unit. Sew a T11 side unit to opposite sides of the pieced center.

7. Sew S19 to opposite ends of the remaining T11 side units; sew these units to the remaining sides of the pieced unit to complete the block.

HARBOR VIEW PIECING INSTRUCTIONS

1. Referring to the Piecing Diagram to piece one block, sew a medium Z56 and Z56R to two adjacent sides of S2; repeat with a light Z56 and Z56R on the two remaining sides of S2 to make a Z unit. Repeat for four Z units.

2. Sew T1 to each side of S2 to complete an S unit; repeat for four S units.

3. Sew a light Z56 and Z56R to the short sides of T33 to make a light T unit; repeat for four light T units. Repeat with medium Z56 and Z56R and T33 to make four medium T units.

4. Sew a medium and light T unit to two adjacent sides of an S unit to complete a corner unit; repeat for four corner units.

5. Join the corner units with the Z units to complete the block.

HARVESTTIME PIECING INSTRUCTIONS

1. Referring to the Piecing Diagram to piece one block, sew a light T7 to a dark T7 on the diagonal to make a square; repeat for six T7 squares.

2. Join three T7 squares to make a strip; repeat for a reverse strip. Sew S5 to one end of one strip.

3. Sew T13 to each long side of Z39; sew to R48.

4. Arrange the pieced units with R46 referring to the Piecing Diagram; join the units to complete the block.

Gretchen
12" x 12" Block

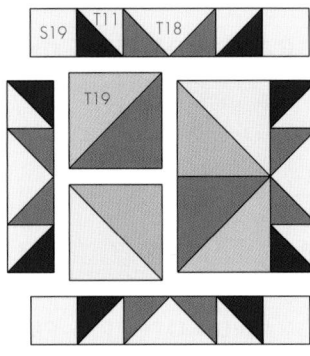

Templates Needed
T19, T11 & Z23

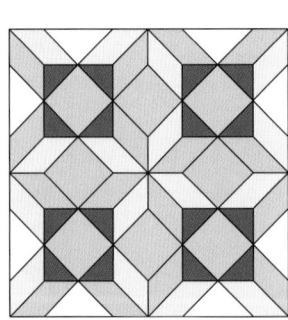

Half-Square Triangle Star
12" x 12" Block

Templates Needed
S19, T11, T18 & T19

Harbor View
12" x 12" Block

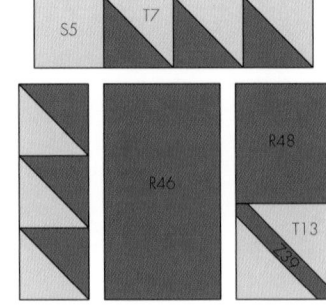

Templates Needed
S2, T1, T33, Z56 & Z56R

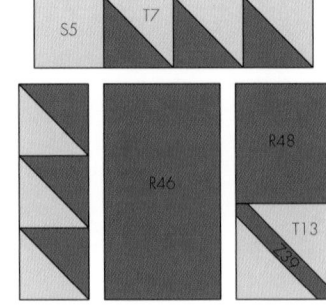

Harvesttime
12" x 12" Block

Templates Needed
R46, R48, S5, T7, T13 & Z39

HAZY DAISY PIECING INSTRUCTIONS

1. Referring to the Piecing Diagram to piece one block, sew T33 to two adjacent sides of S2 to complete a T-S unit; repeat for eight units.

2. Join two T-S units with a light and medium T32 to complete a block quarter; repeat for four quarters.

3. Join the quarter sections to complete the block.

HILL & CRAG PIECING INSTRUCTIONS

1. Referring to the Piecing Diagram to piece one block, sew a dark T42 to each side of S23; add T12 to each side of the pieced unit to complete the center unit.

2. Sew a light T42 to a dark T42 to make a T42 unit; repeat for four units. Sew S24 to the dark end of each T42 unit.

3. Sew a dark T42 to one side of S24; sew this unit to an S24-T42 unit and add a dark T29 to the S24 ends to complete a corner unit.

4. Sew a corner unit to opposite sides of the center unit.

5. Sew a light T29 to each end of each of the remaining corner units; sew these units to the remaining sides of the center unit to complete the block.

HILL & VALLEY PIECING INSTRUCTIONS

1. Referring to the Piecing Diagram to piece one block, sew a light T18 to one side of S29. Sew a light T18 to a dark T18 on the short ends. Join these two units and add T19 to each light T18 side.

2. Sew T39 to the dark sides of the pieced unit to complete half the block; repeat for two halves. Join the two halves to complete the block.

HITHER & YON PIECING INSTRUCTIONS

1. Referring to the Piecing Diagram to piece one block, sew a light T33 to a dark T33 to complete a T2 unit; repeat for eight units. Join four units and add T7 to complete a corner unit. Repeat for two corner units.

2. Sew a corner unit to opposite sides of S22 to complete the center row.

3. Sew a light T7 to a dark T7; repeat for six T7 units.

4. Join three T7 units with two light and one medium T7 triangles to complete a block corner; repeat for two block corners.

5. Sew a block corner to opposite sides of the center row to complete the block.

Hazy Daisy
12" x 12" Block

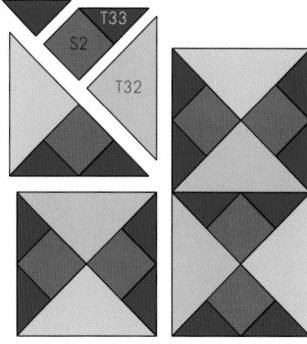

Templates Needed
S2, T32 & T33

Hill & Crag
12" x 12" Block

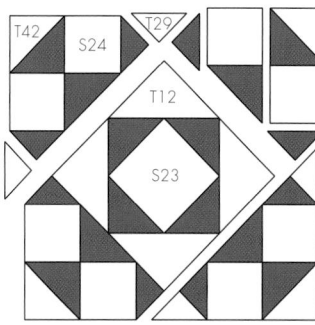

Templates Needed
S23, S24, T12, T29 & T42

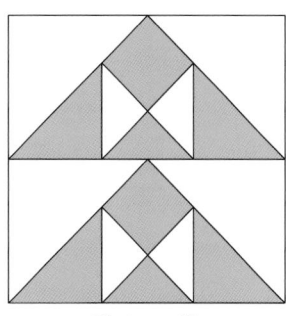

Hill & Valley
12" x 12" Block

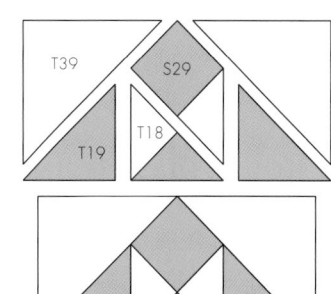

Templates Needed
S29, T18, T19 & T39

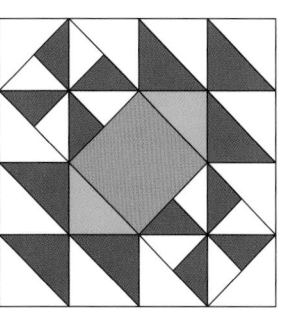

Hither & Yon
12" x 12" Block

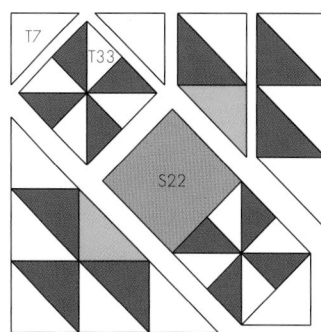

Templates Needed
S22, T7 & T33

HOPE OF HARTFORD PIECING INSTRUCTIONS

1. Referring to the Piecing Diagram to piece one block, sew a dark T22 to a light T22 on the short sides; sew to T40 and add R13 to complete a quarter unit. Repeat for four quarter units.

2. Sew S8 to one end of one quarter unit, leaving the excess unstitched. Add the remaining quarter units to this unit in a clockwise direction, finishing the unstitched edge of the first unit to complete the block.

HOPSCOTCH I PIECING INSTRUCTIONS

1. Referring to the Piecing Diagram to piece one block, sew a light Z26 to T18 and a medium Z26R to T18 to complete light and medium T-Z units; repeat for four of each unit.

2. Sew a medium Z26 and a light Z26R to opposite sides of S19 to make an S-Z unit referring to the Piecing Diagram; repeat for four units.

3. Sew a lightest T18 to a dark T18 on the short sides to make a T18 unit; repeat for four units.

4. Sew a T18 unit to an S-Z unit to complete an S-Z-T unit; repeat for four units.

5. Sew a light and medium T-Z unit to an S-Z-T unit and stitch the corner seam to complete one quarter section; repeat for four quarter sections.

6. Join the four quarter sections to complete the block.

HOPSCOTCH II PIECING INSTRUCTIONS

1. Referring to the Piecing Diagram to piece one block, sew a light T7 to a dark T7 to complete a T unit; repeat for 16 T units.

2. Arrange the T units in four rows of four units each referring to the Piecing Diagram; join in rows and join rows to complete the block.

HOURGLASS PIECING INSTRUCTIONS

1. Referring to the Piecing Diagram to piece one block, sew a light T7 to a dark T7 to complete a T7 unit; repeat for six units.

2. Join two T7 units with two S5 squares to complete an S-T corner unit; repeat for two S-T corner units.

3. Sew a light T7 to the two adjacent dark sides of a T unit; add T39 to complete a T corner unit. Repeat for two T corner units.

4. Join the S-T and T corner units to complete the block.

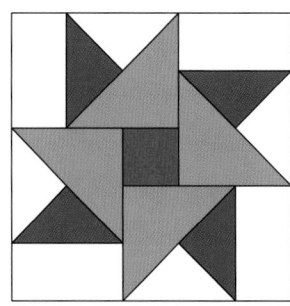

Hope of Hartford
12" x 12" Block

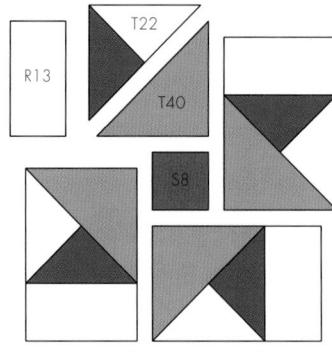

Templates Needed
R13, S8, T22 & T40

Hopscotch I
12" x 12" Block

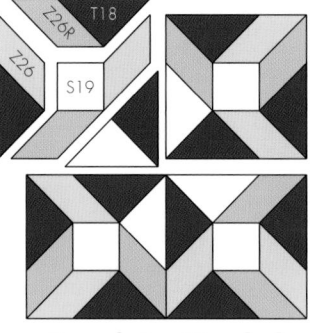

Templates Needed
S19, T18, Z26 & Z26R

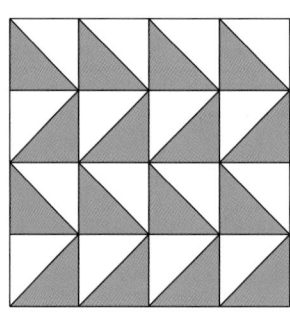

Hopscotch II
12" x 12" Block

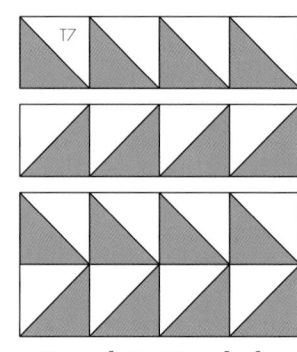

Template Needed
T7

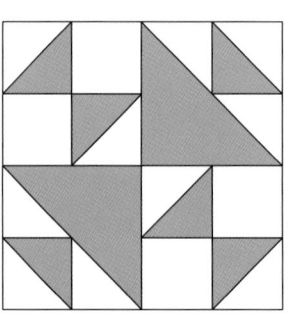

Hourglass
12" x 12" Block

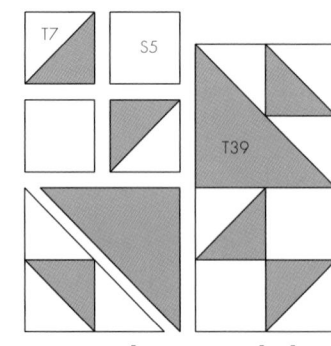

Templates Needed
S5, T7 & T39

HULL'S VICTORY PIECING INSTRUCTIONS

1. Referring to the Piecing Diagram to piece one block, sew T1 to two short sides of a dark T33; repeat for four units. Sew a unit to opposite sides of a light S5.

2. Sew an S30 square to each end of each remaining T1-T33 unit and sew to the remaining sides of S5 to complete the center unit.

3. Sew a light T33 to two adjacent sides of S2; add T7 to the remaining sides of S2 to complete a side unit. Repeat for four side units.

4. Sew a side unit to opposite sides of the center unit; sew a dark S5 square to each end of each of the remaining side units. Sew these units to the remaining sides of the center unit to complete the block.

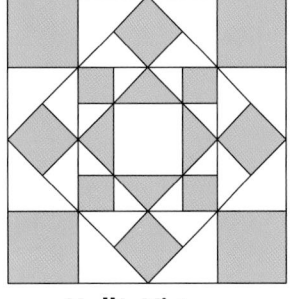

Hull's Victory
12" x 12" Block

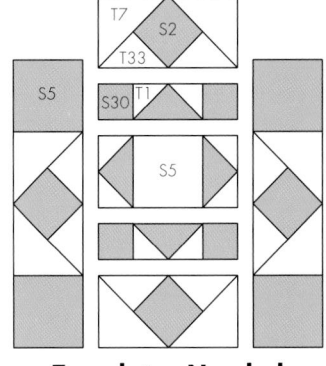

Templates Needed
S2, S5, S30, T1, T7 & T33

ICE CRYSTALS PIECING INSTRUCTIONS

1. Referring to the Piecing Diagram to piece one block, sew a medium T18 to a dark T18; repeat. Join the units to complete the block center.

2. Sew a light T11 to each short side of a lightest T18; add R11 to the T11 side to complete one side unit. Repeat for four side units.

3. Join two lightest and two dark S19 squares to make a corner unit; repeat for four corner units.

4. Arrange the pieced units in rows referring to the Piecing Diagram. Join units in rows; join rows to complete the block.

Ice Crystals
12" x 12" Block

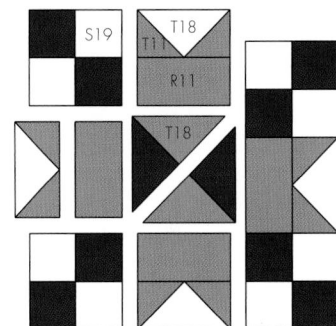

Templates Needed
R11, S19, T11 & T18

INDIAN SQUARES PIECING INSTRUCTIONS

1. Referring to the Piecing Diagram to piece one block, join two dark and one light S2 squares to make a dark S2 strip; repeat for two dark S2 strips. Repeat with one dark and two light S2 squares to make one light S2 strip.

2. Sew the light S2 strip between the two dark S2 strips to complete the center unit.

3. Sew a light T1 to a dark T1 to make a T1 unit; repeat for four T1 units.

4. Sew a T1 unit to one end of R44 and a dark T1 to the opposite end to make an R unit; repeat for four R units.

5. Sew R44 to S5 to Z63 to make a Z unit; repeat for four Z units.

6. Sew T1 to opposite short sides of Z63 to make a T-Z unit; repeat for four T-Z units.

7. Sew T33 to two adjacent sides of a dark S2 to make a side unit; repeat for four side units.

8. Join one R, one Z and one T-Z unit to complete a corner unit referring to the Piecing Diagram; repeat for four corner units.

9. Sew a corner unit to opposite sides of the center unit; sew a side unit to opposite sides of each remaining corner unit and add these units to the remaining sides of the center unit to complete the block.

Indian Squares
12" x 12" Block

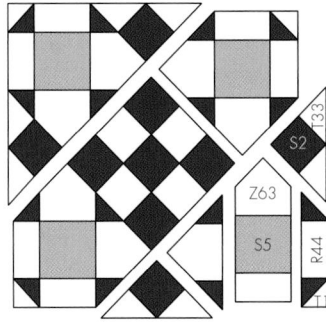

Templates Needed
R44, S2, S5, T1, T33 & Z63

INDIANAPOLIS PIECING INSTRUCTIONS

1. Referring to the Piecing Diagram to piece one block, sew T17 to the angled sides of Z61 to make a T-Z unit; repeat for four units.

2. Sew a T-Z unit to opposite sides of S29.

3. Sew a medium S25 to a dark S25; repeat for eight S25 units. Join two units to make a Four-Patch unit; repeat for four Four-Patch units.

4. Sew a Four-Patch unit to opposite sides of each of the remaining T-Z units to make a row; sew these rows to the remaining sides of S29 to complete the center unit.

5. Sew T53 to one side of T34 and T53R to the other side to complete a corner unit; repeat for four corner units.

6. Sew a corner unit to each side of the center unit to complete the block.

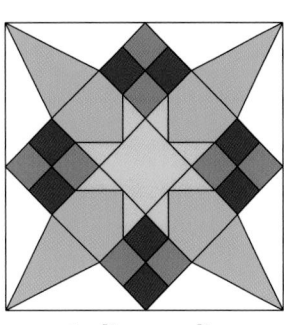

Indianapolis
12" x 12" Block

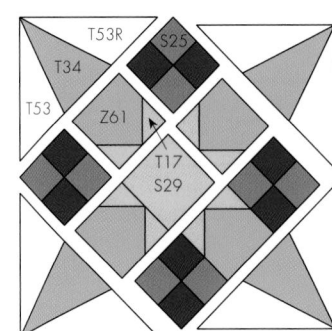

Templates Needed
S25, S29, T17, T34,
T53, T53R & Z61

JACKKNIFE PIECING INSTRUCTIONS

1. Referring to the Piecing Diagram to piece one block, sew a light T11 to a dark Z23; repeat with a dark T11 and a light Z23. Join these two units to complete a corner unit; repeat for four corner units.

2. Sew a light T18 to a dark T18 on the short sides; repeat for two units. Join the two units to complete a side unit; repeat for four side units.

3. Arrange the corner and side units in rows with S14 referring to the Piecing Diagram; join in rows. Join the rows to complete the block.

JACK'S DELIGHT PIECING INSTRUCTIONS

1. Referring to the Piecing Diagram to piece one block, sew a light T18 to a dark T18 to complete a T18 unit; repeat for eight units.

2. Join two units and add T19 to make a corner unit; repeat for four corner units.

3. Sew a corner unit to opposite sides of S27 to complete the center row.

4. Sew a light T18 to the dark end and a dark T18 to the light end of each of the remaining corner units. Sew these corner units to the remaining sides of the center row to complete the block.

JEFFERSON CITY PIECING INSTRUCTIONS

1. Referring to the Piecing Diagram to piece one block, sew a dark T18 to each side of S14 to complete the center unit.

2. Sew a light S29 to a medium S29 to make an S29 unit; repeat for four units.

3. Sew a light T18 to a medium T18 on the short sides; repeat for four T18 units.

4. Sew a T18 unit to each S29 unit to complete a corner unit.

5. Sew a corner unit to opposite sides of the center unit.

6. Sew a dark T18 to each S29 edge of the remaining corner units; sew these units to the remaining sides of the center unit to complete the block.

JOSEPH'S COAT PIECING INSTRUCTIONS

1. Referring to the Piecing Diagram to piece one block, sew a dark T29 to each short side of a light T42 to make a T42 unit; repeat for four units.

2. Sew a T42 unit to opposite sides of S23. Sew S32 to each end of the remaining T42 units; sew these units to the remaining sides of S23 to complete the center unit.

3. Sew a light T29 to each side of S8 and add T42 to one side; sew Z66 and Z66R to two opposite sides of this unit to complete a corner unit; repeat for four corner units.

4. Sew a corner unit to opposite sides of the center unit to complete the center row.

5. Add a light T29 to the Z66 and Z66R sides of the remaining corner units; sew these units to opposite sides of the center row to complete the block.

Jackknife
12" x 12" Block

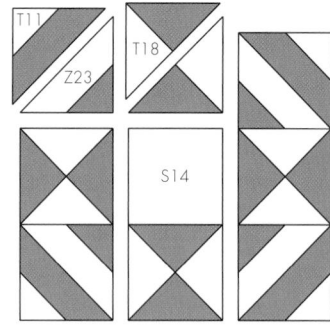

Templates Needed
S14, T11, T18 & Z23

Jack's Delight
12" x 12" Block

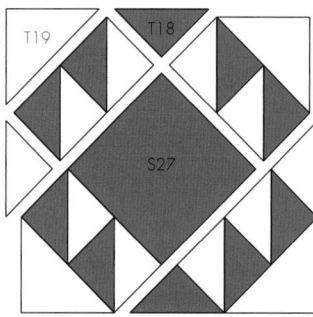

Templates Needed
S27, T18 & T19

Jefferson City
12" x 12" Block

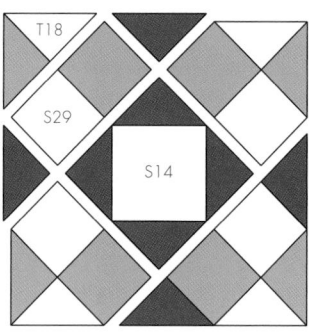

Templates Needed
S14, S29 & T18

Joseph's Coat
12" x 12" Block

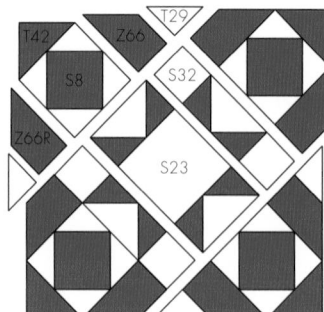

Templates Needed
S8, S23, S32, T29,
T42, Z66 & Z66R

JOY BELLS PIECING INSTRUCTIONS

1. Referring to the Piecing Diagram to piece one block, sew Z26 and Z26R to the short sides of T18; finish seam to join the Z pieces. Add T11 to each Z26 end to complete a side unit; repeat for four side units.

2. Join three dark and two light S28 squares and add T11 to each end to complete the center row.

3. Sew a light S29 to a dark S29 and add T11 to the dark end to complete a corner unit; repeat for two corner units.

4. Join two side units with a corner unit to complete a large corner unit; repeat for two large corner units.

5. Sew a large corner unit to opposite sides of the center row to complete the block.

KALEIDOSCOPE PIECING INSTRUCTIONS

1. Referring to the Piecing Diagram to piece one block, join one light and three medium T49 triangles to complete a side unit; repeat for four side units.

2. Join one light and three dark T49 triangles and add T13 to complete a corner unit; repeat for four corner units.

3. Join two side and two corner units to complete half the block; repeat. Join the two halves to complete the block.

KEYHOLE PIECING INSTRUCTIONS

1. Referring to the Piecing Diagram to piece one block, sew T11 to Z26 and Z26R; repeat for four of each unit. Sew two of each of these units to the sides of S29 to complete a Z-S unit; repeat for two Z-S units.

2. Join three light S19 squares with two R41 pieces to make an S-R strip; repeat for two strips. Join the two Z-S units with the S-R strips referring to the Piecing Diagram to complete the block center.

3. Sew a light S19 to a dark S19; repeat and join with R11 to complete a side strip. Repeat for two side strips.

4. Sew a side strip to opposite sides of the block center to complete the block.

KILIMANJARO PIECING INSTRUCTIONS

1. Referring to the Piecing Diagram to piece one block, sew a dark T18 to each side of S14 to complete the block center.

2. Sew a medium T18 to the short sides of a darkest T19; add a dark T19 to the unit to complete a corner unit.

3. Sew a corner unit to opposite sides of the center unit.

4. Sew a light T18 to each T18 side of each remaining corner unit; sew these units to the remaining sides of the center unit to complete the block.

Joy Bells
12" x 12" Block

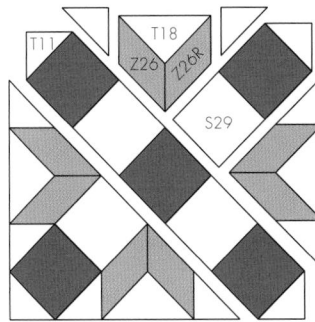

Templates Needed
S29, T11, T18, Z26 & Z26R

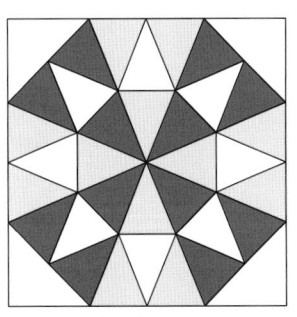

Kaleidoscope
12" x 12" Block

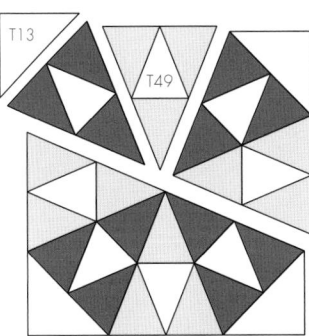

Templates Needed
T13 & T49

Keyhole
12" x 12" Block

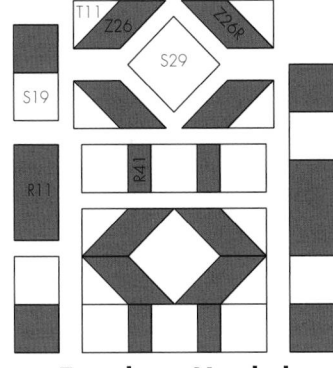

Templates Needed
R11, R41, S19,
S29, T11, Z26 & Z26R

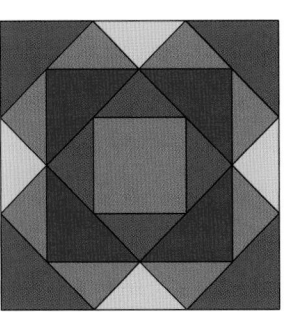

Kilimanjaro
12" x 12" Block

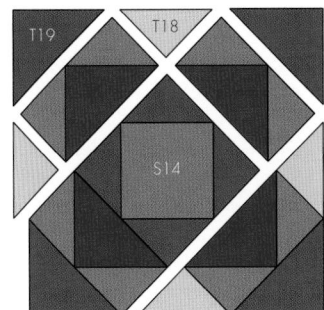

Templates Needed
S14, T18 & T19

KING DAVID'S CROWN PIECING INSTRUCTIONS

1. Referring to the Piecing Diagram to piece one block, sew a light T29 to Z24; repeat for four units. Sew a unit to each side of S10 to complete the center unit.

2. Sew a light T42 to a dark T42 to make a T unit; repeat for eight T units. Sew S8 to the dark side of a T unit. Sew a light T42 to the dark side of a T unit.

3. Join the pieced units and add a medium T29 to two light T unit edges to complete a corner unit; repeat for four corner units.

4. Sew a corner unit to opposite sides of the center unit.

5. Sew a light T29 triangle to each medium T29 end of the remaining corner units; sew these units to the remaining sides of the pieced center to complete the block.

King David's Crown
12" x 12" Block

Templates Needed
S8, S10, T29, T42 & Z24

KISSING LANES PIECING INSTRUCTIONS

1. Referring to the Piecing Diagram to piece one block, sew a light T11 to a dark T11 to complete a T11 unit; repeat for 12 units.

2. Join three T11 units with S19 to complete one T corner unit; repeat for two T corner units.

3. Join two T11 units with two S19 squares to complete an S-T unit; repeat for three S-T units.

4. Sew a dark T11 to each side of S29 to make a side unit; repeat for four side units.

5. Arrange the pieced units in rows and join referring to the Piecing Diagram to complete the block.

Kissing Lanes
12" x 12" Block

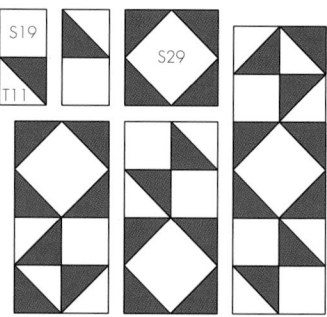

Templates Needed
S19, S29 & T11

LAWYER'S PUZZLE PIECING INSTRUCTIONS

1. Referring to the Piecing Diagram to piece one block, sew a light T1 to a dark T1 to make a T1 unit; repeat for 24 T1 units.

2. Join three T1 units; repeat for four joined T1 units and four reversed joined T1 units

3. Sew a light T31 to a medium T31 to make a T31 unit; repeat for four units.

4. Sew a joined T1 unit to the medium sides of a T31 unit. Add S30 to the dark end of a reversed joined T1 unit and sew to the remaining dark side of the T31 unit to complete a quarter section; repeat for four quarter sections.

5. Join the quarter sections to complete the block.

Lawyer's Puzzle
12" x 12" Block

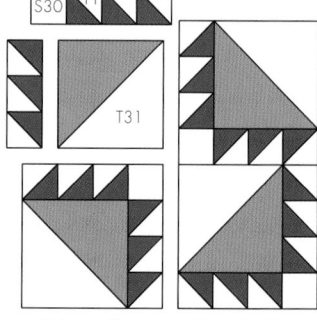

Templates Needed
S30, T1 & T31

LIGHTNING IN THE HILLS PIECING INSTRUCTIONS

1. Referring to the Piecing Diagram to piece one block, sew a light T11 to each side of S29 to complete the center unit.

2. Sew a light T11 to a darkest T11 to complete a T11 unit; repeat for 12 units.

3. Sew a light T11 to opposite sides of Z26R to complete a Z unit; repeat for four units.

4. Sew S19 to the darkest side of a T11 unit; join with a Z unit to complete a corner unit. Repeat for four corner units.

5. Sew a medium T11 to each short side of T18; repeat for four T-T units.

6. Join two T11 units; add a T-T unit to complete a side unit. Repeat for four side units.

7. Sew a side unit to opposite sides of the center unit to complete the center row. Sew a side unit between two corner units to complete a side row; repeat for two side rows.

8. Sew the center row between the side rows to complete the block.

Lightning in the Hills
12" x 12" Block

Templates Needed
S19, S29, T11, T18 & Z26R

LILY PIECING INSTRUCTIONS

1. Referring to the Piecing Diagram to piece one block, sew a dark S2 between two light S2 squares; repeat for two units. Sew an S2 unit to opposite sides of R19; sew T31 to each side of this unit to complete the center unit.

2. Sew a medium T1 to each short side of T33 to make a T unit; repeat for eight T units.

3. Join two T units with R44 to complete a side unit; repeat for four side units. Sew a side unit to opposite sides of the center unit.

4. Sew S30 to each end of the remaining side units; sew these units to the remaining sides of the center unit to complete the block.

LILY QUILT PIECING INSTRUCTIONS

1. Referring to the Piecing Diagram to piece one block, join two light S19 and one dark S19 to make a strip; repeat for two strips. Sew a strip to opposite sides of R6 and add T32 to each side of this unit to complete the center unit.

2. Sew a dark T29 to the short sides of T42; repeat for eight units. Join two units with S32 to complete a side unit; repeat for four side units.

3. Sew a side unit to opposite sides of the center unit.

4. Sew S32 to each end of each of the remaining side units; sew these units to the remaining sides of the center unit to complete the block.

LOG CABIN STAR PIECING INSTRUCTIONS

1. Referring to the Piecing Diagram to piece one block, sew a light T11 to a medium T11 on the diagonal to make the block center.

2. Beginning with the R41 strip, sew the R strips to the center referring to the Piecing Diagram for placement of pieces by color and template number to complete the block center.

3. Sew a dark T11 to a light T11 on the diagonal; repeat for eight T11 units.

4. Sew a medium T11 to the short sides of T18 to make a side unit; repeat for four side units.

5. Sew a T11 unit to each short end of a side unit. Sew a T11 side unit to opposite sides of the pieced center.

6. Sew S19 to opposite ends of the remaining T11 side units; sew these units to the remaining sides of the pieced unit to complete the block.

LUCKY CLOVER PIECING INSTRUCTIONS

1. Referring to the Piecing Diagram to piece one block, sew a medium T11 to the angled side of Z2 and Z2R; join these two units to complete a side unit.

2. Sew a light S19 to a medium S19 to complete an S19 unit; repeat for eight units.

3. Join two S19 units to complete a corner unit; repeat for four corner units.

4. Sew a side unit to opposite sides of S14 to complete the center row.

5. Sew a side unit between two corner units to complete a side row.

6. Sew the center row between the two side rows to complete the block.

Lily
12" x 12" Block

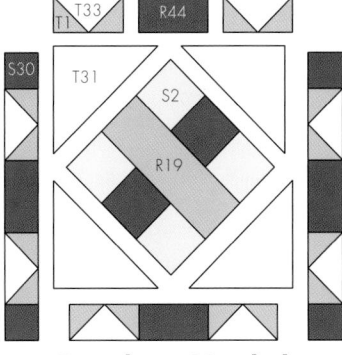

Templates Needed
R19, R44, S2, S30,
T1, T31 & T33

Lily Quilt
12" x 12" Block

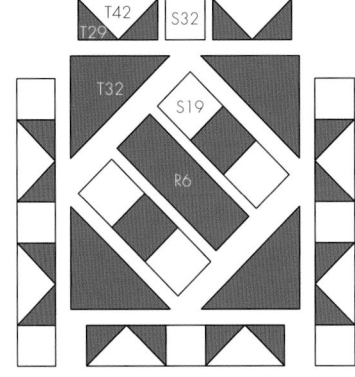

Templates Needed
R6, S19, S32, T29, T32 & T42

Log Cabin Star
12" x 12" Block

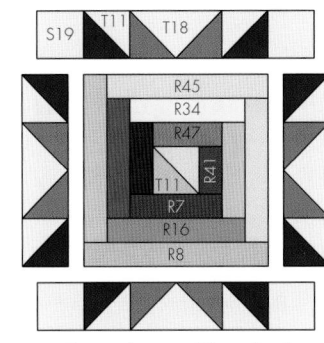

Templates Needed
R7, R8, R16, R34, R41,
R45, R47, S19, T11 & T18

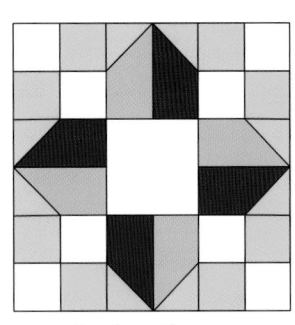

Lucky Clover
12" x 12" Block

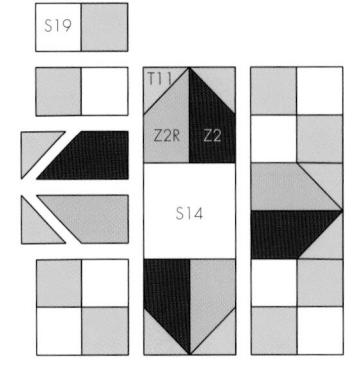

Templates Needed
S14, S19, T11, Z2 & Z2R

MARE'S NEST PIECING INSTRUCTIONS

1. Referring to the Piecing Diagram to piece one block, sew T4 to opposite sides of Z44 to complete a T-Z unit; repeat for eight units.

2. Join two T-Z units to make a side unit; repeat for four side units.

3. Sew a side unit to opposite sides of a lightest S8 to complete the center row.

4. Sew T42 to two adjacent sides of a dark S8; add T40 to complete a corner unit. Repeat for four corner units.

5. Join two corner units with a side unit to complete a side row; repeat for two side rows.

6. Sew the center row between the side rows to complete the block.

MAY BASKET PIECING INSTRUCTIONS

1. Referring to the Piecing Diagram to piece one block, sew a colored T42 to a light T42 to make a T42 unit; repeat for seven units.

2. Sew a colored T42 to the two short sides of T22; repeat for two T22 units.

3. Sew a dark T40 to a colored T40 to make a T40 unit.

4. Sew a dark T42 to one end of R1; repeat for a reversed R1 unit.

5. Join S8 with one T42 and one T22 unit to make a row.

6. Join four T42 units to make a row.

7. Join two T42 units; join with a T22 and a T40 unit to make a row.

8. Arrange the rows and join referring to the Piecing Diagram; add R1 and R1 reversed units and a light T40 to complete the block.

MEGAN'S GARDEN PIECING INSTRUCTIONS

1. Referring to the Piecing Diagram to piece one block, join one each light and medium and two dark T33 triangles to complete a T unit; repeat for four units.

2. Sew a T unit to each side of S21 to complete the center unit.

3. Sew a light T33 to two sides of Z57; repeat for Z57R; join these two units to complete a corner unit. Repeat for four corner units.

4. Sew a corner unit to each side of the center unit to complete the block.

MEMORY BLOCK PIECING INSTRUCTIONS

1. Referring to the Piecing Diagram to piece one block, sew a light T33 to two adjacent sides of S5 and add R43 to complete a corner unit; repeat for four corner units.

2. Sew a corner unit to opposite sides of S22 to complete the center row.

3. Join one light, one dark and two medium T33 triangles to make a side unit; repeat for four side units.

4. Sew a side unit to each side of the remaining corner units; sew these larger corner units to opposite sides of the center row to complete the block.

Mare's Nest
12" x 12" Block

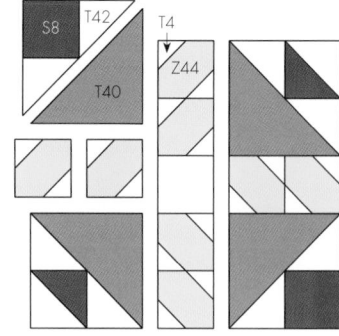

Templates Needed
S8, T4, T40, T42 & Z44

May Basket
12" x 12" Block

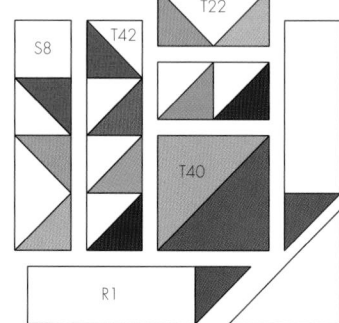

Templates Needed
R1, S8, T22, T40 & T42

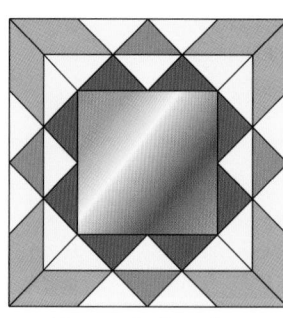

Megan's Garden
12" x 12" Block

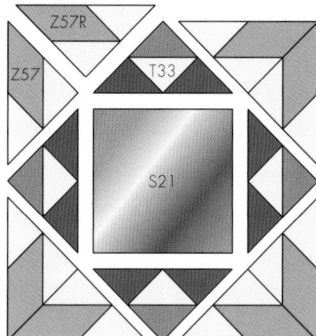

Templates Needed
S21, T33, Z57 & Z57R

Memory Block
12" x 12" Block

Templates Needed
R43, S5, S22 & T33

MEMORY VARIATION PIECING INSTRUCTIONS

1. Referring to the Piecing Diagram to piece one block, center and sew a Z59 to a Z42 piece; repeat for four units; join these four units to complete the center unit.

2. Sew a dark T33 to two adjacent sides of S5 to make an S-T unit; repeat for four units.

3. Sew R43 to the dark T33 sides of two S-T units; sew these units to opposite sides of the center unit to complete the center row.

4. Sew a light T33 to the dark T33 ends of the remaining S-T units to complete an S-T corner unit.

5. Sew a dark T33 to each angled end of Z30; add a light T33 to each end to complete a Z corner unit. Repeat for two units.

6. Sew a Z corner unit to each S-T corner unit to complete the block corners. Sew a block corner to opposite sides of the center row to complete the block.

MEMORY'S CHAIN PIECING INSTRUCTIONS

1. Referring to the Piecing Diagram to piece one block, sew a medium T1 to the short sides of a light T33 to complete a light T33 unit; repeat for two units.

2. Sew a light T1 to the short sides of a dark T33 to complete a dark T33 unit; repeat for four units.

3. Join a light and dark T33 unit with a medium R44; repeat. Sew these units to opposite sides of S5 to complete the center row.

4. Sew a light T1 to a medium T1 to make a T1 unit; repeat for 12 T1 units.

5. Sew a light S30 to the light side of a T1 unit; repeat for a reverse unit. Sew these units to opposite ends of R33 to make a row; repeat for two rows. Sew these rows to opposite sides of the center row.

6. Join one light and two medium R44 pieces with two T1 units to make a row; repeat for two rows. Sew these rows to opposite sides of the center row.

7. Join two T1 units with two light and two medium S30 squares and a dark T33 unit to make an outside row; repeat for two outside rows. Sew the outside rows to opposite sides of the center row to complete the block.

MERRY KITE PIECING INSTRUCTIONS

1. Referring to the Piecing Diagram to piece one block, sew a dark T11 to the short sides of a lightest T18 to make a lightest T18 unit; repeat for four units.

2. Sew a light T11 to the short sides of a dark T18 to make a dark T18 unit; repeat for four units.

3. Join a lightest and dark T18 unit to complete a side unit; repeat for four side units. Sew a side unit to opposite sides of S14 to complete the center row.

4. Sew a medium S19 to a light S19 to complete a light S19 unit; repeat for four units.

5. Sew a dark S19 to a medium S19 to complete a dark S19 unit; repeat for four units. Join a light S19 unit with a dark S19 unit to complete a corner unit; repeat for four corner units.

6. Join two corner units with a side unit to complete a side row; repeat for two side rows. Sew the center row between the side rows to complete the block.

MEXICAN STAR PIECING INSTRUCTIONS

1. Referring to the Piecing Diagram to piece one block, sew a medium T29 to two adjacent sides of S8 to make an S unit; repeat for four units.

2. Sew a lightest T29 to each T29 side of the S units. Sew T42 to Z29; sew this unit to the S8-T29 unit to complete a corner unit.

Memory Variation
12" x 12" Block

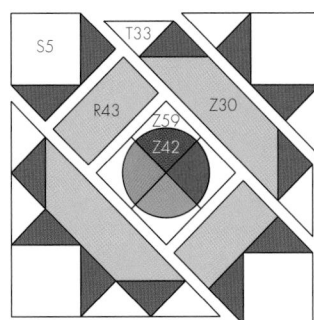

Templates Needed
R43, S5, T33, Z30, Z42 & Z59

Memory's Chain
12" x 12" Block

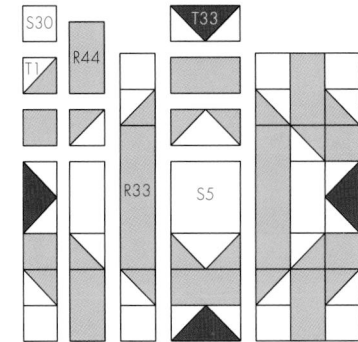

Templates Needed
R33, R44, S5, S30, T1 & T33

Merry Kite
12" x 12" Block

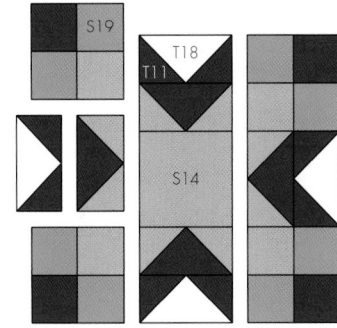

Templates Needed
S14, S19, T11 & T18

Mexican Star
12" x 12" Block

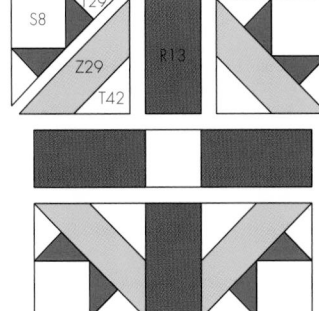

Templates Needed
R13, S8, T29, T42 & Z29

Repeat for four corner units. Join two corner units with R13 to make a row; repeat for two rows.

3. Sew R13 to opposite sides of S8 to make the center row. Sew the center row between the two previously pieced rows to complete the block.

MIDNIGHT IN THE GARDEN PIECING INSTRUCTIONS

1. Referring to the Piecing Diagram to piece one block, sew R44 to opposite sides of S5. Sew a medium S30 to each end of R44; repeat for two units. Join the units to complete the center unit.

2. Sew a dark T1 to each short side of T33; add a dark S30 to each end. Join a light and dark T1 on the diagonal to make a square; repeat for two squares. Sew a T1 square to each end of R44. Join a T33 and R44 unit to make a side unit; repeat for four side units.

3. Join two light and two medium S30 squares to make a corner unit; repeat for four corner units.

4. Arrange the pieced units in rows referring to the Piecing Diagram. Join units in rows; join rows to complete the block.

MILL WHEEL PIECING INSTRUCTIONS

1. Referring to the Piecing Diagram to piece one block, center and stitch a dark Z8 piece in the curved area of a light Z52; repeat for eight light Z52 units.

2. Repeat step 1 with a light Z8 and a dark Z52 to complete eight dark Z52 units.

3. Join four light Z52 units to complete a light quarter section; repeat for two light quarter sections. Repeat with four dark Z52 units to complete two dark quarter sections.

4. Join the quarter sections to complete one block.

MIXED T PIECING INSTRUCTIONS

1. Referring to the Piecing Diagram to piece one block, sew a dark Z17R to a light Z17R to complete a ZR unit; repeat for eight units.

2. Sew a light Z17 to a dark Z17 to make a Z unit; repeat for seven units.

3. Join two ZR units and one Z unit to make a row; repeat for three rows.

4. Join two Z units and one ZR unit to make a row; repeat for two rows.

5. Join one dark and two light R20 pieces to make a row; repeat for two rows.

6. Join one light and two dark R20 pieces to make a row; repeat for two rows.

7. Arrange the rows referring to the Piecing Diagram; join the rows to complete the block.

MOLLIE'S CHOICE PIECING INSTRUCTIONS

1. Referring to the Piecing Diagram to piece one block, sew T55 and T55R to the angled sides of T52 to complete a T52 unit; repeat for eight units.

2. Join two T52 units with R20 to complete a side unit; repeat for four side units.

3. Sew a light T10 to each side of a dark T10 to complete a T10 unit; repeat for four units.

4. Sew a T10 unit to Z28 and add T19 to complete a corner unit; repeat for four corner units.

5. Sew a side unit to opposite sides of S14 to complete the center row.

6. Sew a side unit between two corner units to complete a side row; repeat for two side rows.

7. Sew the center row between two side rows to complete the block.

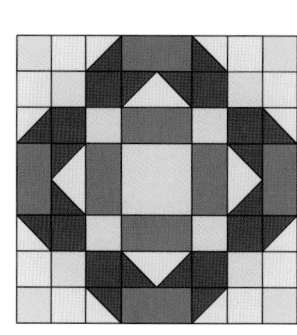

Midnight in the Garden
12" x 12" Block

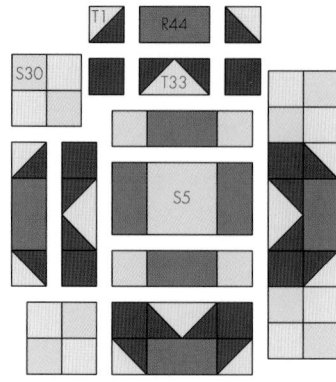

Templates Needed
R44, S5, S30, T1 & T33

Mill Wheel
12" x 12" Block

Templates Needed
Z8 & Z52

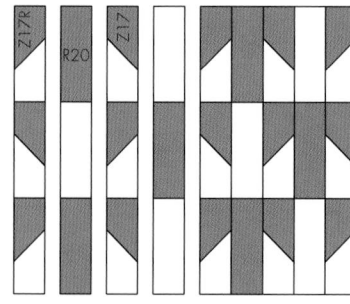

Mixed T
12" x 12" Block

Templates Needed
R20, Z17 & Z17R

Mollie's Choice
12" x 12" Block

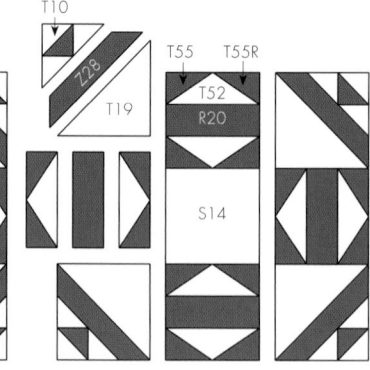

Templates Needed
R20, S14, T10, T19, T52,
T55, T55R & Z28

MOSAIC I PIECING INSTRUCTIONS

1. Referring to the Piecing Diagram to piece one block, sew a light T7 to each side of S22 to complete the center unit.

2. Sew a light T7 to a dark T7 to complete a corner unit; repeat for four corner units.

3. Sew a light T7 to each short side of T32 to complete a side unit; repeat for four side units.

5. Sew a side unit to opposite sides of the center unit to complete the center row.

6. Sew a side unit between two corner units to complete a side row; repeat for two side rows.

7. Sew the center row between two side rows to complete the block.

MOSAIC II PIECING INSTRUCTIONS

1. Referring to the Piecing Diagram to piece one block, sew T11 to each side of S29 to complete the center unit.

2. Sew a dark T18 to a light T18 on the short sides to make a T18 unit; repeat for eight units.

3. Join two T18 units to make a side unit; repeat for four side units.

4. Sew a light T19 to a dark T19 to complete a corner unit; repeat for four corner units.

5. Sew a side unit to opposite sides of the center unit to complete the center row.

6. Sew a side unit between two corner units to complete a side row; repeat for two side rows.

7. Sew a center row between two side rows to complete the block.

MOSAIC III PIECING INSTRUCTIONS

1. Referring to the Piecing Diagram to piece one block, sew a light T7 to a medium T7 and add T32 to complete a T32 unit; repeat for four units.

2. Add a medium T7 to each T32 unit to complete the corner units. Sew a corner unit to opposite sides of S22 to complete the center row.

3. Sew T33 to two adjacent sides of S2 to complete a side unit; repeat for four side units.

4. Sew a side unit to opposite sides of each of the remaining corner units; sew these units to opposite sides of the center row to complete the block.

MOSAIC X PIECING INSTRUCTIONS

1. Referring to the Piecing Diagram to piece one block, sew a dark T7 to each side of S22 to complete the center unit.

2. Sew a light T7 to the short sides of a dark T32 to complete a side unit; repeat for two side units. Sew a side unit to opposite sides of the center unit to complete the center row.

3. Join one dark and two light T32 triangles; add a dark T7 to each end to complete a side row. Repeat for two side rows.

4. Sew the center row between the two side rows to complete the block.

Mosaic I
12" x 12" Block

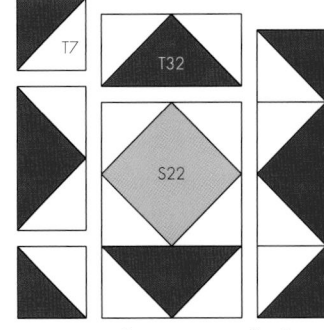

Templates Needed
S22, T7 & T32

Mosaic II
12" x 12" Block

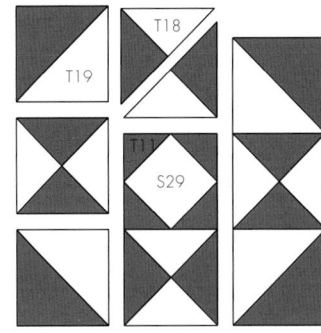

Templates Needed
S29, T11, T18 & T19

Mosaic III
12" x 12" Block

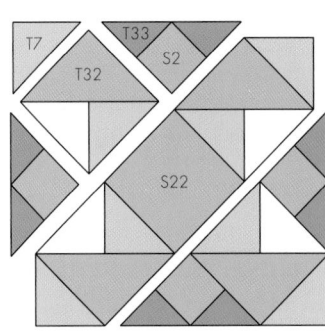

Templates Needed
S2, S22, T7, T32 & T33

Mosaic X
12" x 12" Block

Templates Needed
S22, T7 & T32

MRS. CLEVELAND'S CHOICE PIECING INSTRUCTIONS

1. Referring to the Piecing Diagram to piece one block, sew T23 to each side of S12; add R55 to opposite sides and R5 to the remaining sides.

2. Join three light and one dark T17 triangle to make a T17 unit; repeat for four units. Sew a T17 unit to opposite sides of the previously pieced unit to complete the center unit.

3. Sew a light T11 to a dark T11 to make a T11 unit; repeat for 12 units.

4. Join two T11 units and add a light T11; sew a light T11 to one T11 unit. Join these two units with another T11 and add Z27 to complete a corner unit; repeat for four corner units.

5. Sew a corner unit to each side of the center unit; join side seams to complete the block.

NECKTIE PIECING INSTRUCTIONS

1. Referring to the Piecing Diagram to piece one block, sew T1 to the angled edge of Z14; add S5 to a T1 side to complete one unit. Repeat for eight units.

2. Join two units to complete a quarter section; repeat for four quarter sections.

3. Join the quarter sections to complete the block.

NEXT-DOOR NEIGHBOR PIECING INSTRUCTIONS

1. Referring to the Piecing Diagram to piece one block, sew a medium T7 to a dark T7 on the short sides to make a T7 unit; repeat for two units. Join the two units to complete the center unit.

2. Sew a light T32 to a dark T32 to make a T32 unit; repeat for four units.

3. Sew a light T7 to the dark side of each T32 unit to make the corner units. Sew a corner unit to opposite sides of the center unit to complete the center row.

4. Sew a medium T32 to two opposite sides of each of the remaining corner units; sew these units to opposite sides of the center row to complete the block.

NINE-PATCH PLAID PIECING INSTRUCTIONS

1. Referring to the Piecing Diagram to piece one block, sew a dark S19 between two light S19 squares to make a light row; repeat for two light rows. Repeat with one light and two dark S19 squares to make a dark row. Join the rows to complete the center unit.

2. Sew R6 to opposite sides of the center unit. Sew a light S19 to each end of the remaining R6 pieces; sew these units to the remaining sides of the center unit.

3. Sew R24 to the top of the center unit. Sew a medium S19 to one end of the remaining R24 piece; sew this unit to the left side of the center unit to complete the block.

Mrs. Cleveland's Choice
12" x 12" Block

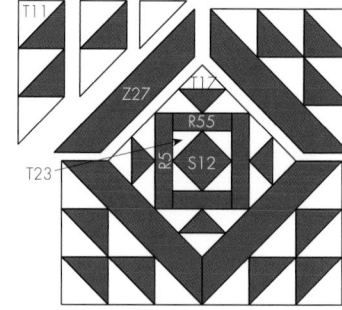

Templates Needed
R5, R55, S12, T11,
T17, T23 & Z27

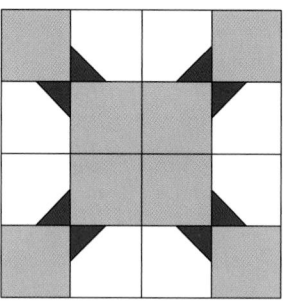

Necktie
12" x 12" Block

Templates Needed
S5, T1 & Z14

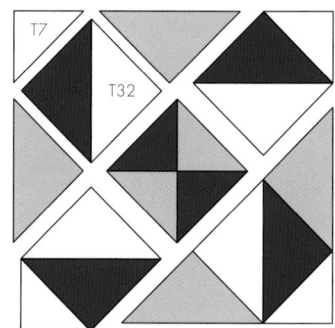

Next-Door Neighbor
12" x 12" Block

Templates Needed
T7 & T32

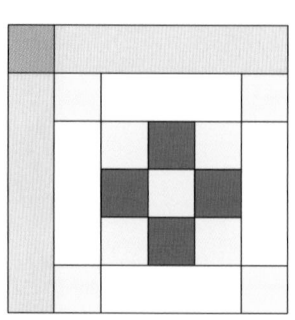

Nine-Patch Plaid
12" x 12" Block

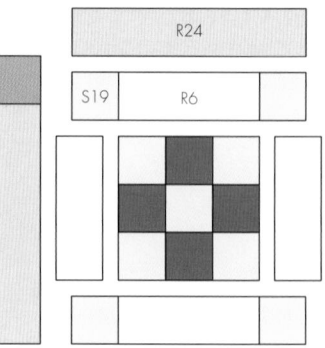

Templates Needed
R6, R24 & S19

NO PLACE LIKE HOME PIECING INSTRUCTIONS

1. Referring to the Piecing Diagram to piece one block, sew a light T8 to a dark T8 on a short side; repeat for two units. Join the two units.

2. Sew R11 to opposite sides of the pieced unit. Sew S19 to opposite ends of R11; repeat for two units.

3. Sew an S19-R11 unit to the remaining sides of the pieced unit.

4. Sew R15 to opposite sides of the pieced unit. Sew S19 to opposite ends of R15; repeat for two units.

5. Sew an S19-R15 unit to the remaining sides of the pieced unit to complete the block.

NORTH CAROLINA STAR PIECING INSTRUCTIONS

1. Referring to the Piecing Diagram to piece one block, sew R57 to each side of S29 and set in Z36 to complete the center unit.

2. Sew Z35 and Z35R to opposite sides of T57 and add T19 to complete a corner unit; repeat for four corner units.

3. Sew the corner units between the Z36 points of the center units to complete the block.

OHIO STAR PIECING INSTRUCTIONS

1. Referring to the Piecing Diagram to piece one block, sew Z57 to Z57R and set in S2 to complete a star unit; repeat for four star units.

2. Join four star units to complete the center unit.

3. Sew Z57 and Z57R to two adjacent sides of S5 and add T7 to complete a corner unit; repeat for four corner units.

4. Set a corner unit into the center unit to complete the block.

OHIO STAR-IN-A-STAR PIECING INSTRUCTIONS

1. Referring to the Piecing Diagram to piece one block, sew a dark 2 T11 to each side of S29.

2. Sew a dark 1 T11 to each short side of T18; repeat for four units. Sew a unit to opposite sides of the T11-S29 unit.

3. Sew an S19 to each end of the remaining T11-T18 units; sew these units to the remaining sides of the pieced unit to complete the block center.

4. Sew a dark T11 to a light T11 on the diagonal; repeat for eight T11 units.

5. Sew a medium T11 to the short sides of T18 to make a side unit; repeat for four side units.

6. Sew a T11 unit to each short end of a side unit. Sew a T11 side unit to opposite sides of the pieced center.

7. Sew S19 to opposite ends of the remaining T11 side units; sew these units to the remaining sides of the pieced unit to complete the block.

No Place Like Home
12" x 12" Block

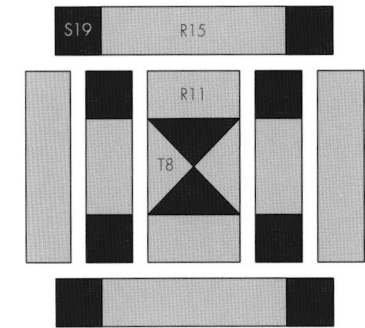

Templates Needed
R11, R15, S19 & T8

North Carolina Star
12" x 12" Block

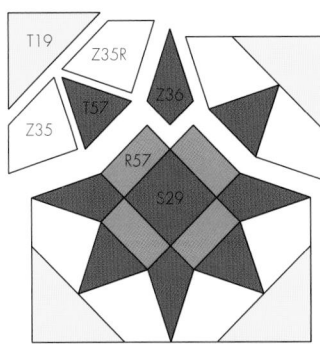

Templates Needed
R57, S29, T19, T57,
Z35, Z35R & Z36

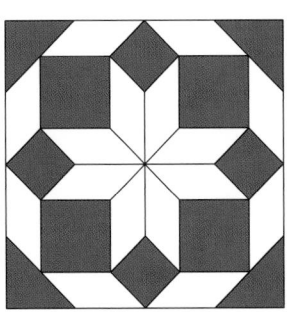

Ohio Star
12" x 12" Block

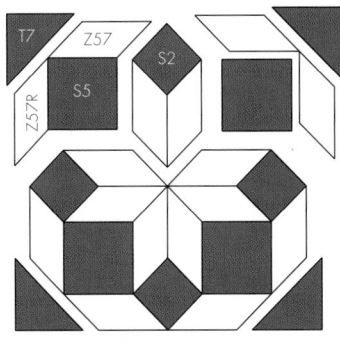

Templates Needed
S2, S5, T7, Z57 & Z57R

Ohio Star-in-a-Star
12" x 12" Block

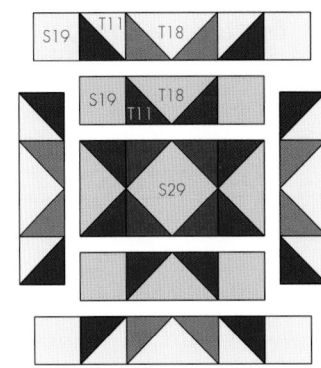

Templates Needed
S19, S29, T11 & T18

OLD MAID'S PUZZLE PIECING INSTRUCTIONS

1. Referring to the Piecing Diagram to piece one block, sew a light T1 to a dark T1 and add S30; repeat for two units and join to complete a T-S unit. Repeat for four T-S units.

2. Sew a light T1 to each side of a dark T1 triangle and add T7 to complete a T unit; repeat for eight T units. Sew a medium T1 to each side of S2; add R44 to opposite sides.

3. Sew a light T1 to a medium T1; repeat for four T1 units. Sew R44 between two T1 units; repeat. Sew a unit to the remaining side of the S2-T1 unit to complete the center unit.

4. Join two T units to make a side unit; repeat for four units.

5. Sew a side unit to opposite sides of the center unit to complete the center row.

6. Sew a side unit between two T-S units to complete a side row; repeat. Sew a side row to each side of the center row to complete the block.

OMBRE PIECING INSTRUCTIONS

1. Referring to the Piecing Diagram to piece one block, sew a light S8 to a medium S8 to complete a side unit; repeat for four side units.

2. Join two side units with the lightest S8 to complete the center row.

3. Sew a dark T42 to a medium Z29 and a dark T42 to a lightest Z29; join these units to complete a corner unit. Repeat for four corner units.

4. Join two corner units with a side unit to make a side row; repeat for two side rows. Sew the center row between the side rows to complete the block.

ON THE SQUARE PIECING INSTRUCTIONS

1. Referring to the Piecing Diagram to piece one block, sew a medium S9 to each side of a dark S9; repeat for two S9 units. Sew these units to opposite sides of S14.

2. Join two medium and three dark S9 squares; repeat for two units. Sew these units to the remaining sides of S14 to complete the center unit.

3. Sew a medium S9 to each end of R20; repeat for four R20 units. Sew R51 to each R20 unit to complete four side units.

4. Sew a side unit to the top and bottom of the center unit.

5. Sew a medium S9 to a dark S9; repeat for eight units. Join two units to complete a corner unit; repeat for four corner units.

6. Sew a corner unit to each end of the remaining sides units; sew these units to opposite sides of the center unit to complete the block.

OPTICAL ILLUSION PIECING INSTRUCTIONS

1. Referring to the Piecing Diagram to piece one block, sew a medium T11 to a darkest T11 to make a T11 unit; repeat for four units. Join the four T11 units to complete the center unit.

2. Sew a light T16R to a dark T16R to complete a unit; repeat with a light T16 and a darkest T16 to complete a unit. Join the two units to complete a side unit; repeat for four side units.

3. Sew a medium T18 to a short side of a dark T18; repeat with a medium T18 and a darkest T18. Join these two units to complete a corner unit; repeat for four corner units.

4. Sew a side unit to opposite sides of the center unit to complete the center row.

5. Sew a side unit between two corner units to complete a side row; repeat for two side rows. Sew the center row between two side rows to complete the block.

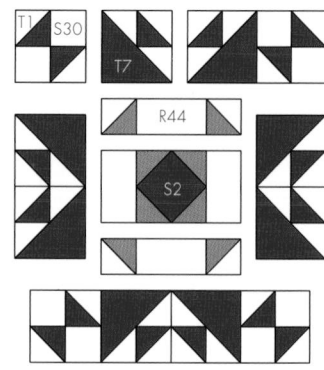

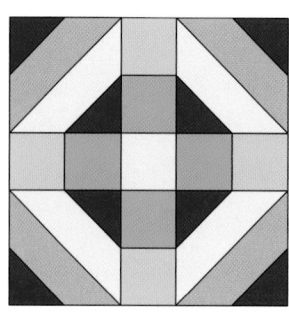

Old Maid's Puzzle
12" x 12" Block

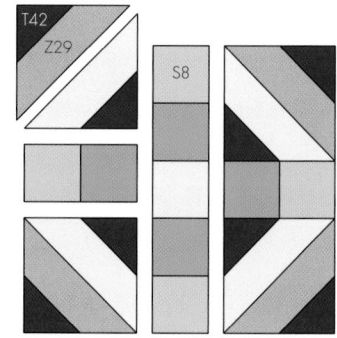

Templates Needed
R44, S2, S30, T1 & T7

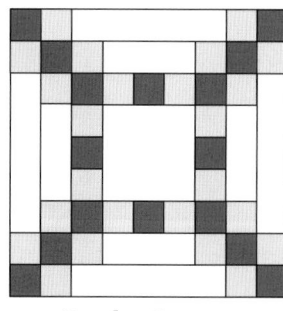

Ombre
12" x 12" Block

Templates Needed
S8, T42 & Z29

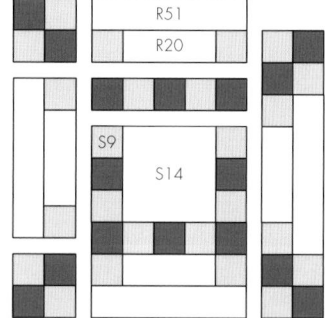

On the Square
12" x 12" Block

Templates Needed
R20, R51, S9 & S14

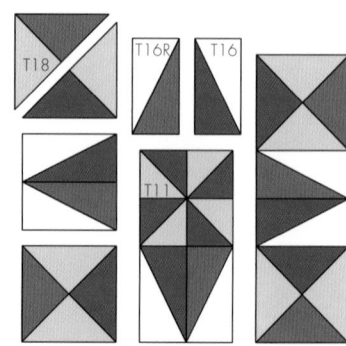

Optical Illusion
12" x 12" Block

Templates Needed
T11, T16, T16R & T18

OZARK MOUNTAINS PIECING INSTRUCTIONS

1. Referring to the Piecing Diagram to piece one block, sew a light T33 to the short sides of a medium T7 and add a lightest T7 to the T33 side. Sew a lightest T33 to the light T33 ends to complete a corner unit; repeat for four corner units.

2. Sew a dark T33 to two adjacent sides of S2 and add two lightest T7 pieces to the pieced unit to complete an S2 unit; repeat for two S2 units.

3. Sew a dark T7 to each end and a T32 to the light T7 side of an S2 unit to complete a center unit; repeat for two center units.

4. Sew a corner unit to the T32 sides of a center unit to complete half the block; repeat for two halves.

5. Join the two half-blocks to complete the block.

PAISLEY LILIES PIECING INSTRUCTIONS

1. Referring to the Piecing Diagram to piece one block, join one darkest and two light S19 squares to make a row; repeat for two rows. Join one dark and two darkest S19 squares to make a row. Sew this row between the two previously pieced rows to complete the center unit.

2. Sew T32 to each side of the center unit to complete the block center.

3. Sew T29 to two short sides of T42 to complete a T unit; repeat for eight T units. Join two T units with an S32 to complete a side unit; repeat for four side units.

4. Sew a side unit to opposite sides of the block center. Sew S32 to each end of the remaining side units; sew these units to the remaining sides of the block center to complete the block.

PASTEL PINWHEEL PIECING INSTRUCTIONS

1. Referring to the Piecing Diagram to piece one block, turn under the curved edges of the Z20 pieces; baste to hold.

2. Align the straight edge of a Z20 piece with one edge of an S14 square to make a center unit; stitch along straight edge to hold. Appliqué curved edge in place to complete one center square. Repeat for four center squares.

3. Join the four center squares to complete the center; sew an R15 rectangle to opposite sides.

4. Sew a light T11 to a medium T11 along the diagonal to make a corner unit; repeat for four corner units.

5. Sew a corner unit to each end of the remaining R15 pieces. Sew these units to the remaining sides of the center to complete the block.

PATCHES OF SUNSHINE PIECING INSTRUCTIONS

1. Referring to the Piecing Diagram to piece one block, sew a light S3 to a dark S3; repeat for two units. Join the units to complete a corner unit; repeat for four corner units.

2. Sew a dark T16 and T16R to the short sides of a medium T35 to make a side unit; repeat for four side units.

3. Sew a medium T19 to a light T19 along the diagonal to make a medium T19 unit. Repeat for two units.

4. Sew a dark T19 to a light T19 along the diagonal to make a dark T19 unit; repeat for two units.

5. Join the T19 units to complete the center; sew a side unit to opposite sides of the center.

6. Sew a corner unit to each end of the remaining side units; sew these side units to the remaining sides of the center to complete the block.

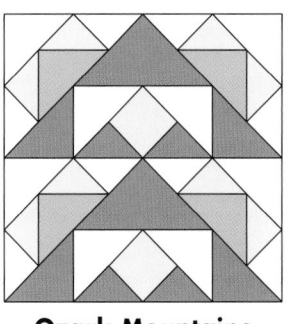
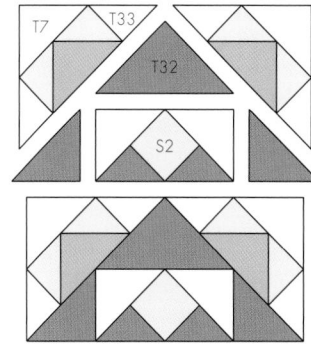

Ozark Mountains
12" x 12" Block

Templates Needed
S2, T7, T32 & T33

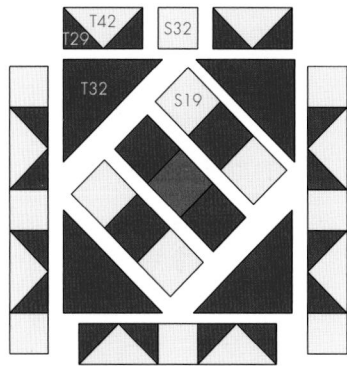

Paisley Lilies
12" x 12" Block

Templates Needed
S19, S32, T29, T32 & T42

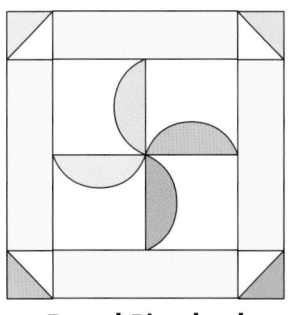
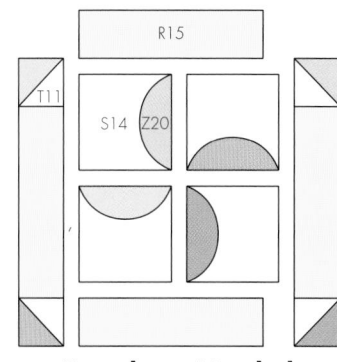

Pastel Pinwheel
12" x 12" Block

Templates Needed
R15, S14, T11 & Z20

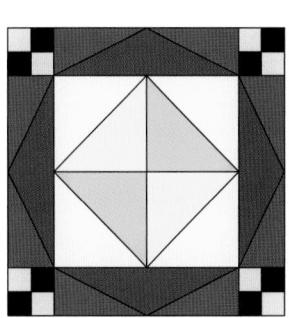
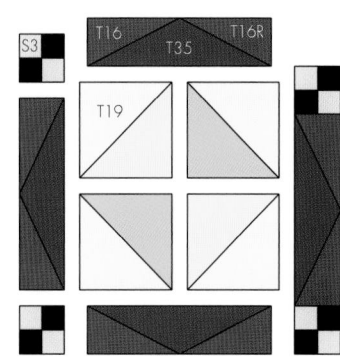

Patches of Sunshine
12" x 12" Block

Templates Needed
S3, T16, T16R, T19 & T35

113

PATCHWORK POSY PIECING INSTRUCTIONS

1. Referring to the Piecing Diagram to piece one block, sew a light S9 between two darkest S9 squares to make a row; repeat for two rows. Repeat with one dark and two light S9 squares to make a row; join this row with the previously pieced rows to complete the center unit.
2. Sew a light R54 piece between two darkest R54 pieces to complete an R54 unit; repeat for four units.
3. Sew a lightest T59 and T59R to each angled side of T50; add T10 to each end to complete a T50 unit. Repeat for four T50 units. Sew a T50 unit to one long side of an R54 unit to complete a side unit; repeat for four side units.
4. Sew a side unit to opposite sides of the center unit to complete the center row.
5. Sew a medium S9 to one end of a lightest R54 piece; sew this unit to R40 to complete a corner unit. Repeat for four corner units.
6. Sew a corner unit to each side of each of the remaining side units to complete the side rows. Sew the center row between the side rows to complete the block.

PATIENCE CORNER PIECING INSTRUCTIONS

1. Referring to the Piecing Diagram to piece one block, sew R11 to one side of S14 and add R6 to complete a block quarter section; repeat for four quarter sections.
2. Arrange and join the quarter sections to complete the block.

PEACE & PLENTY PIECING INSTRUCTIONS

1. Referring to the Piecing Diagram to piece one block, sew a light T7 to a dark T7 to complete a T7 unit; repeat for four units. Join the four units to complete the center unit.
2. Sew a dark T7 to a light T7 on the short sides to complete a T unit; repeat for four T units. Sew one of these units to each side of the center unit.
3. Join a dark T32 and a light T32 on the short sides to complete a T32 unit; repeat for four units.
4. Sew a T32 unit to each side of the center unit to complete the block.

PERSHING PIECING INSTRUCTIONS

1. Referring to the Piecing Diagram to piece one block, sew T11 to each side of S29; add a lightest T18 to each side of this pieced unit to complete the center unit.
2. Sew a dark T18 to the short sides of a light T19 and add a lightest T19 to the T18 side to complete a corner unit; repeat for four corner units.
3. Sew a corner unit to opposite sides of the center unit.
4. Sew a light T18 to each end of each remaining corner unit; sew one of these units to the remaining sides of the center unit to complete the block.

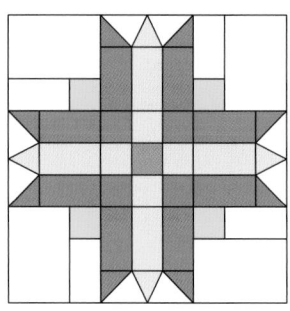

Patchwork Posy
12" x 12" Block

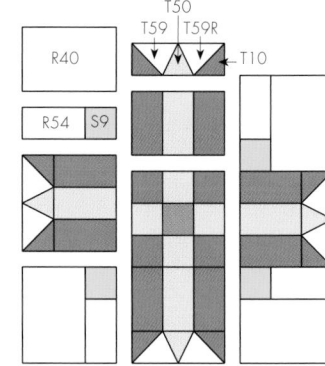

Templates Needed
R40, R54, S9, T10,
T50, T59 & T59R

Patience Corner
12" x 12" Block

Templates Needed
R6, R11 & S14

Peace & Plenty
12" x 12" Block

Templates Needed
T7 & T32

Pershing
12" x 12" Block

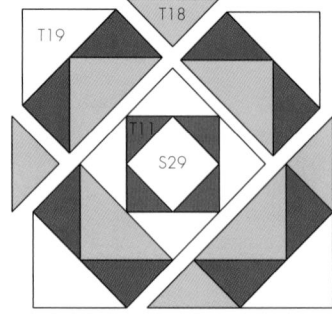

Templates Needed
S29, T11, T18 & T19

PINWHEEL SQUARE PIECING INSTRUCTIONS

1. Referring to the Piecing Diagram to piece one block, sew a light T27 to a dark T27 to complete a T27 unit; repeat for four units.

2. Join two T27 units with S8 to complete the center row.

3. Sew a light T12 to a dark T12 to complete a T12 unit; repeat for four units.

4. Sew a light T42 to two adjacent sides of S8 to complete an S unit; repeat for four S units.

5. Sew an S unit to a T12 unit to complete a corner unit; repeat for four corner units.

6. Join two corner units with a T27 unit to complete a side row; repeat for two side rows.

7. Sew the center row between the two side rows to complete the block.

PINWHEEL STAR PIECING INSTRUCTIONS

1. Referring to the Piecing Diagram to piece one block, sew a light T11 to a dark T11 along the diagonal; repeat for 16 units. Join four same-fabric units to complete a pinwheel unit; repeat for four units.

2. Join the pinwheel units to complete the block center.

3. Sew a dark T11 to a light T11 on the diagonal; repeat for eight T11 units.

4. Sew a medium T11 to the short sides of T18 to make a side unit; repeat for four side units.

5. Sew a T11 unit to each short end of a side unit. Sew a T11 side unit to opposite sides of the pieced center.

6. Sew S19 to opposite ends of the remaining T11 side units; sew these units to the remaining sides of the pieced unit to complete the block.

PINWHEELS PIECING INSTRUCTIONS

1. Referring to the Piecing Diagram to piece one block, sew a light T7 to a medium T7 to complete a medium T7 unit; repeat for eight medium units.

2. Sew a light T7 to a dark T7 to complete a dark T7 unit; repeat for four dark T7 units.

3. Join one dark T7 with S5; join two medium T7 units. Join these two units to complete a quarter section; repeat for four quarter sections.

4. Join the quarter sections to complete the block.

PINWHEELS & SQUARES PIECING INSTRUCTIONS

1. Referring to the Piecing Diagram to piece one block, sew T7 to two adjacent sides of S5 to complete an S unit; repeat for four S units.

2. Sew a light T32 to a medium T32 to complete a T unit; repeat for four T units.

3. Sew a T unit to an S unit to complete a quarter section; repeat for four quarter sections.

4. Join the quarter sections to complete the block.

Pinwheel Square
12" x 12" Block

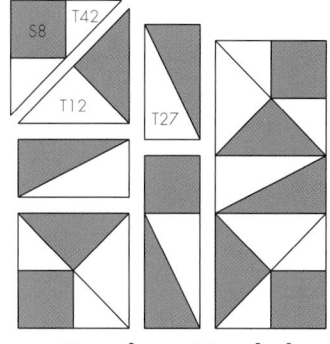

Templates Needed
S8, T12, T27 & T42

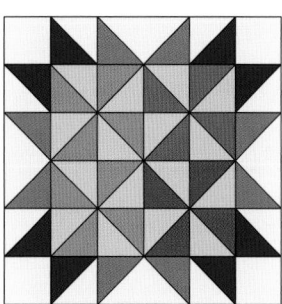

Pinwheel Star
12" x 12" Block

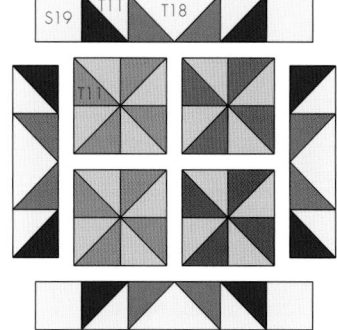

Templates Needed
S19, T11 & T18

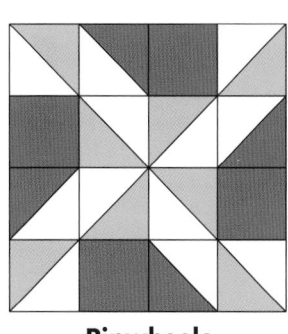

Pinwheels
12" x 12" Block

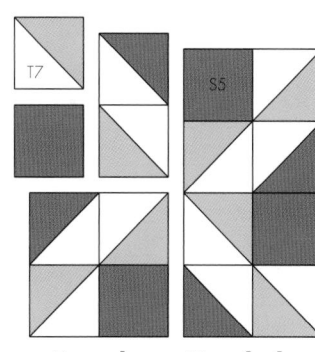

Templates Needed
S5 & T7

Pinwheels & Squares
12" x 12" Block

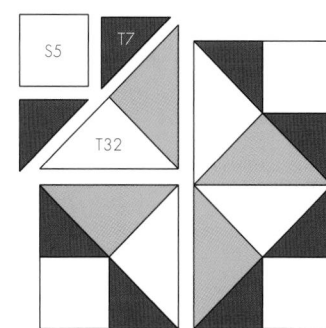

Templates Needed
S5, T7 & T32

POINSETTIA PIECING INSTRUCTIONS

1. Referring to the Piecing Diagram to piece one block, sew a light T7 to a medium T7; repeat for four units. Join the units to complete the center unit.

2. Sew a light T7 to T32 and a light T7 to Z58; join these two units to complete a side unit; repeat for four side units.

3. Sew a side unit to the center unit, matching the medium T7 end and leaving excess loose at the opposite end. Sew the remaining side units to the center unit; finish the seam on the first unit to complete the block.

PRAIRIE CLAW PIECING INSTRUCTIONS

1. Referring to the Piecing Diagram to piece one block, sew T1 to each side of S2 to make an S-T unit; repeat for five units.

2. Sew a dark S5 to opposite sides of one S-T unit to complete the center row.

3. Join two S-T units with a light S5 to complete a row; repeat for two rows. Sew a row to opposite sides of the center row to complete the center unit.

4. Sew T1 to the short sides of T33 to complete a T unit; repeat for four T units. Sew R44 to each end of two T units; sew these units to opposite sides of the center unit.

5. Sew R44 and S30 to each end of the remaining two T units; sew these units to the remaining sides of the center unit to complete the block.

PRIMROSE CLUSTER 1 PIECING INSTRUCTIONS

1. Referring to the Piecing Diagram to piece one block, sew a darkest T7 to a dark T7 along the diagonal to make a corner unit; repeat for four corner units.

2. Sew a dark T7 to each short side of a medium T32 to make a side unit; repeat for four side units.

3. Sew a light T7 to each side of the darkest S22 to complete the center.

4. Sew a side unit to opposite sides of the pieced center.

5. Sew a corner unit to each end of the remaining two side units; sew these units to the remaining sides of the pieced center to complete the block.

PRIMROSE CLUSTER 2 PIECING INSTRUCTIONS

1. Referring to the Piecing Diagram to piece one block, sew a medium T7 to each short side of a darkest T32 to make a side unit; repeat for four side units.

2. Sew a darkest T7 to each side of the lightest S22 to make the center unit.

3. Sew a side unit to opposite sides of the center unit.

4. Sew a lightest S5 to each end of the remaining two side units; sew these units to the remaining sides of the center unit to complete the block.

Poinsettia
12" x 12" Block

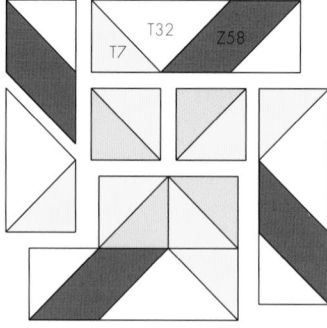

Templates Needed
T7, T32 & Z58

Prairie Claw
12" x 12" Block

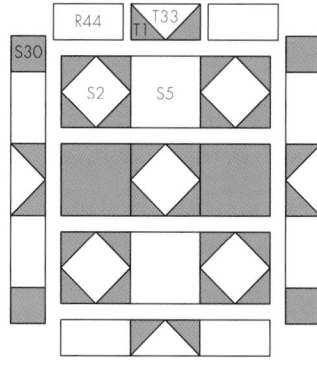

Templates Needed
R44, S2, S5, S30, T1 & T33

Primrose Cluster 1
12" x 12" Block

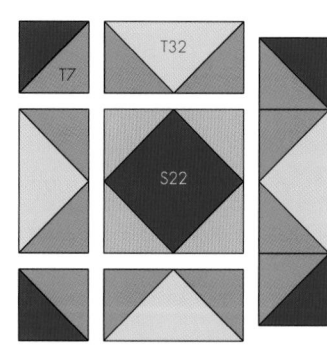

Templates Needed
S22, T7 & T32

Primrose Cluster 2
12" x 12" Block

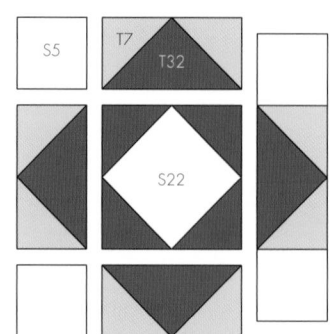

Templates Needed
S5, S22, T7 & T32

PROVIDENCE PIECING INSTRUCTIONS

1. Referring to the Piecing Diagram to piece one block, sew a light T29 to a medium T29 on the short sides; repeat for eight units. Join two units to complete a T29 unit; repeat for four units.

2. Join two T29 units with one light and two medium S8 squares to complete the center row.

3. Join one T29 unit with one dark S8 to complete a side row; repeat for two side rows.

4. Sew a light T42 to a dark T42 to complete a T42 unit; repeat for eight units. Join two T42 units with two light S8 squares to complete a corner unit; repeat for four corner units.

5. Join two corner units with a side unit to complete a side row; repeat for two side rows.

6. Sew the center row between the two side rows to complete the block.

PUERTO RICO PIECING INSTRUCTIONS

1. Referring to the Piecing Diagram to piece one block, sew a medium T7 to two opposite sides of S22; repeat with dark T7 pieces on the remaining sides to complete the center unit.

2. Sew a light T7 to a dark T7 and a light T7 to a medium T7; join the two units to complete a side unit; repeat for four side units.

3. Sew a side unit to opposite sides of the center unit to complete the center row.

4. Sew a medium S30 to a dark S30; repeat for eight units. Join two units to complete a corner unit; repeat for four corner units.

5. Join the corner units with a side unit to complete a side row; repeat for two side rows.

6. Sew the center row between the two side rows to complete the block.

PYRAMIDS PIECING INSTRUCTIONS

1. Referring to the Piecing Diagram to piece one block, sew a medium T33 to each side of S5; add a dark T7 to each side of this unit to complete the center unit.

2. Sew a medium T33 to two adjacent sides of S2 to complete a side unit; repeat for four side units.

3. Sew a side unit to each side of the center unit.

4. Sew a medium T33 to each short side of a light T7; add a dark T7 to the T33 side and add a light T33 to the T33 ends to complete a corner unit; repeat for four corner units.

5. Sew a corner unit to each side of the pieced center unit to complete the block.

QUARTER-SQUARE TRIANGLE STAR PIECING INSTRUCTIONS

1. Referring to the Piecing Diagram to piece one block, join a medium T18 with a dark T18 on a short side; repeat for eight units.

2. Join two units to complete one T18 unit; repeat for four units. Join the units to complete the block center.

3. Sew a dark T11 to a light T11 on the diagonal; repeat for eight T11 units. Sew a medium T11 to the short sides of T18 to make a side unit; repeat for four side units.

4. Sew a T11 unit to each short end of a side unit. Sew a T11 side unit to opposite sides of the pieced center.

5. Sew S19 to opposite ends of the remaining T11 side units; sew these units to the remaining sides of the pieced unit to complete the block.

Providence
12" x 12" Block

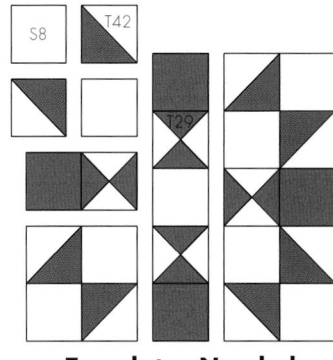

Templates Needed
S8, T29 & T42

Puerto Rico
12" x 12" Block

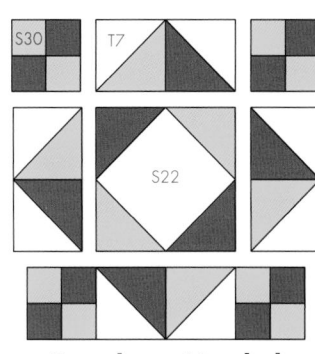

Templates Needed
S22, S30 & T7

Pyramids
12" x 12" Block

Templates Needed
S2, S5, T7 & T33

Quarter-Square Triangle Star
12" x 12" Block

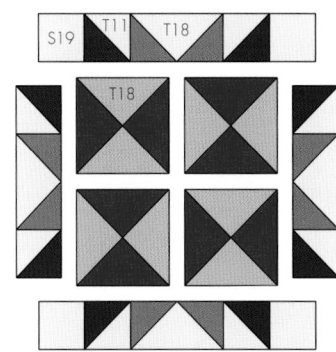

Templates Needed
S19, T11 & T18

QUEEN'S CROWN PIECING INSTRUCTIONS

1. Referring to the Piecing Diagram to piece one block, sew a dark T42 to a light T42 to complete a T42 unit; repeat for 12 units.

2. Join four T42 units with a dark S24 to complete the center row.

3. Sew a light T40 to a dark T40 to complete a T corner unit; repeat for two T corner units.

4. Join two T42 units with two light S24 squares to make an S corner unit; repeat for two S corner units.

5. Join two T42 units to make a side unit; sew a side unit between one each S and T corner units to complete a side row. Repeat for two side rows.

6. Sew the center row between two side rows to complete the block.

Queen's Crown
12" x 12" Block

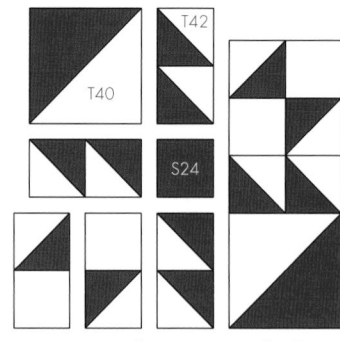

Templates Needed
S24, T40 & T42

RAIL FENCE VARIATION STAR PIECING INSTRUCTIONS

1. Referring to the Piecing Diagram to piece one block, sew a light R11 to a medium R11; repeat for two light units.

2. Sew a dark R11 to a medium R11; repeat for two dark units.

3. Sew a light unit to a dark unit; repeat. Join the two pieced units to complete the center unit.

4. Sew a dark T11 to a light T11 on the diagonal; repeat for eight T11 units.

5. Sew a medium T11 to the short sides of T18 to make a side unit; repeat for four side units.

6. Sew a T11 unit to each short end of a side unit. Sew a T11 side unit to opposite sides of the pieced center.

7. Sew S19 to opposite ends of the remaining T11 side units; sew these units to the remaining sides of the pieced unit to complete the block.

Rail Fence Variation Star
12" x 12" Block

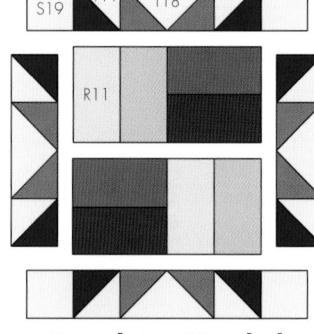

Templates Needed
R11, S19, T11 & T18

RAILROAD CROSSING PIECING INSTRUCTIONS

1. Referring to the Piecing Diagram to piece one block, sew T33 to each short side of a light T7 to complete a T7 unit; repeat for 10 units.

2. Join six T7 units to make a strip; add a light T7 to the T33 end and a dark T7 to the light T7 end to complete the center row.

3. Join two T7 units; repeat for two units. Add a dark T7 to the light end of one unit and a light T7 to the dark end of the remaining unit. Add T32 to each dark side of each unit to complete a corner unit.

4. Sew the corner units to opposite sides of the center row to complete the block.

Railroad Crossing
12" x 12" Block

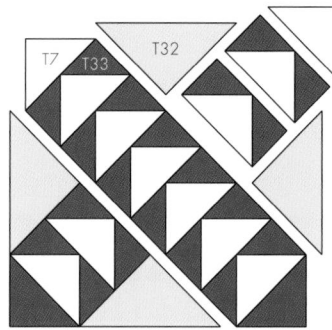

Templates Needed
T7, T32 & T33

RAMBLER PIECING INSTRUCTIONS

1. Referring to the Piecing Diagram to piece one block, sew T33 to each side of S5 to complete the center unit.

2. Sew T33 to each short side of four light and four dark T7 triangles to make light and dark T7 units.

3. Join one light and one dark T7 unit with one dark T7 to make a corner unit; repeat for four corner units.

4. Sew a corner unit to opposite sides of the center unit to complete the center row.

5. Sew T32 to the sides of each remaining corner unit to complete the corner rows. Sew a corner row to opposite sides of the center row to complete the block.

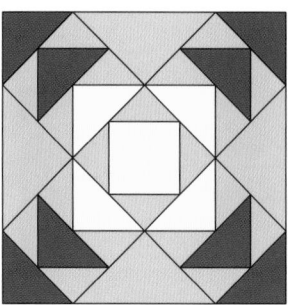

Rambler
12" x 12" Block

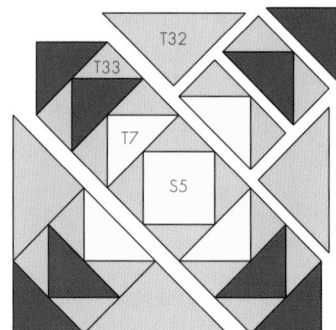

Templates Needed
S5, T7, T32 & T33

RED CROSS I PIECING INSTRUCTIONS

1. Referring to the Piecing Diagram to piece one block, sew a light T42 to a dark T42; repeat for 16 units.

2. Join four T42 units to complete a corner unit; repeat for four corner units.

3. Join two corner units with R13 to complete a side unit; repeat for two side units.

4. Sew R13 to opposite sides of S8 to complete the center row; sew this row between the side rows to complete the block.

RED CROSS II PIECING INSTRUCTIONS

1. Referring to the Piecing Diagram to piece one block, join three dark and two light S24 squares to complete the center row.

2. Join one medium and three light T42 triangles to complete a T42 unit; repeat for four units.

3. Sew a light T42 to Z29 to complete a Z unit; repeat for four Z units. Sew a Z unit to a T42 unit to complete a corner unit; repeat for four corner units.

4. Sew a light S24 to a dark S24; sew this unit between two corner units to complete a side unit. Repeat for two side units.

5. Sew the center unit between the side units to complete the block.

RHODE ISLAND PIECING INSTRUCTIONS

1. Referring to the Piecing Diagram to piece one block, sew T17 to the two short sides of T11 to complete a T11 unit; repeat for four units.

2. Sew a T11 unit to opposite sides of S29. Sew an S25 square to each end of the remaining T11 units; sew these units to the remaining sides of S29 to complete the center unit.

3. Sew a light T18 to two adjacent sides of S14 to complete a corner unit; repeat for four units. Sew a unit to opposite sides of the center unit to complete the center row.

4. Sew a dark T18 to the light T18 ends of the remaining corner units; sew these units to opposite sides of the center row to complete the block.

ROAD TO BERLIN PIECING INSTRUCTIONS

1. Referring to the Piecing Diagram to piece one block, sew T54 to Z19 to make a side unit; repeat for four side units.

2. Sew a side unit to each side of S21 and finish corner seams to complete the block.

Red Cross I
12" x 12" Block

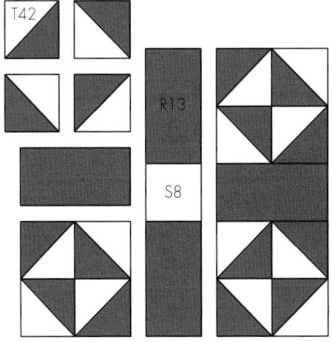

Templates Needed
R13, S8 & T42

Red Cross II
12" x 12" Block

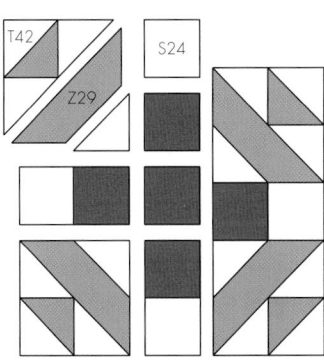

Templates Needed
S24, T42 & Z29

Rhode Island
12" x 12" Block

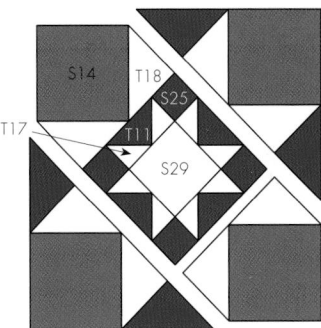

Templates Needed
S14, S25, S29,
T11, T17 & T18

Road to Berlin
12" x 12" Block

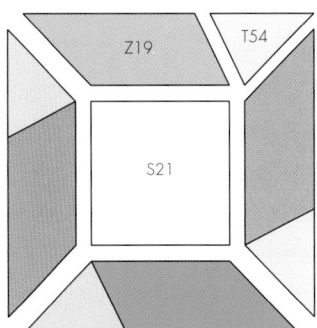

Templates Needed
S21, T54 & Z19

ROAD TO CALIFORNIA PIECING INSTRUCTIONS

1. Referring to the Piecing Diagram to piece one block, sew T29 to the short sides of T42 to complete a T42 unit; repeat for 12 units.

2. Join two S23 squares with three T42 units to make a row; repeat for two rows.

3. Join two T42 units with three S32 squares to make a row; repeat for three rows.

4. Join the rows referring to the Piecing Diagram to complete the block.

ROAD TO DAMASCUS PIECING INSTRUCTIONS

1. Referring to the Piecing Diagram to piece one block, sew T33 to two adjacent sides of S2 to make an S-T unit; repeat for two units.

2. Sew a dark T32 to one side of each S-T unit; join these two units to complete the center unit.

3. Sew T7 to the short sides of a medium T32; repeat for two units. Sew these units to opposite sides of the center unit to complete the center row.

4. Sew T7 to the short sides of each dark T32 and add S5 to each end to make the side rows.

5. Sew the center row between the two side rows to complete the block.

ROAD TO HEAVEN PIECING INSTRUCTIONS

1. Referring to the Piecing Diagram to piece one block, sew a light T7 to a medium T7 to complete a T7 unit; repeat for four units. Join two units with two S5 squares to complete an S5 unit; repeat for two units.

2. Join one medium and three light T7 triangles and add T39 to complete a T7 unit; repeat for two units.

3. Join the pieced units to complete the block.

ROCKY ROAD TO DUBLIN PIECING INSTRUCTIONS

1. Referring to the Piecing Diagram to piece one block, center and sew a light Z9 into a dark Z60 to complete a dark Z unit; repeat for eight units.

2. Center and sew a medium Z9 into a light Z60 to make a light Z unit; repeat for four units.

3. Center and sew a light Z9 into a medium Z60 to make a medium Z unit; repeat for four units.

4. Arrange and join the Z units in corner units referring to the Piecing Diagram; join the units to complete the block.

Road to California
12" x 12" Block

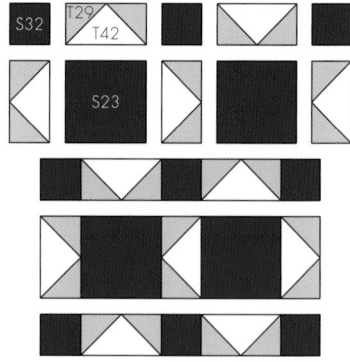

Templates Needed
S23, S32, T29 & T42

Road To Damascus
12" x 12" Block

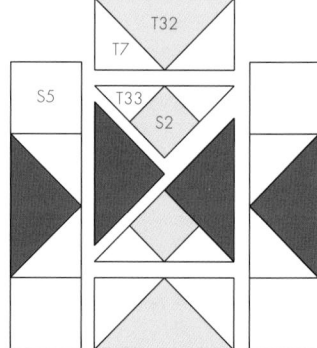

Templates Needed
S2, S5, T7, T32 & T33

Road to Heaven
12" x 12" Block

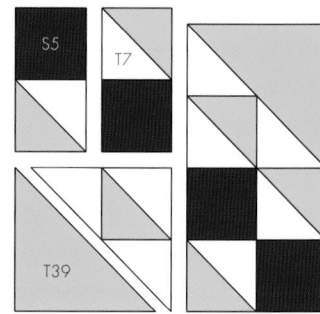

Templates Needed
S5, T7 & T39

Rocky Road to Dublin
12" x 12" Block

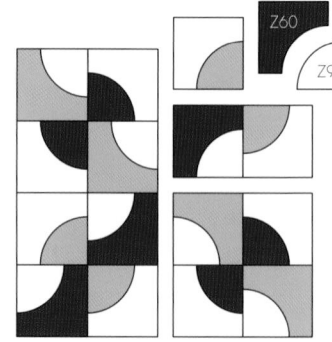

Templates Needed
Z9 & Z60

ROLLING STAR PIECING INSTRUCTIONS

1. Referring to the Piecing Diagram to piece one block, sew a dark Z57 to a light Z57R and set in S2 to complete an S-Z unit; repeat for four units. Join the four S-Z units to complete the center unit.

2. Sew a dark Z57R and a dark Z57 to two adjacent sides of S5; add T7 to the Z side to complete a corner unit. Repeat for four corner units.

3. Sew a corner unit between the points of the center unit to complete the block.

ROSEBUD PIECING INSTRUCTIONS

1. Referring to the Piecing Diagram to piece one block, sew a light T29 to a medium T29 to complete a medium T29 unit; repeat for eight units. Repeat with a light T29 and a dark T29 to complete eight dark T29 units.

2. Join a dark and darkest S32; repeat for eight S2 units. Join two S32 units to complete an S unit; repeat for four S units.

3. Sew a medium T29 unit to a dark T29 unit to make a T unit; repeat to make a reversed T unit. Sew the T unit to an S unit. Sew a medium S32 to the medium end of the reversed T unit and sew to the medium end of the stitched S unit to complete a corner unit; repeat for four corner units.

4. Join two corner units with R22 to complete a row; repeat for two rows.

5. Join two R22 pieces with a dark S32 to complete the center row.

6. Join the two previously pieced rows with the center row to complete the block.

SALT LAKE CITY PIECING INSTRUCTIONS

1. Referring to the Piecing Diagram to piece one block, sew a medium T7 triangle to each side of S22 to complete the center unit.

2. Sew T33 to two adjacent sides of S2 and add a dark T7 to the remaining sides of S2 to create a side unit; repeat for two side units. Sew a side unit to opposite sides of the center unit.

3. Sew T33 to two adjacent sides of S2; add T32 and a light T7 to each end of the pieced unit to complete a side row; repeat for two rows.

4. Sew the side rows to opposite sides of the center unit to complete the block.

SAWTOOTH PATCH PIECING INSTRUCTIONS

1. Referring to the Piecing Diagram to piece one block, sew T11 to each side of S29 to make an S-T unit; repeat for five units.

2. Join three S-T units to complete the center row.

3. Sew a light T19 to a medium T19 to complete a corner unit; repeat for four corner units.

4. Join two corner units with an S-T unit to complete a side row; repeat for two side rows.

5. Sew the center row between the two side rows to complete the block.

Rolling Star
12" x 12" Block

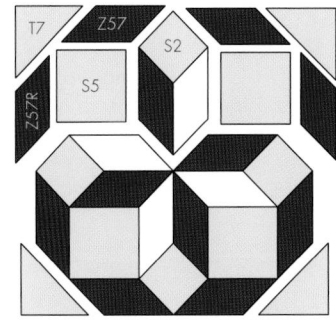

Templates Needed
S2, S5, T7, Z57 & Z57R

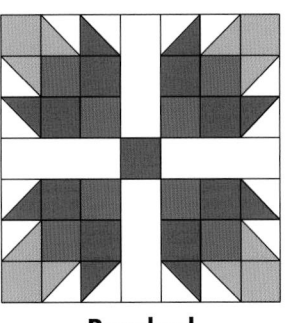

Rosebud
12" x 12" Block

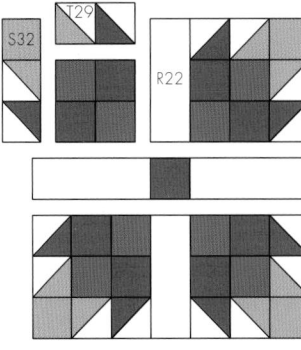

Templates Needed
R22, S32 & T29

Salt Lake City
12" x 12" Block

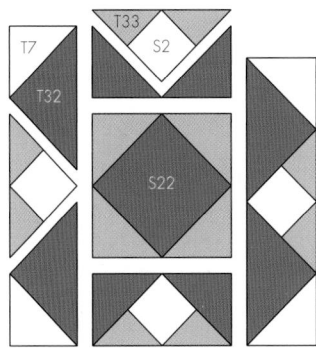

Templates Needed
S2, S22, T7, T32 & T33

Sawtooth Patch
12" x 12" Block

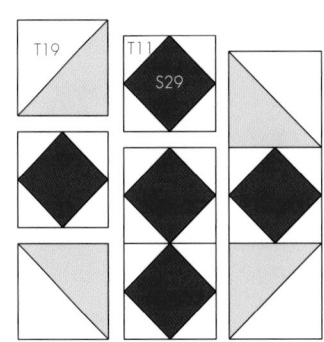

Templates Needed
S29, T11 & T19

SCOTCH PLAID PIECING INSTRUCTIONS

1. Referring to the Piecing Diagram to piece one block, sew R43 to opposite sides of S22.

2. Sew a light T33 to a dark T33; repeat for four units. Sew a T33 unit to each end of the remaining R43 pieces; sew these units to the remaining sides of S22 to complete the center unit.

3. Join one dark and three light T7 squares to make a corner unit; repeat for four corner units.

4. Sew a corner unit to each side of the center unit to complete the block.

SEDONA ILLUSION PIECING INSTRUCTIONS

1. Referring to the Piecing Diagram to piece one block, sew a lightest T7 to a light T7 on the diagonal; repeat for two top end units. Repeat with a medium T7 and a light T7 to make two bottom end units.

2. Sew a top end unit to the top and a bottom end unit to the bottom of R21 to complete a side unit; repeat for two side units.

3. Join a dark T32 and a darkest T32 on the short sides; repeat for two T32 units.

4. Sew a darkest T32 to opposite sides of the dark S22 square; join with the two T32 units to complete the block center.

5. Sew a side unit to opposite sides of the block center to complete the block.

SHINING STAR PIECING INSTRUCTIONS

1. Referring to the Piecing Diagram to piece one block, join two T45 pieces; add Z47 and Z47R to the sides of the pieced unit.

2. Sew Z32 to opposite sides of the pieced unit.

3. Sew T7 to each corner of the pieced unit to complete the block.

SHOOTING STAR PIECING INSTRUCTIONS

1. Referring to the Piecing Diagram to piece one block, sew a medium T47 to a dark T47 and add a lightest T49 to two adjacent sides of the unit to complete a center unit; repeat for four center units.

2. Join one light, one medium and two dark T49 pieces; add T13 to the dark end to complete a corner unit; repeat for four corner units.

3. Alternate the units and join in a clockwise direction to complete the block.

Scotch Plaid
12" x 12" Block

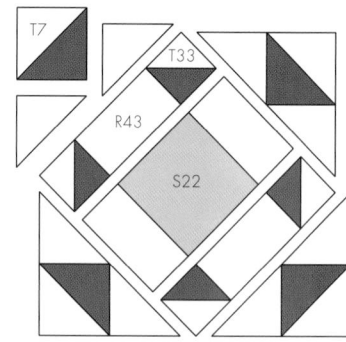

Templates Needed
R43, S22, T7 & T33

Sedona Illusion
12" x 12" Block

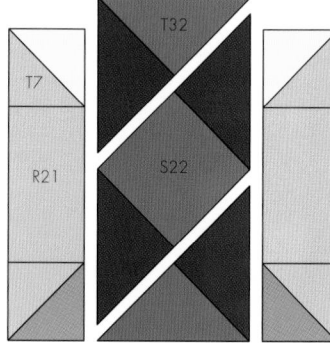

Templates Needed
R21, S22, T7 & T32

Shining Star
12" x 12" Block

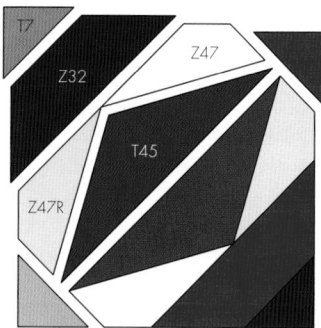

Templates Needed
T7, T45, Z32, Z47 & Z47R

Shooting Star
12" x 12" Block

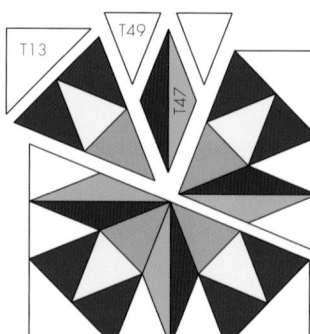

Templates Needed
T13, T47 & T49

SINGLE CHAIN & KNOT PIECING INSTRUCTIONS

1. Referring to the Piecing Diagram to piece one block, join one light and two dark S8 squares to make a row; repeat for two rows. Join one dark and two lights to make a row. Join the rows to complete the center unit.

2. Sew R1 to opposite sides of the center unit to complete the center row.

3. Sew a light S16 to a dark S16; repeat for eight units; join two of these units to complete a corner unit.

4. Sew a corner unit to each end of the remaining R1 pieces to make the side rows. Sew these rows to opposite sides of the center row to complete the block.

SISTER'S CHOICE PIECING INSTRUCTIONS

1. Referring to the Piecing Diagram to piece one block, join two light and three dark S8 squares to complete the center row.

2. Join one light and one dark S8 to complete a side unit; repeat for two side units.

3. Sew a light T42 to a dark T42 to complete a T42 unit; repeat for eight T42 units.

4. Join two T42 units with one light and one dark S8 square to complete a corner unit; repeat for four corner units.

5. Join two corner units with one side unit to complete a side row; repeat for two side rows.

6. Sew the center row between the two side rows to complete the block.

SNOWBALL PIECING INSTRUCTIONS

1. Referring to the Piecing Diagram to piece one block, center and sew Z10 into Z51 to complete a Z unit; repeat for 16 Z units.

2. Arrange and join the Z units in rows referring to the Piecing Diagram; join the rows to complete the block.

SNOWBALL STAR PIECING INSTRUCTIONS

1. Referring to the Piecing Diagram to piece one block, sew T5 to each angled side of Z64; repeat for four units.

2. Join the four pieced units to complete the block center.

3. Sew a dark T11 to a light T11 on the diagonal; repeat for eight T11 units.

4. Sew a medium T11 to the short sides of T18 to make a side unit; repeat for four side units.

5. Sew a T11 unit to each short end of two side units. Sew a T11 side unit to opposite sides of the pieced center.

6. Sew S19 to opposite ends of the remaining T11 side units; sew these units to the remaining sides of the pieced unit to complete the block.

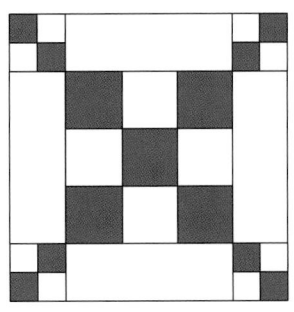

Single Chain & Knot
12" x 12" Block

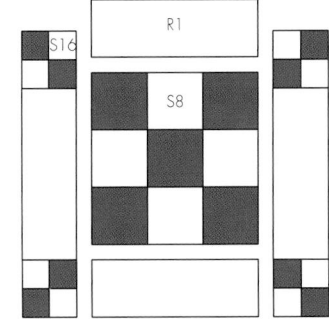

Templates Needed
R1, S8 & S16

Sister's Choice
12" x 12" Block

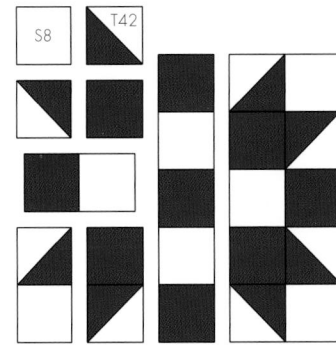

Templates Needed
S8 & T42

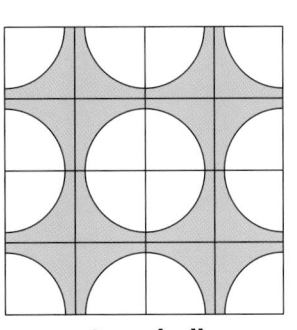

Snowball
12" x 12" Block

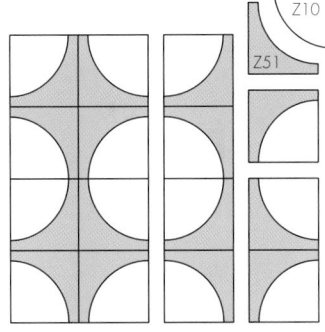

Templates Needed
Z10 & Z51

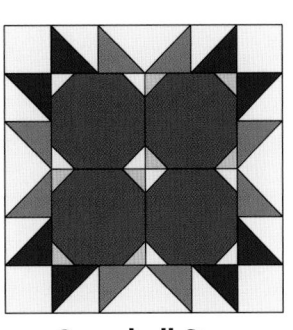

Snowball Star
12" x 12" Block

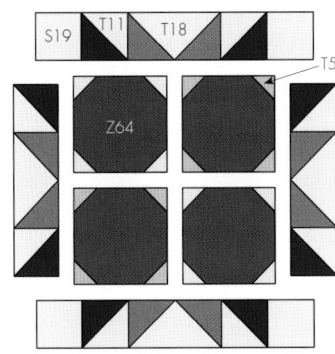

Templates Needed
S19, T5, T11, T18 & Z64

SOUTH CAROLINA PIECING INSTRUCTIONS

1. Referring to the Piecing Diagram to piece one block, join Z56 and Z56R. Sew a light T1 to one side of S30 and set into the Z unit to make a Z–S unit. Sew a light T1 to a medium T1 and sew the medium side to a light S2. Sew this unit to the Z–S unit to complete a corner unit; repeat for four corner units.

2. Sew a light T1 to each side of a dark S2; add T33 to one side and T7 to two sides to complete a side unit; repeat for four side units.

3. Join two corner units with a dark S2 square to complete the center row.

4. Sew a side unit to opposite sides of each of the remaining corner units to complete the block corners.

5. Sew a block corner to opposite sides of the center row to complete the block.

SPINNING PINWHEELS PIECING INSTRUCTIONS

1. Referring to the Piecing Diagram to piece one block, sew T7 to T32 and Z68 to a dark T11. Join the two units to make a T unit; repeat for four T units.

2. Sew a light T11 to Z67 and add T19 to complete a Z unit; repeat for four Z units.

3. Sew a T unit to a Z unit to make a quarter unit; repeat for four quarter units.

4. Join the four quarter units to complete the block.

SPRING GARDEN PATH PIECING INSTRUCTIONS

1. Referring to the Piecing Diagram to piece one block, join four R44 pieces to make an R44 unit; repeat for four units.

2. Sew two same-color R33 pieces to opposite long sides of an R44 unit to complete a block quarter; repeat for four block quarters.

3. Join the block quarters to complete the block.

SQUARE DANCE PIECING INSTRUCTIONS

1. Referring to the Piecing Diagram to piece one block, join three light S8 and two medium S8 squares to make the center row.

2. Join one light, one medium and two dark T42 triangles to create a T42 unit; repeat for four units.

3. Sew a dark T42 to Z29 to make a Z unit; repeat for four Z units. Sew a Z unit to a T42 unit to complete a corner unit; repeat for four corner units.

4. Join one light and one medium S8 square and sew between two corner units to complete a side row; repeat for two side rows.

5. Sew the center row between the side rows to complete the block.

South Carolina
12" x 12" Block

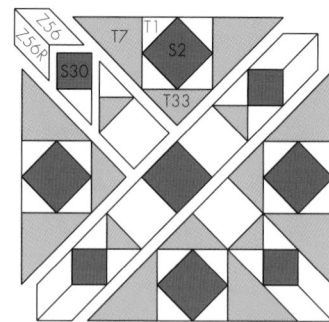

Templates Needed
S2, S30, T1, T7,
T33, Z56 & Z56R

Spinning Pinwheel
12" x 12" Block

Templates Needed
T7, T11, T19,
T32, Z67 & Z68

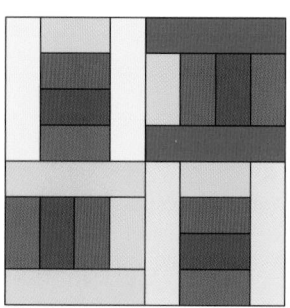

Spring Garden Path
12" x 12" Block

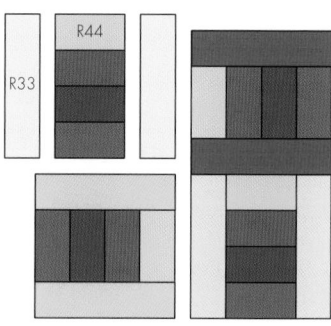

Templates Needed
R33 & R44

Square Dance
12" x 12" Block

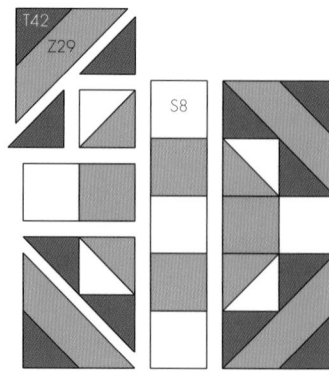

Templates Needed
S8, T42 & Z29

SQUARE-IN-A-SQUARE STAR PIECING INSTRUCTIONS

1. Referring to the Piecing Diagram to piece one block, sew T11 to each side of S29; repeat for four units.

2. Join the four pieced units to complete the block center.

3. Sew a dark T11 to a light T11 on the diagonal; repeat for eight T11 units.

4. Sew a medium T11 to the short sides of T18 to make a side unit; repeat for four side units.

5. Sew a T11 unit to each short end of a side unit. Sew a T11 side unit to opposite sides of the pieced center.

6. Sew S19 to opposite ends of the remaining T11 side units; sew these units to the remaining sides of the pieced unit to complete the block.

STAR PIECING INSTRUCTIONS

1. Referring to the Piecing Diagram to piece one block, sew a dark T7 to each short side of T32 to complete a side unit; repeat for four side units.

2. Sew a light T7 to a dark T7 to complete a corner unit; repeat for four corner units.

3. Sew a side unit to opposite sides of the center unit to complete the center row.

4. Sew a corner unit to each side of the side units to complete the side rows. Sew the center row between the two side rows to complete the block.

STAR LIGHT, STAR BRIGHT PIECING INSTRUCTIONS

1. Referring to the Piecing Diagram to piece one block, sew a darkest T16 to a dark T16 to complete a T16 unit; repeat for four T16 units.

2. Sew a light T16R to a darkest T16R to make a T16R unit; repeat for four T16R units.

3. Join a T16 unit with a T16R unit to make a side unit; repeat for four side units.

4. Join four S19 squares to complete the block center.

5. Sew a side unit to opposite sides of the block center.

6. Sew S14 to opposite sides of each of the remaining two side units; sew these units to opposite sides of the block center to complete the block.

STAR OF THE MILKY WAY PIECING INSTRUCTIONS

1. Referring to the Piecing Diagram to piece one block, sew a light T7 to Z58 and a medium T7 to Z58R; join these two units on the Z sides to complete a Z unit.

2. Sew a light T7 to a medium T7 to complete a T7 unit; set this unit into the Z unit to complete a block quarter section; repeat for four quarter sections.

3. Join the quarter sections to complete the block.

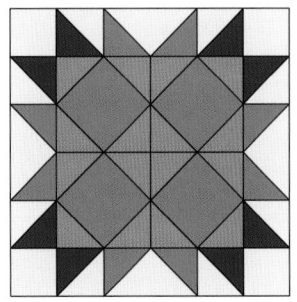

Square-in-a-Square Star
12" x 12" Block

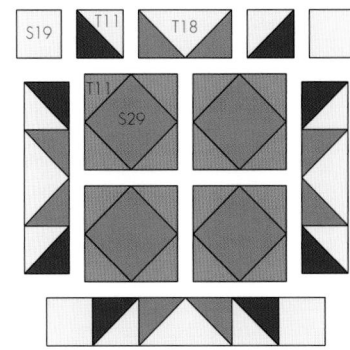

Templates Needed
S19, S29, T11 & T18

Star
12" x 12" Block

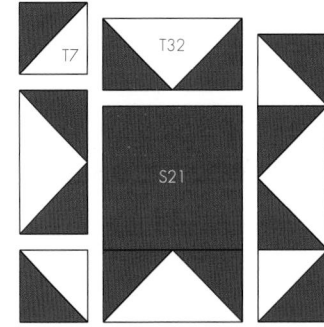

Templates Needed
S21, T7 & T32

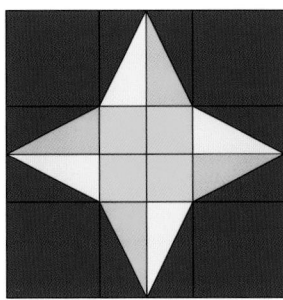

Star Light, Star Bright
12" x 12" Block

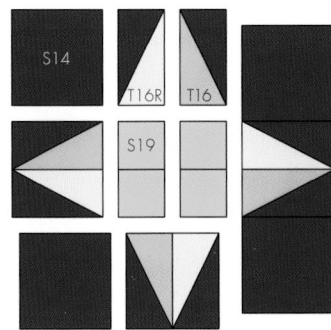

Templates Needed
S14, S19, T16 & T16R

Star of the Milky Way
12" x 12" Block

Templates Needed
T7, Z58 & Z58R

STAR X PIECING INSTRUCTIONS

1. Referring to the Piecing Diagram to piece one block, sew a medium and dark T18 to opposite sides of S29; repeat for two units. Join these units to complete an S29 unit.

2. Join a light T18 to a medium T18 on the short sides; repeat for six T units. Sew two of these units on the ends of the S29 unit to complete the center row.

3. Join two T units to complete a side unit; repeat for two side units.

4. Sew a light T19 to a darkest T19 to complete a corner unit; repeat for four corner units.

5. Sew a side unit between two corner units to complete a side row; repeat for two side rows.

6. Sew the center row between the side rows to complete the block.

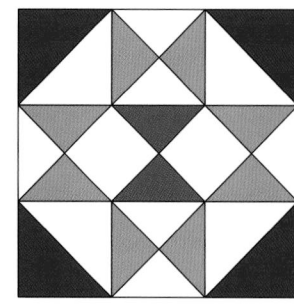

Star X
12" x 12" Block

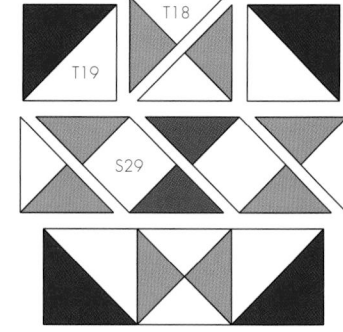

Templates Needed
S29, T18 & T19

STARRY LANE A PIECING INSTRUCTIONS

1. Referring to the Piecing Diagram to piece one block, sew a light T3 to a medium T3 along the diagonal; repeat for four units. Join the units to complete the T3 unit.

2. Sew R34 to opposite sides of the T3 unit. Sew S3 to opposite ends of each remaining R34; sew to the remaining sides of the T3 unit to complete the center unit.

3. Sew Z12 and Z12R to the short sides of T13 to make a side unit; repeat for four side units.

4. Sew a side unit to opposite sides of the pieced center unit; sew S15 to each end of the remaining side units.

5. Sew the S15 side units to the remaining sides of the pieced unit to complete the block.

Starry Lane A
12" x 12" Block

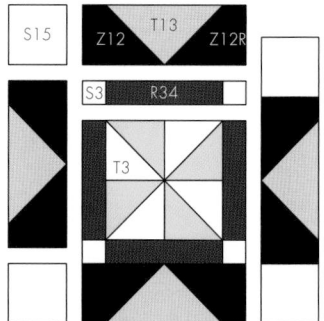

Templates Needed
R34, S3, S15, T3,
T13, Z12 & Z12R

STARRY LANE B PIECING INSTRUCTIONS

1. Referring to the Piecing Diagram to piece one block, sew R39 to opposite sides of S28.

2. Sew a medium S20 to each end of the remaining R39 pieces; sew these units to the remaining sides of the pieced unit to complete the center unit.

3. Sew a medium S20 to a dark S20; repeat for eight units. Join two units to complete a corner unit; repeat for four corner units.

4. Sew R38 to opposite sides of the center unit.

5. Sew a corner unit to each end of the remaining R38 pieces; sew these units to the pieced unit to complete the block.

Starry Lane B
12" x 12" Block

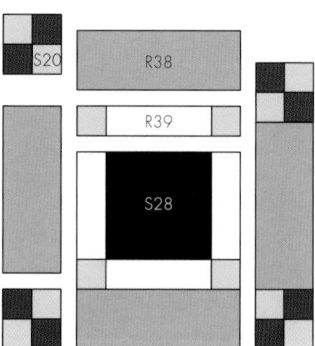

Templates Needed
R38, R39, S20 & S28

STATE OF GEORGIA PIECING INSTRUCTIONS

1. Referring to the Piecing Diagram to piece one block, join one medium, two light and two dark S8 squares to complete the center row.

2. Sew a light S8 to a medium S8; sew a medium T42 to a dark T42 and add a medium S8 to the medium side. Join these two pieced units to complete a corner unit; repeat for four corner units.

3. Sew a dark S8 to a light S8; sew this unit between two corner units to complete a side row; repeat for two side rows.

4. Sew the center row between the side rows to complete the block.

State of Georgia
12" x 12" Block

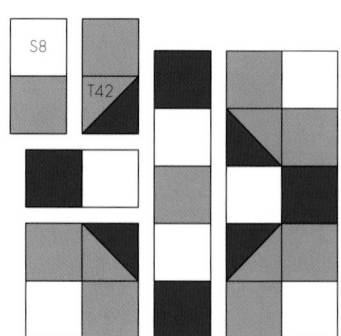

Templates Needed
S8 & T42

STATE HOUSE PIECING INSTRUCTIONS

1. Referring to the Piecing Diagram to piece one block, sew a light S30 to a medium S30 to complete a medium S30 unit; repeat for eight medium units. Repeat for eight dark S30 units.
2. Join two medium S30 units to complete a medium S unit; repeat for four medium S units. Repeat with two dark S30 units to complete a dark S unit; repeat for four dark S units.
3. Sew a light T7 to a dark T7 to complete a T7 unit; repeat for four dark units. Repeat with light and medium T7 pieces to complete four medium units.
4. Join two medium S units with two dark T7 units to complete a dark corner unit; repeat for two dark corner units. Repeat with medium T7 units and dark S units to complete two medium corner units.
5. Join the medium and dark corner units to complete the block.

ST. ELMO'S CROSS PIECING INSTRUCTIONS

1. Referring to the Piecing Diagram to piece one block, sew Z6 to opposite sides of S23; sew T29 to each short side of each remaining Z6. Sew these units to the remaining sides of S23 to complete the center unit.
2. Sew a dark S8 between two light S8 squares to make a side unit; repeat for four side units. Sew a side unit to opposite sides of the center unit.
3. Sew a dark T42 to a medium T42 to complete a corner unit; repeat for four corner units.
4. Sew a corner unit to each end of the remaining side units; sew these units to the remaining sides of the center unit to complete the block.

STEPS TO THE ALTAR PIECING INSTRUCTIONS

1. Referring to the Piecing Diagram to piece one block, join two lightest, one light and one medium S19 squares to make a row.
2. Join two lightest, one light and one dark S19 square to make a row.
3. Join one light, one lightest and one dark S19 square with T11 to make a row.
4. Join one lightest and one dark S19 square with T11 to make a row.
5. Join the rows as stitched and add T19 to the T11 side to complete the block corner.
6. Sew a dark S19 to the end of R6 and add R15; repeat for two units. Sew one unit to one T19 side of the block corner; sew the S14 square to the R-only end of the remaining unit and sew to the remaining T19 side of the block center to complete the block.

STILES & PATHS PIECING INSTRUCTIONS

1. Referring to the Piecing Diagram to piece one block, sew a light S9 between two dark S9 squares to make a row; repeat for two rows. Sew a dark S9 between two light S9 squares to make a row. Join the rows to complete the center unit.
2. Sew a dark R20 between two light R20 pieces to complete a side unit; repeat for four side units.
3. Sew a light T19 to a dark T19 to complete a corner unit; repeat for four corner units.
4. Sew a side unit between two corner units to complete a side row; repeat for two side rows.
5. Sew the center row between the side rows to complete the block.

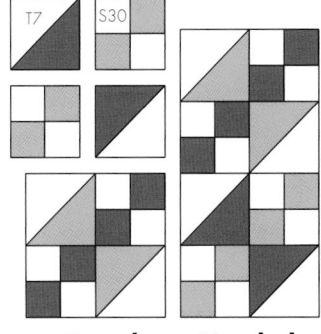

State House
12" x 12" Block

Templates Needed
S30 & T7

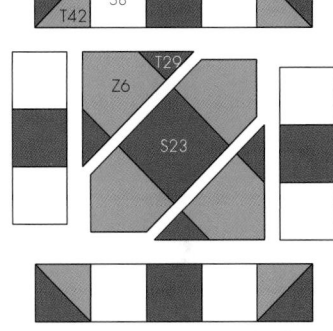

St. Elmo's Cross
12" x 12" Block

Templates Needed
S8, S23, T29, T42 & Z6

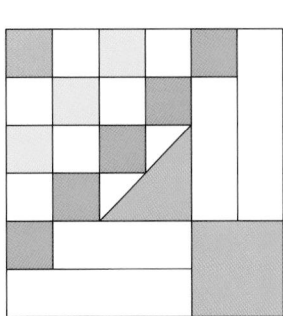
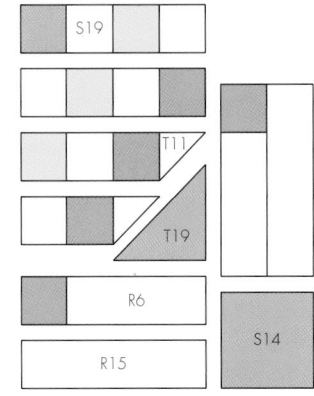

Steps to the Altar
12" x 12" Block

Templates Needed
R6, R15, S14, S19, T11 & T19

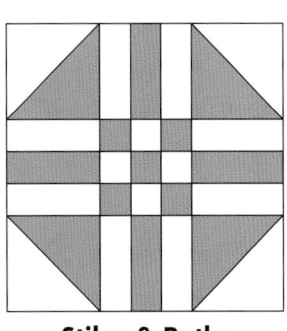
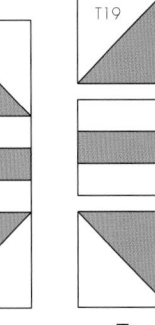
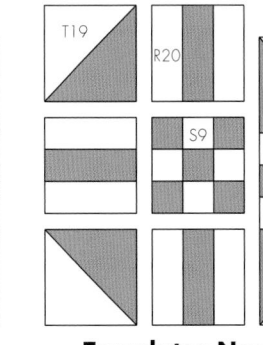

Stiles & Paths
12" x 12" Block

Templates Needed
R20, S9 & T19

ST. LOUIS PIECING INSTRUCTIONS

1. Referring to the Piecing Diagram to piece one block, sew T26 to one short side of T13; sew T26R to one short side of Z40. Join the units to complete a side unit; repeat for four side units.

2. Sew T26 to one short side of Z40; sew T26R to one side of S18. Join the units to complete a corner unit; repeat for four corner units.

3. Join two side and two corner units to complete half the block; repeat. Join the two halves to complete the block.

STREAK OF LIGHTNING PIECING INSTRUCTIONS

1. Referring to the Piecing Diagram to piece one block and starting with the top row and working down, join one light and one dark R11 with one light and one dark S19 to complete a row; repeat for two rows.

2. Join one dark S19 with one light and one dark R11 to make a row. Repeat with a light S19 and one light and one dark R11 to make a second row; join the rows and add a dark R11 to the dark S19 end to complete a double row.

3. Join one dark and two light R11 pieces to complete a row.

4. Join one light and two dark R11 pieces to complete a row.

5. Arrange and join the rows referring to the Piecing Diagram to complete the block.

SUNFLOWER PIECING INSTRUCTIONS

1. Referring to the Piecing Diagram to piece one block, sew Z53 to two adjacent same-size sides of Z46R to make a ZR unit; repeat for four ZR units.

2. Alternate and join the ZR units with Z46 pieces; set in T38 at the sides and S5 at the corners.

3. Appliqué the Z65 circle to the center to complete the block.

SUNNY LANES PIECING INSTRUCTIONS

1. Referring to the Piecing Diagram to piece one block, sew a light S30 to a medium S30; repeat for 16 units. Join two units to complete an S30 unit; repeat for eight units.

2. Sew a lightest T7 to a dark T7 to complete a T7 unit; repeat for eight T7 units.

3. Join two S30 units with two T7 units to complete a quarter section; repeat for four quarter sections.

4. Join the quarter sections to complete the block.

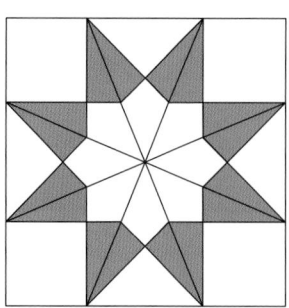

St. Louis
12" x 12" Block

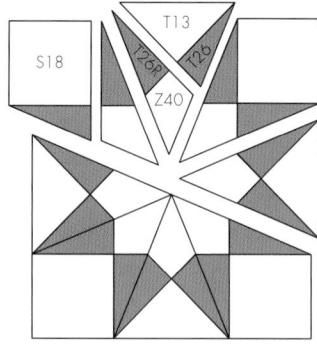

Templates Needed
S18, T13, T26, T26R & Z40

Streak of Lightning
12" x 12" Block

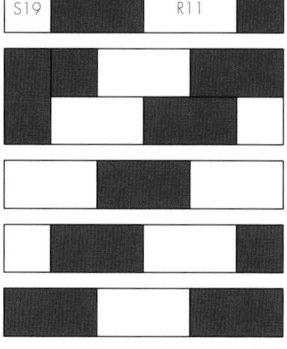

Templates Needed
R11 & S19

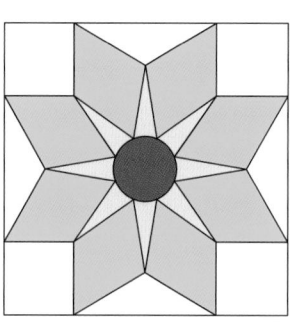

Sunflower
12" x 12" Block

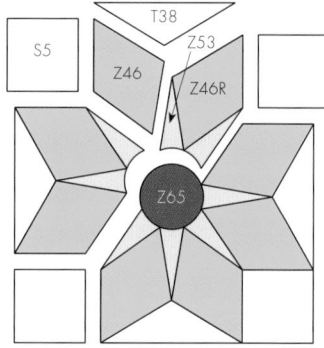

Templates Needed
S5, T38, Z46,
Z46R, Z53 & Z65

Sunny Lanes
12" x 12" Block

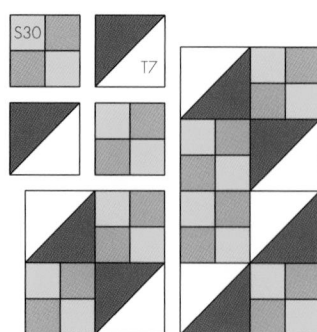

Templates Needed
S30 & T7

SWING IN THE CENTER I PIECING INSTRUCTIONS

1. Referring to the Piecing Diagram to piece one block, join two light and three dark S29 squares; add a light T11 to the dark ends to complete the center row.

2. Sew a medium T11 to the short sides of a light T18; repeat for four units. Sew a light T11 to each short end and a medium T18 to the medium side of each unit to complete a side unit; repeat for four side units.

3. Sew a light S29 to a dark S29 and add a light T11 to the dark end to complete a corner unit; repeat for four corner units.

4. Sew a side unit to each side of a corner unit to complete a block corner; repeat for two block corners.

5. Sew a block corner to opposite sides of the center row to complete the block.

Swing in the Center I
12" x 12" Block

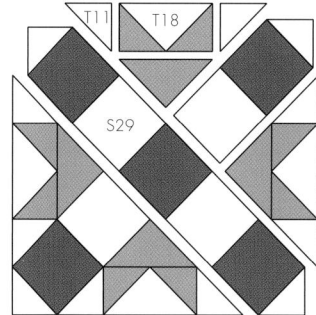

Templates Needed
S29, T11 & T18

SWING IN THE CENTER II PIECING INSTRUCTIONS

1. Referring to the Piecing Diagram to piece one block, sew S23 between two R53 pieces; add T42 to each end to complete the center row.

2. Sew T42 to one end of each of the remaining R53 pieces to complete a corner unit; repeat for two corner units.

3. Join Z48 and Z48R and set in T29; add T42 to the Z sides to complete a side unit. Repeat for four side units.

4. Sew a side unit to opposite sides of a corner unit to make a block corner; repeat for two block corners.

5. Sew a block corner to opposite sides of the center row to complete the block.

Swing in the Center II
12" x 12" Block

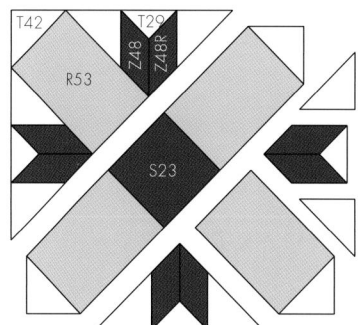

Templates Needed
R53, S23, T29,
T42, Z48 & Z48R

SWIRLS PIECING INSTRUCTIONS

1. Referring to the Piecing Diagram to piece one block, center and sew Z43 into Z45 to complete a Z unit; repeat for four different-color Z units.

2. Arrange and join the Z units in rows; join the rows to complete the block.

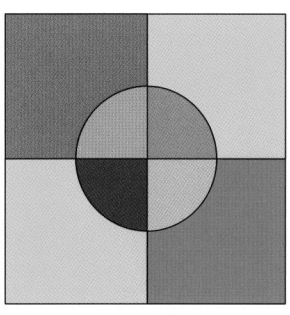

Swirls
12" x 12" Block

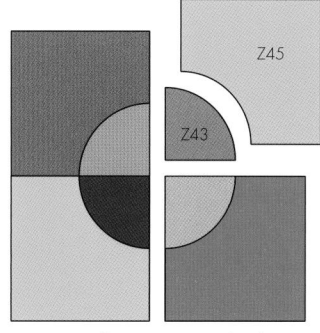

Templates Needed
Z43 & Z45

TEMPERANCE TREE PIECING INSTRUCTIONS

1. Referring to the Piecing Diagram to piece one block, sew a light T11 to a dark T11 to complete a T unit; repeat for 18 T units.

2. Join four T units to make a row; repeat for two rows and two reversed rows. Join two rows to complete a side unit; repeat with reversed rows to complete two side units.

3. Join two T units with S19 to complete a corner unit.

4. Cut one 8⅞" x 8⅞" medium square; cut in half on one diagonal to make two A triangles. Set aside one triangle for another project or block.

5. Sew T21 to opposite sides of Z55 and add A to complete the tree unit; sew a side unit to one A side of the tree unit.

6. Sew the corner unit to the end of the remaining side unit; sew this unit to the remaining A side of the tree unit to complete the block.

Temperance Tree
12" x 12" Block

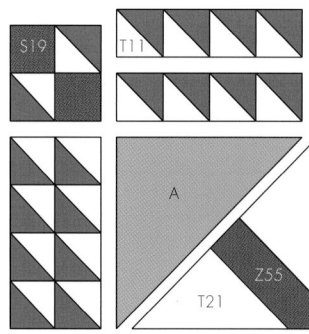

Templates Needed
S19, T11, T21 & Z55

THE ARKANSAS CROSSROADS
PIECING INSTRUCTIONS

1. Referring to the Piecing Diagram to piece one block, sew a light S5 to a dark S5 to complete an S5 unit; repeat for four S5 units. Join two S5 units to complete a quarter section; repeat for two quarter sections.
2. Sew a lightest T7 to a medium T7 to complete a T7 unit; repeat for four units. Join two T7 units with two lightest S5 squares to make a quarter section. Repeat for two quarter sections.
3. Arrange and join the quarter sections referring to the Piecing Diagram to complete the block.

THE HOUSE THAT JACK BUILT
PIECING INSTRUCTIONS

1. Referring to the Piecing Diagram to piece one block, join three R2 pieces and add T7 to one end to make a corner unit; repeat for four corner units.
2. Sew a corner unit to opposite sides of S22 to complete the center row.
3. Add T32 to each R2 side of the remaining corner units; sew one of these corner units to the remaining sides of the center row to complete the block.

THE PRIDE OF OHIO PIECING INSTRUCTIONS

1. Referring to the Piecing Diagram to piece one block, sew S2 between two R49 pieces to make a row. Sew an R49 piece between two S34 squares to make a row; repeat for two rows. Join the rows to complete the center unit.
2. Join two dark and one light S30 square and add T1 to make a row; sew a light S30 to a dark S30 and add T1 to make a row. Sew T1 to a dark S30 to make a row. Join the rows with one T1 triangle to complete a corner triangle referring to the Piecing Diagram.
3. Sew a corner triangle to each side of the center unit to complete the block.

TIME & TIDE PIECING INSTRUCTIONS

1. Referring to the Piecing Diagram to piece one block, join a medium T18 to a dark T18 on the short ends to make a T18 unit; repeat for two units. Join the units to complete the center unit.
2. Sew T16 and T16R to T56 to complete a side unit; repeat for four side units. Sew a side unit to opposite sides of the center unit to complete the center row.
3. Sew T16 and T16R to Z37 to complete a corner unit; repeat for four corner units.
4. Sew a side unit between two corner units to complete a side row; repeat for two side rows.
5. Sew the center row between the side rows to complete the block.

The Arkansas Crossroads
12" x 12" Block

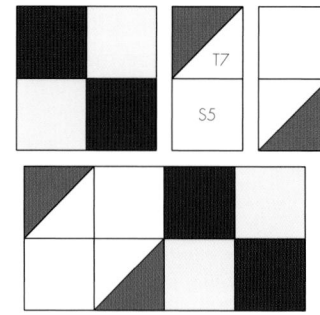

Templates Needed
S5 & T7

The House That Jack Built
12" x 12" Block

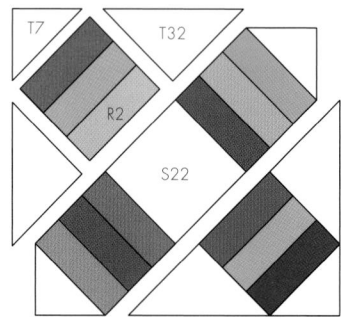

Templates Needed
R2, S22, T7 & T32

The Pride of Ohio
12" x 12" Block

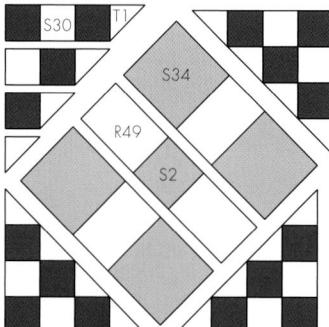

Templates Needed
R49, S2, S30, S34 & T1

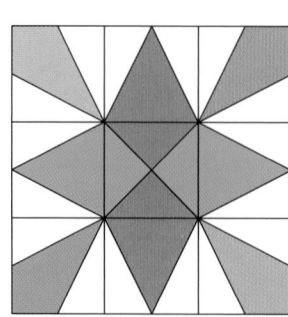

Time & Tide
12" x 12" Block

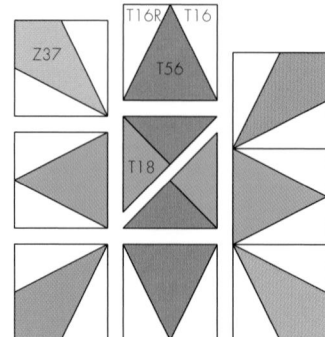

Templates Needed
T16, T16R, T18, T56 & Z37

TINTED CHAINS PIECING INSTRUCTIONS

1. Referring to the Piecing Diagram to piece one block, sew one dark and one lightest T33 triangle to opposite sides of a medium S2; add T11 to complete a corner unit; repeat for four corner units.

2. Join one each light, medium and dark S2 squares to make a row; sew a lightest T33 to each end. Repeat for two corner rows.

3. Arrange and join the remaining S2 squares in three rows of five squares each referring to the Piecing Diagram for positioning of colors. Join the rows to complete the center unit.

4. Sew a corner unit to opposite ends of the center unit.

5. Sew the remaining corner units to the corner rows to make block corners. Sew the block corners to the sides of the center unit to complete the block.

TIPSY STAR PIECING INSTRUCTIONS

1. Referring to the Piecing Diagram to piece one block, sew a light T14 to a medium T14 to complete a T14 unit; repeat for four T14 units.

2. Sew Z31 and Z31R to the two light sides of each T14 unit to complete a Z unit; repeat for four Z units. Sew a Z unit to opposite sides of S1. Sew a light T14 to the Z sides of each of the remaining two Z units; sew these units to the remaining sides of S1 to complete the center unit.

3. Sew T36 to each short side of a medium T14 and add T13 to complete a corner unit; repeat for four corner units.

4. Sew a corner unit to each side of the center unit to complete the block.

TOMBSTONE PIECING INSTRUCTIONS

1. Referring to the Piecing Diagram to piece one block, sew T7 to each side of S22 to complete the center unit.

2. Sew T33 to two adjacent sides of S2 to complete a side unit; sew a side unit to each side of the center unit to complete the block center.

3. Sew T13 to Z16 to complete a corner unit; repeat for four corner units. Sew a corner unit to each side of the block center to complete the block.

TOPSY-TURVY PIECING INSTRUCTIONS

1. Referring to the Piecing Diagram to piece one block, sew a light T58 to a medium T58 on the short ends to make a light T58 unit; repeat for four units. Repeat with a light T58 and a dark T58 to make four dark T58 units.

2. Join a light and dark T58 unit and set in T13 to complete the star units; repeat for four star units.

3. Join the star units to complete the block center.

4. Sew a medium T13 to a dark T13 to complete a corner unit; repeat for four corner units. Sew these units into the corners of the block center to complete the block.

Tinted Chains
12" x 12" Block

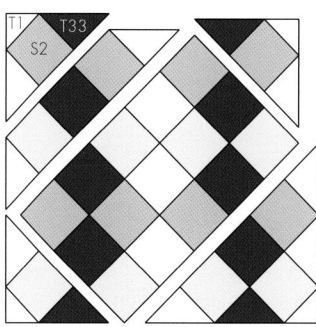

Templates Needed
S2, T1 & T33

Tipsy Star
12" x 12" Block

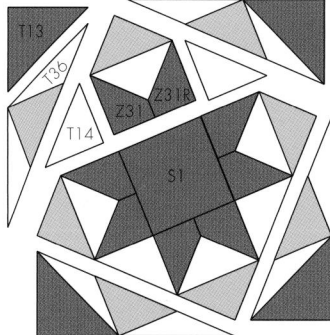

Templates Needed
S1, T13, T14, T36, Z31 & Z31R

Tombstone
12" x 12" Block

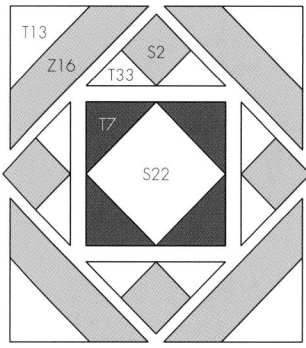

Templates Needed
S2, S22, T7, T13, T33 & Z16

Topsy-Turvy
12" x 12" Block

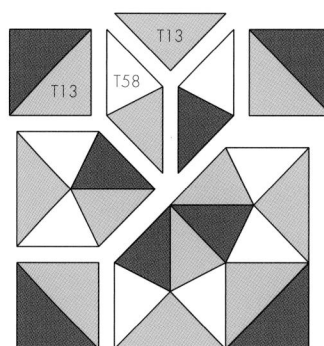

Templates Needed
T13 & T58

TROPICAL BUTTERFLIES PIECING INSTRUCTIONS

1. Referring to the Piecing Diagram to piece one block, cut a 12½" x 12½" background A square; fold and crease the square horizontally, vertically and diagonally to mark the center.

2. Cut one 8½" x 8½" square appliqué fabric. Refer to Tropical Butterflies quilt instructions on page 43 to cut the Z50 piece.

3. Center prepared appliqué shape on A and hand- or machine-appliqué in place to complete the block.

TUMBLEWEED PIECING INSTRUCTIONS

1. Referring to the Piecing Diagram to piece one block, sew T5 to the end of Z15 to make a Z unit; repeat for four Z units. Sew a Z unit to one short side of T20 to complete one T-Z unit; repeat for four T-Z units.

2. Sew Z15 to T18 and add T32 to complete a T unit; repeat for four T units.

3. Sew a T unit to a T-Z unit to complete a quarter section; repeat for four quarter sections.

4. Join the quarter sections to complete the block.

TURKEY IN THE STRAW PIECING INSTRUCTIONS

1. Referring to the Piecing Diagram to piece one block, sew a light R43 to a dark R43 and add T7 to the dark end to make a corner unit; repeat for four corner units.

2. Sew a corner unit to opposite sides of S22 to complete the center row.

3. Sew Z56 and Z56R to the short sides of T33; add T1 to each Z end to complete a side unit. Repeat for four side units.

4. Sew a side unit to opposite sides of each remaining corner unit to complete block corners.

5. Sew a block corner to opposite sides of the center row to complete the block.

TWISTER PIECING INSTRUCTIONS

1. Referring to the Piecing Diagram to piece one block, sew a light T42 to a dark T42 to complete a T42 unit; repeat for 12 units.

2. Sew a T42 unit to opposite sides of S8 to make an S8 row. Join three T42 units to make a row referring to the Piecing Diagram; repeat for two rows. Sew these rows to opposite sides of the S8 row to complete the center unit.

3. Sew R1 to opposite sides of the center unit to complete the center row.

4. Sew a T42 unit to each end of the remaining R1 pieces to make side rows.

5. Sew the center row between the side rows to complete the block.

Tropical Butterflies
12" x 12" Block

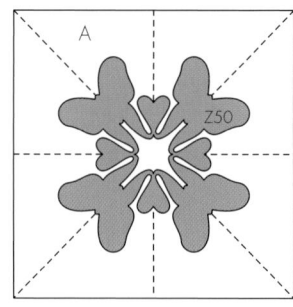

Template Needed
Z50

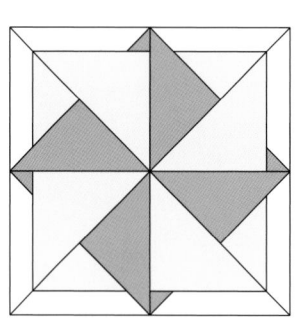

Tumbleweed
12" x 12" Block

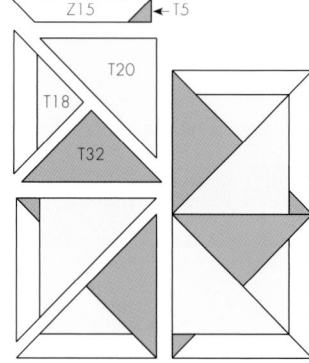

Templates Needed
T5, T18, T20, T32 & Z15

Turkey in the Straw
12" x 12" Block

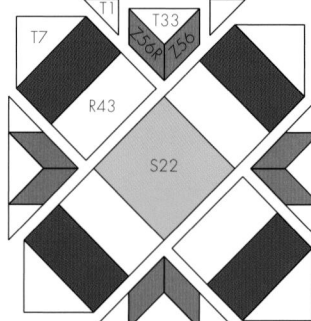

Templates Needed
R43, S22, T1, T7,
T33, Z56 & Z56R

Twister
12" x 12" Block

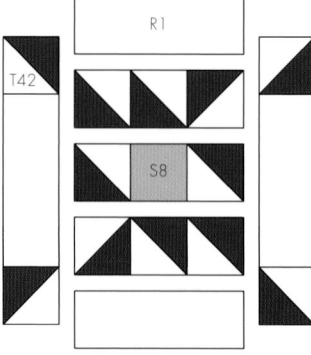

Templates Needed
R1, S8 & T42

UNEVEN NINE-PATCH STAR PIECING INSTRUCTIONS

1. Referring to the Piecing Diagram to piece one block, sew R11 to opposite sides of S14.

2. Sew a dark S19 to each end of the remaining R11 pieces; sew these units to the remaining sides of the R11-S14 unit to complete the block center.

3. Sew a dark T11 to a light T11 on the diagonal; repeat for eight T11 units.

4. Sew a medium T11 to the short sides of T18 to make a side unit; repeat for four side units.

5. Sew a T11 unit to each short end of a side unit. Sew a T11 side unit to opposite sides of the pieced center.

6. Sew S19 to opposite ends of the remaining T11 side units; sew these units to the remaining sides of the pieced unit to complete the block.

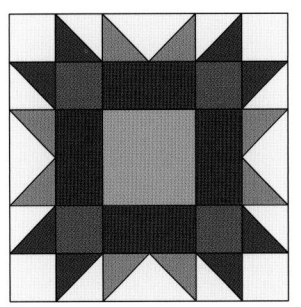

Uneven Nine-Patch Star
12" x 12" Block

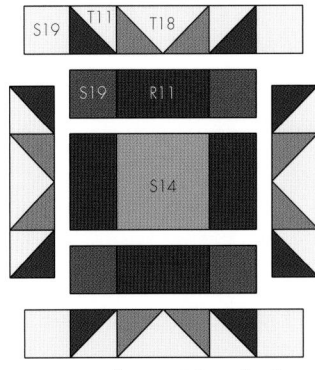

Templates Needed
R11, S14, S19, T11 & T18

UNNAMED PIECING INSTRUCTIONS

1. Referring to the Piecing Diagram to piece one block, sew a dark S19 square to the square end of a light Z2; repeat with Z2R to make light Z and ZR units.

2. Join a light Z2 and Z2R with an angled seam and set in a dark S19 to complete a dark S unit.

3. Sew a light Z unit and light ZR unit to the S19 sides of the S unit to complete a light corner unit; repeat for two units.

4. Repeat steps 1–3 with dark Z2 and Z2R and light S19 squares to complete two dark corner units.

5. Join the light and dark corner units to complete the block.

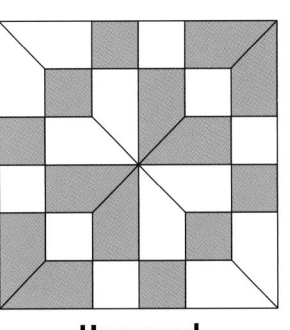

Unnamed
12" x 12" Block

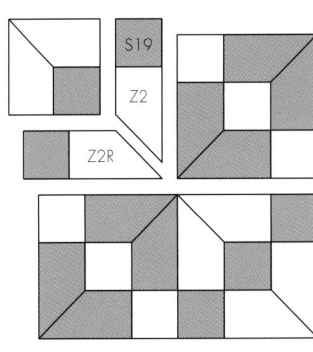

Templates Needed
S19, Z2 & Z2R

VINE OF FRIENDSHIP PIECING INSTRUCTIONS

1. Referring to the Piecing Diagram to piece one block, sew a dark Z9 into a light Z60 to complete a light Z unit; repeat for eight light Z units.

2. Center and sew a light Z9 into a dark Z60 unit to complete a dark Z unit; repeat for eight dark Z units.

3. Arrange and join the light and dark Z units in rows referring to the Piecing Diagram; join the rows to complete the block.

Vine of Friendship
12" x 12" Block

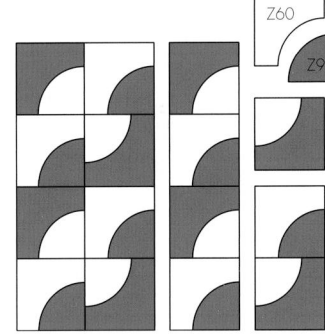

Templates Needed
Z9 & Z60

VINTAGE MEMORIES PIECING INSTRUCTIONS

1. Referring to the Piecing Diagram to piece one block, sew three medium T13 triangles to R10; repeat for two units.

2. Sew a dark T39 to the short sides of one pieced unit and a light T39 to the short sides of the remaining unit.

3. Join the two pieced units to complete the block.

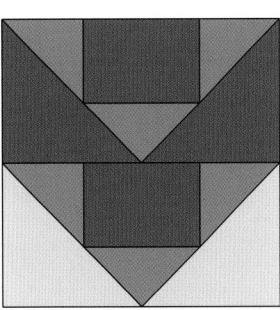

Vintage Memories
12" x 12" Block

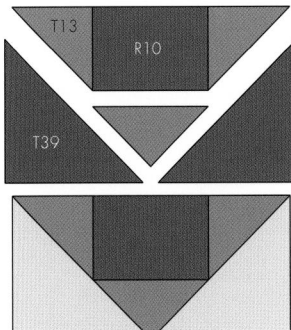

Templates Needed
R10, T13 & T39

WAGON TRACKS PIECING INSTRUCTIONS

1. Referring to the Piecing Diagram to piece one block, sew a light S19 to a medium S19 to make an S19 unit; repeat for 10 units.

2. Join two S19 units to complete an S unit; repeat for five S units.

3. Sew a light T19 to a dark T19 to complete a T unit; repeat for four T units.

4. Join two S units with a T unit to complete a side row; repeat for two side rows.

5. Join two T units with an S unit to complete the center row; sew the center row between the side rows to complete the block.

WEDDING RING PIECING INSTRUCTIONS

1. Referring to the Piecing Diagram to piece one block, join two dark and three light S8 squares to complete the center row.

2. Sew T42 to Z29 and add T40 to complete a corner unit; repeat for four corner units.

3. Sew a light S8 to a dark S8; sew this unit between two corner units to complete a side row. Repeat for two side rows.

4. Sew the center row between the side rows to complete the block.

WILD GOOSE CHASE PIECING INSTRUCTIONS

1. Referring to the Piecing Diagram to piece one block, sew T1 to the short sides of a medium T33 to complete a medium T unit; repeat for eight units. Repeat with the dark T33 pieces to complete eight dark T units.

2. Join four medium T units to make a strip; repeat for two strips. Sew these strips to opposite sides of S21 to complete the center row.

3. Join four dark T units to make a side unit; repeat for two side units.

4. Sew a medium T33 to a dark T33 on the short sides; repeat for four units. Join two units to complete a corner unit; repeat for two corner units.

5. Sew a corner unit to one end and S5 to the other end of each side unit to make a side row; repeat for two rows.

6. Sew the center row between the side rows to complete the block.

WILD WAVES PIECING INSTRUCTIONS

1. Referring to the Piecing Diagram to piece one block, sew a light T33 to a dark T33 on a short side; sew T7 to the pieced unit to complete a T unit. Repeat for 16 T units.

2. Arrange the T units in four rows of four units each referring to the Piecing Diagram; join the units to make rows. Join the rows to complete the block.

Wagon Tracks
12" x 12" Block

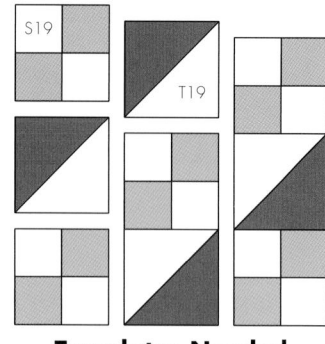

Templates Needed
S19 & T19

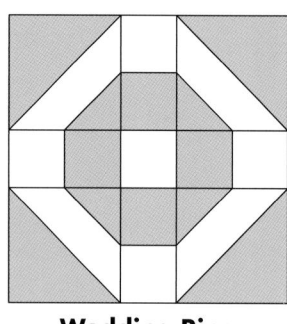

Wedding Ring
12" x 12" Block

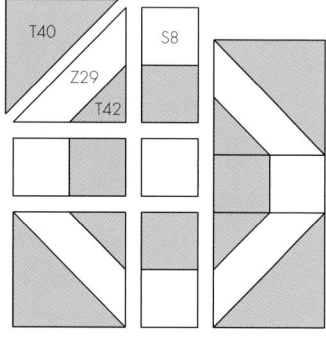

Templates Needed
S8, T40, T42 & Z29

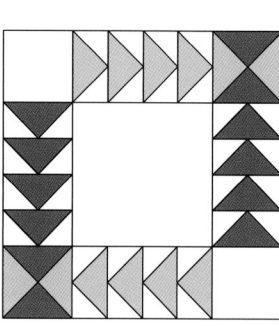

Wild Goose Chase
12" x 12" Block

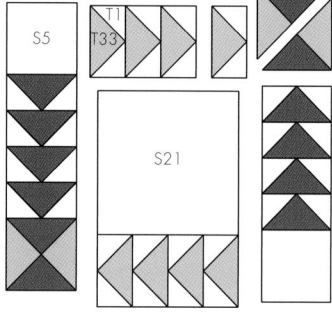

Templates Needed
S5, S21, T1 & T33

Wild Waves
12" x 12" Block

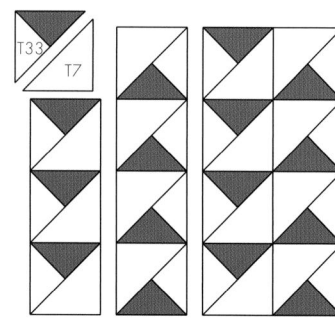

Templates Needed
T7 & T33

WINDBLOWN SQUARE PIECING INSTRUCTIONS

1. Referring to the Piecing Diagram to piece one block, sew two medium and two dark T7 triangles to the sides of S22 to complete the center unit.

2. Sew a light T7 to a medium T7 on the short sides; repeat for two medium T7 units. Repeat with a light T7 and a dark T7 to complete two dark T7 units. Sew these units to the sides of the center unit to complete the block center.

3. Sew a light T32 to a medium T32 to complete a medium corner unit; repeat for two medium corner units. Repeat with light and dark T32 pieces to complete two dark corner units.

4. Sew the corner units to the block center to complete the block.

Windblown Square
12" x 12" Block

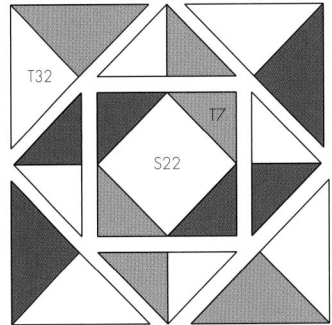

Templates Needed
S22, T7 & T32

WOVEN THREADS PIECING INSTRUCTIONS

1. Referring to the Piecing Diagram to piece one block, sew a light S19 to a medium S19; add R11 and R7 to complete a corner unit. Repeat for four corner units.

2. Sew an R30 to each long side of R34 to make a side sashing unit; repeat for two side sashing units.

3. Sew an R28 to each long side of R29 to make a center sashing unit.

4. Join two corner units with a side sashing unit to make a row; repeat for two rows.

5. Join the rows with the center sashing unit; sew R37 to opposite sides of the pieced unit to complete one block.

Woven Threads
12" x 12" Block

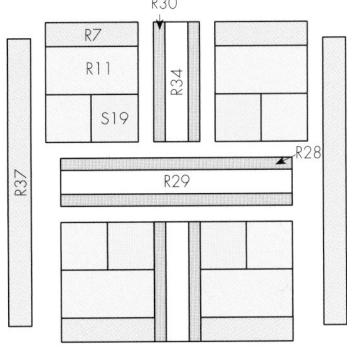

Templates Needed
R7, R11, R28, R29, R30, R34, R37 & S19

YELLOW LILIES PIECING INSTRUCTIONS

1. Referring to the Piecing Diagram to piece one block, join one dark and two light S16 squares to make a light S16 row; repeat for six light S16 rows.

2. Join one light and two dark S16 squares to make a center row. Sew this row between two light S16 rows to complete the center unit.

3. Sew a light T30 to a dark T30 on the short sides; repeat for eight units. Join two units to complete a T30 unit; repeat for four T30 units.

4. Sew a light S16 row to the dark side of an T30 unit; add a light T30 to the S16 row side of the unit to complete a corner unit. Repeat for four corner units.

5. Sew a corner unit to opposite sides of the center unit to complete the center row.

6. Sew R3 between Z11 and Z11R and add to T41 to make a side unit; repeat for four side units.

7. Sew a side unit to opposite sides of each remaining corner unit to complete the block corners.

8. Sew the block corners to opposite sides of the center row.

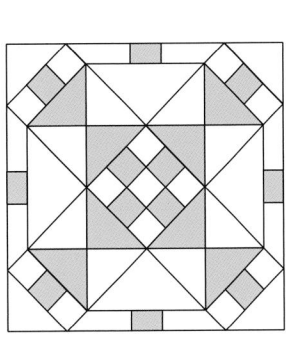

Yellow Lilies
12" x 12" Block

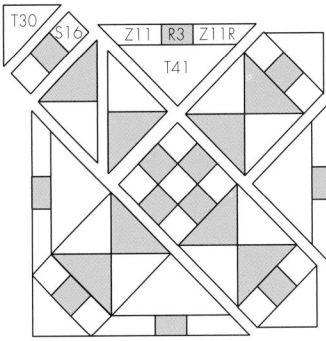

Templates Needed
R3, S16, T30, T41, Z11 & Z11R

YREKA SQUARE PIECING INSTRUCTIONS

1. Referring to the Piecing Diagram to piece one block, sew a light S32 to a medium S32; repeat for eight units. Join two units to complete an S unit; repeat for four S units.

2. Sew a medium S32 to a dark S32 to complete an S32 unit; repeat for four units. Join two S units with an S32 unit to make a row; repeat for two rows. Join the remaining S32 units with a dark S32 to make a row. Sew this row between the previously pieced rows to complete the center unit.

3. Sew T29 to each short side of Z7 to complete a corner unit; repeat for four corner units. Sew a corner unit to each side of the center unit to complete the block.

Yreka Square
12" x 12" Block

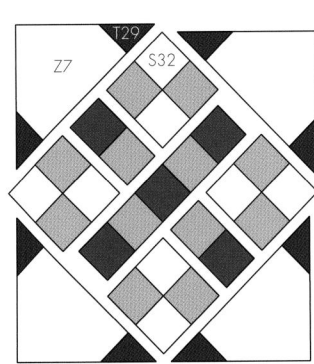

Templates Needed
S32, T29 & Z7

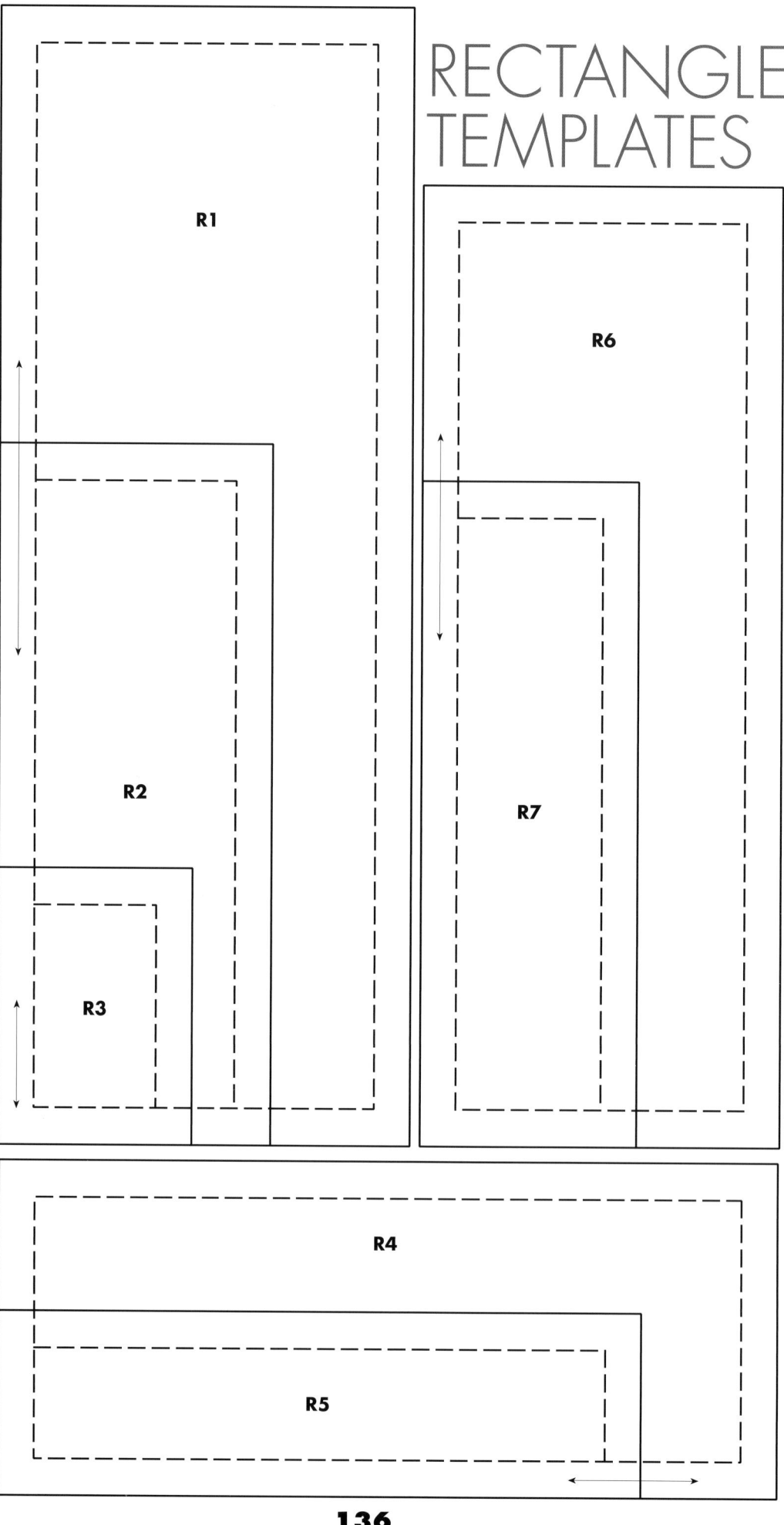

RECTANGLE
TEMPLATES

R1

R2

R3

R4

R5

R6

R7

136

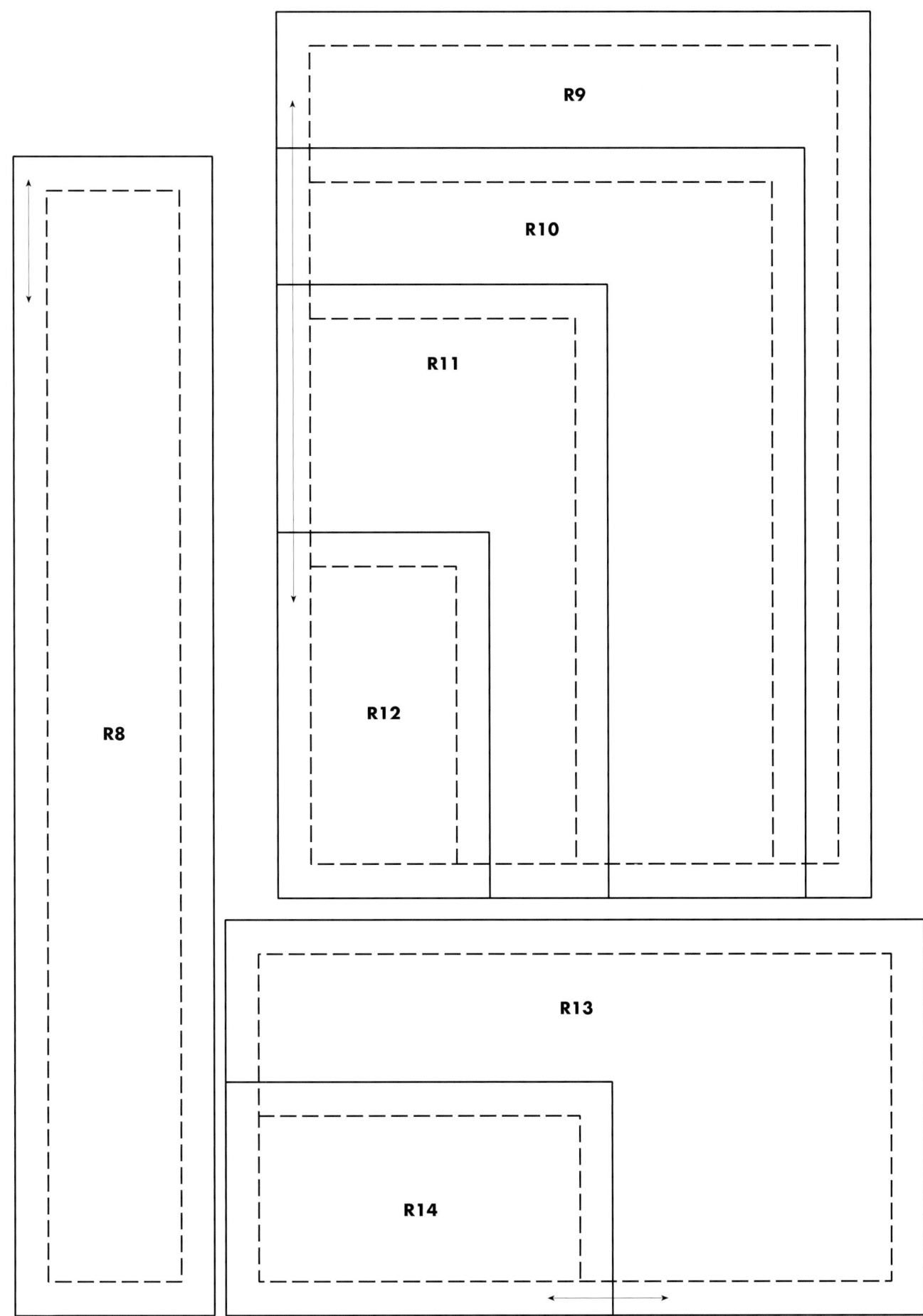

R8

R9

R10

R11

R12

R13

R14

137

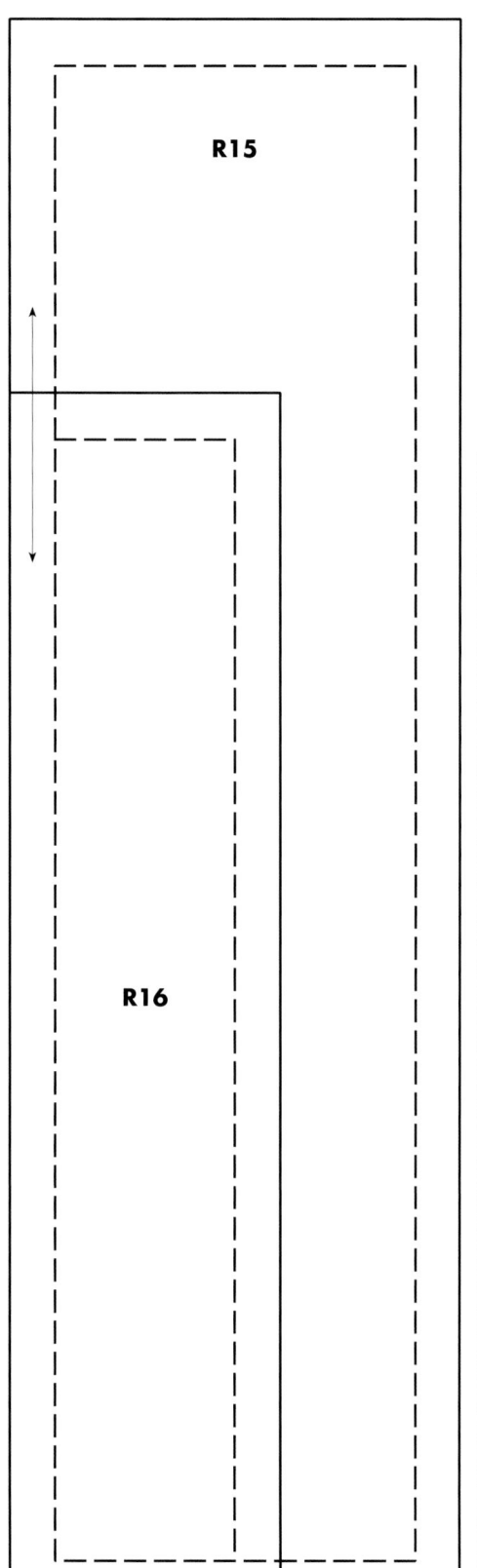

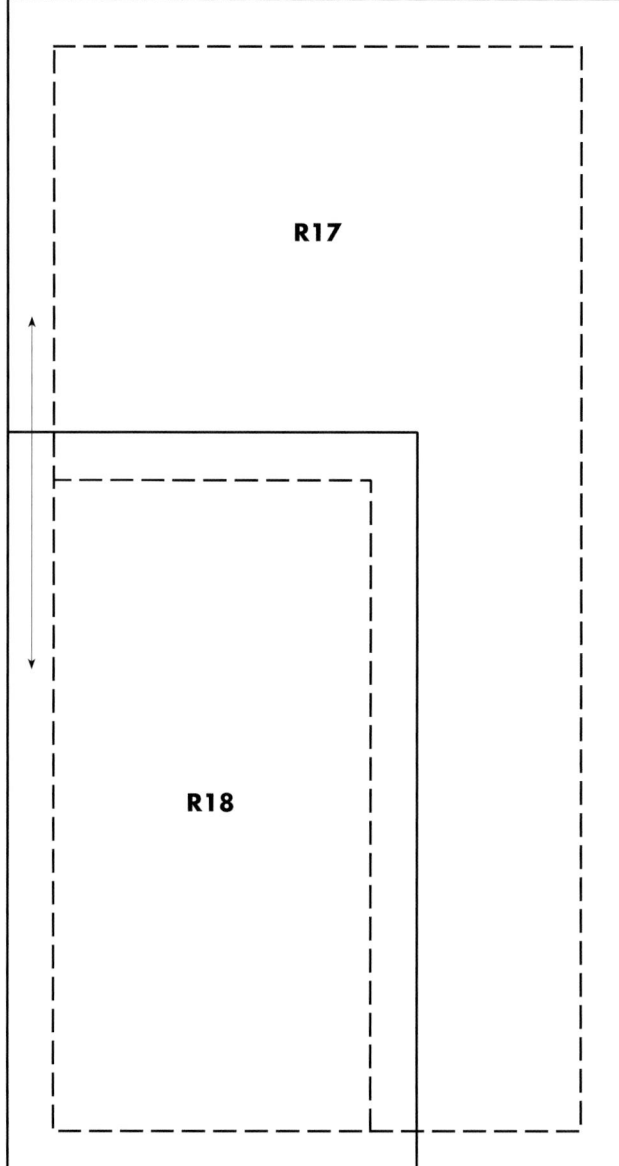

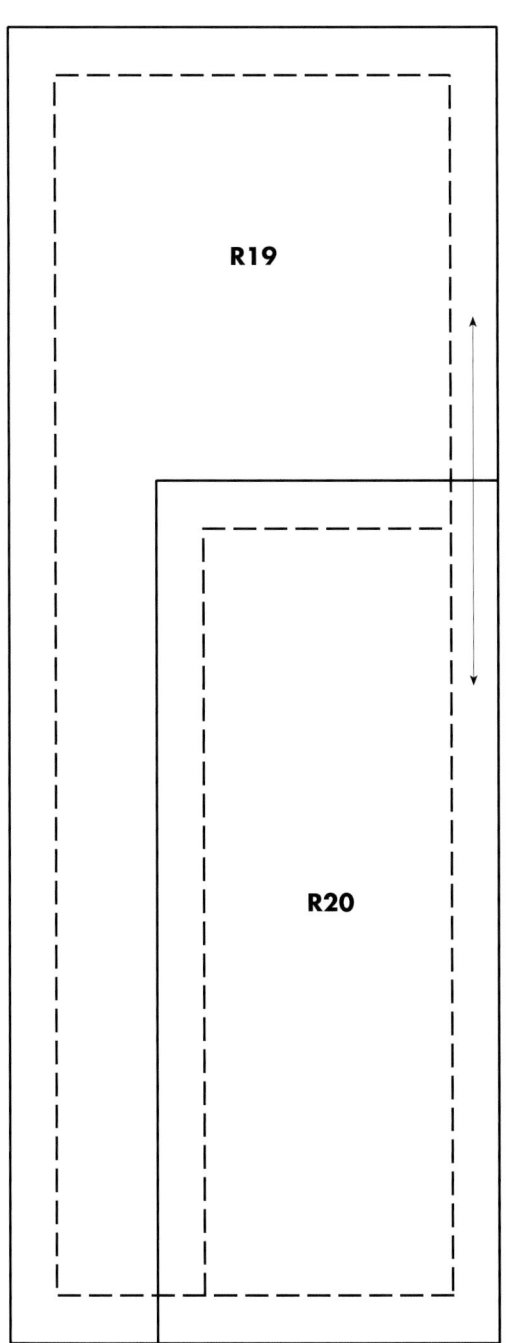

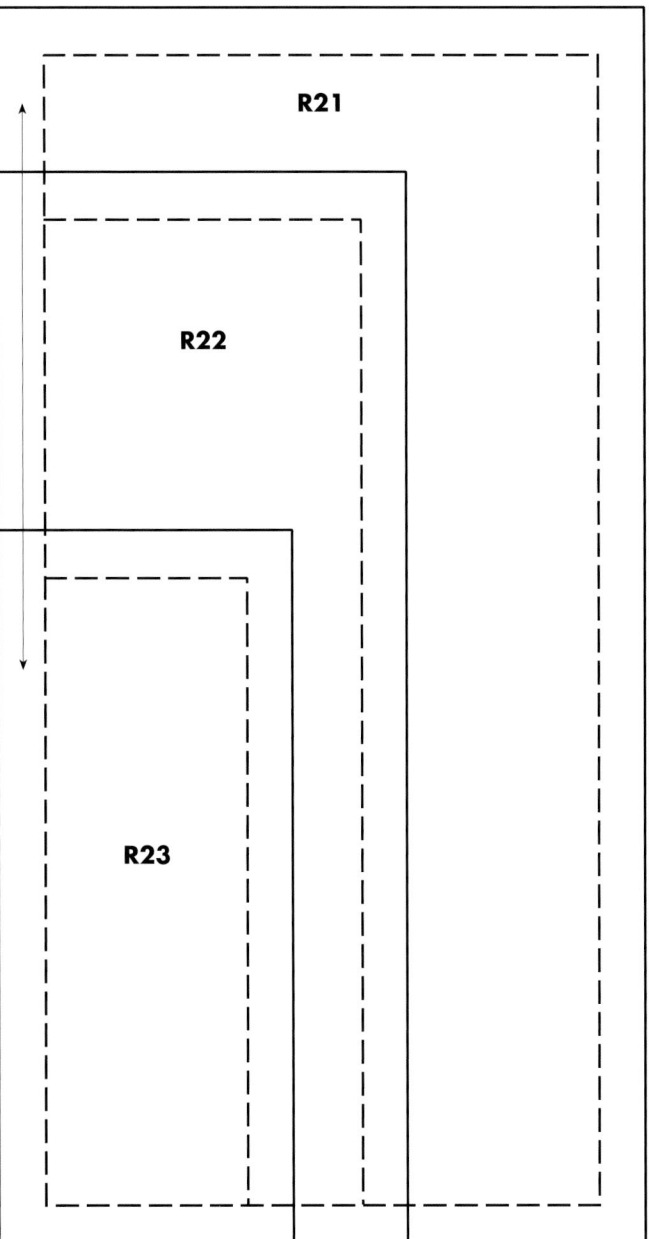

R19

R20

R21

R22

R23

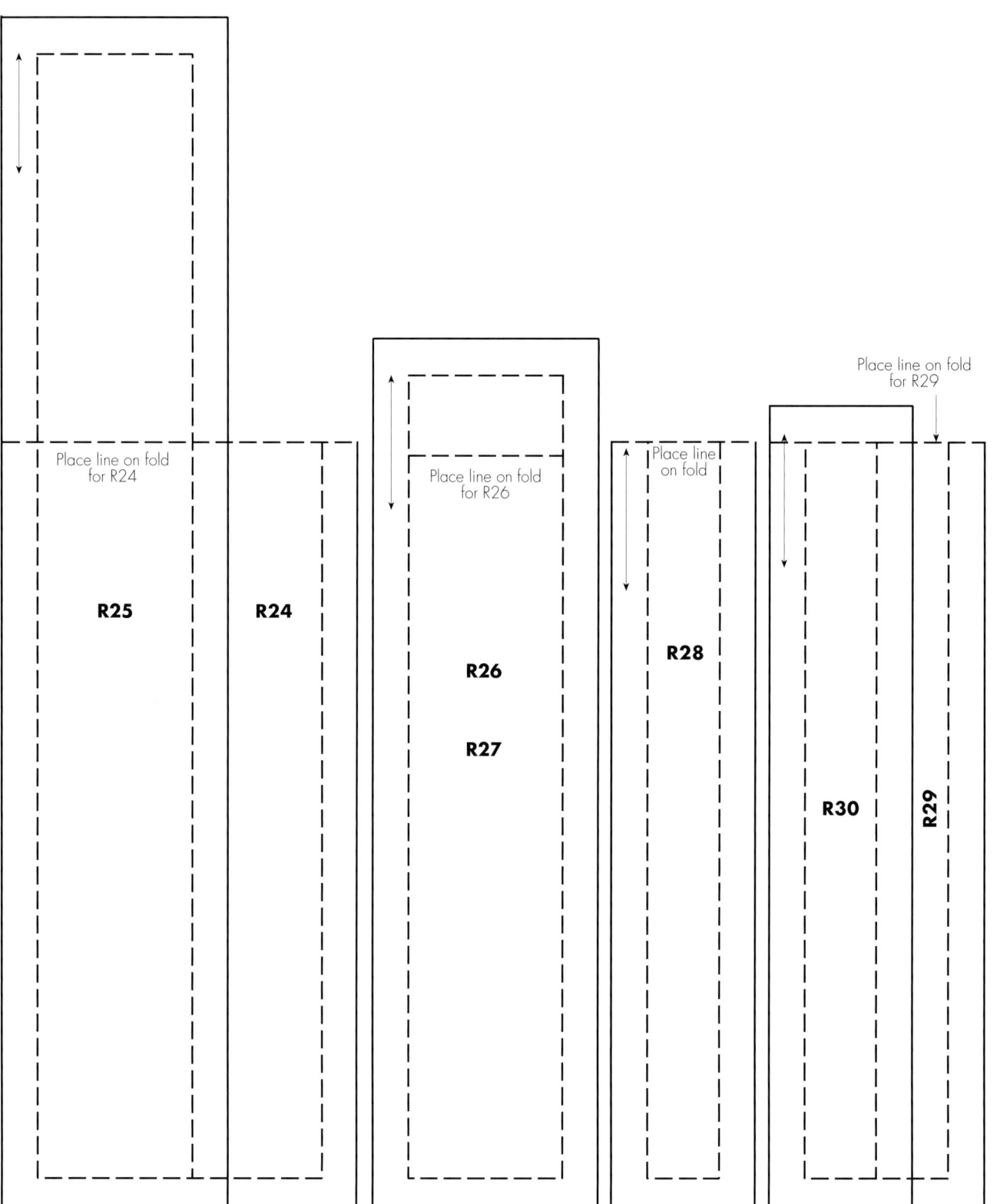

Place line on fold for R24

R25

R24

Place line on fold for R26

R26

R27

Place line on fold

R28

Place line on fold for R29

R30

R29

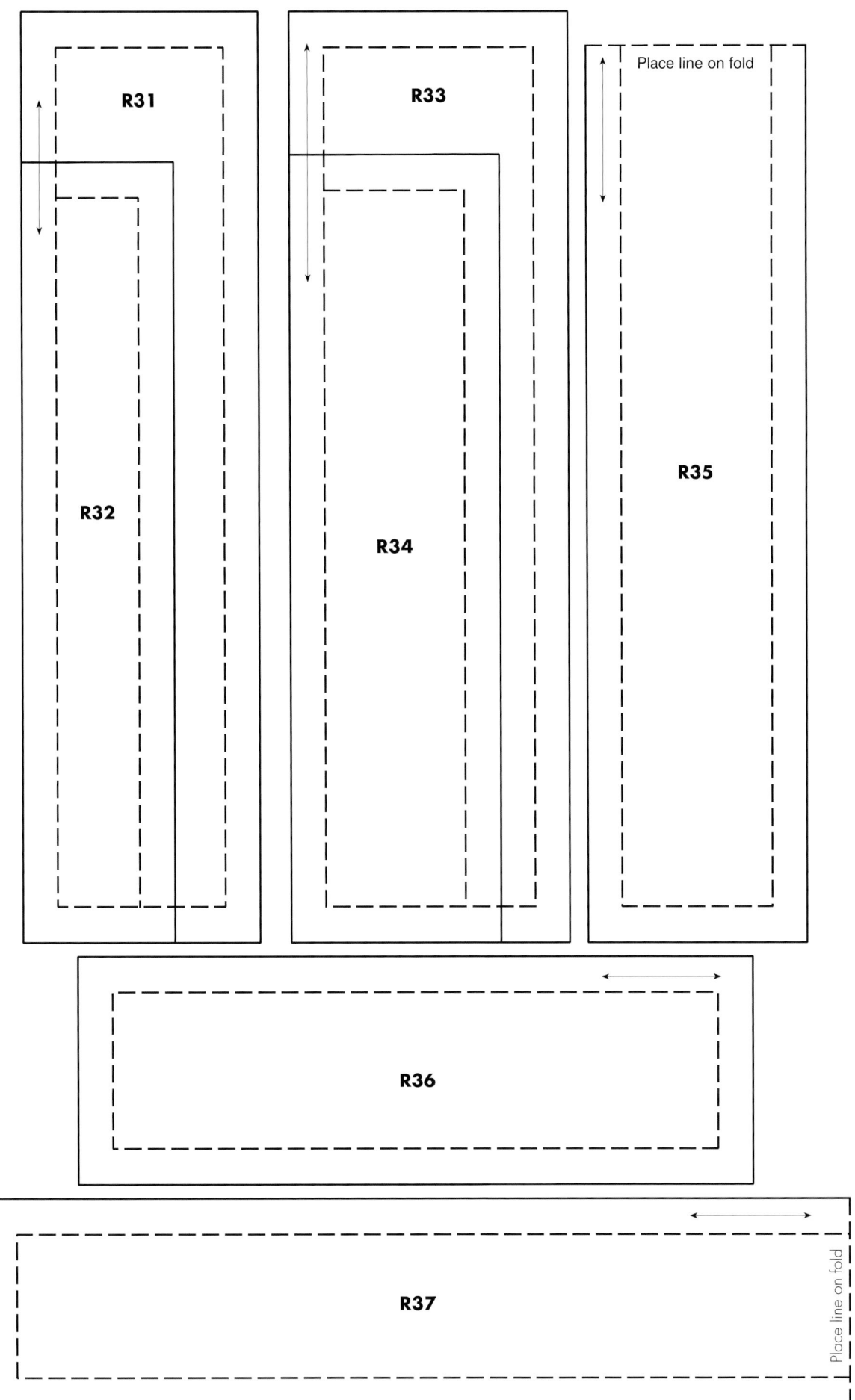

R31

R32

R33

R34

R35

Place line on fold

R36

R37

Place line on fold

141

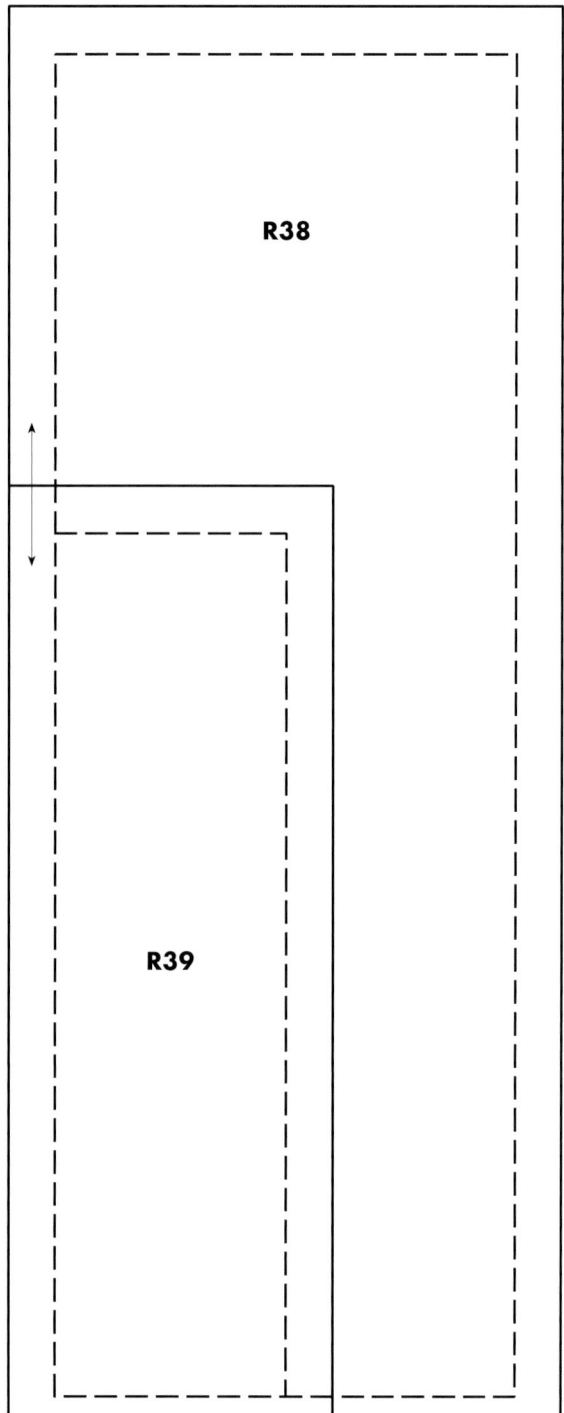

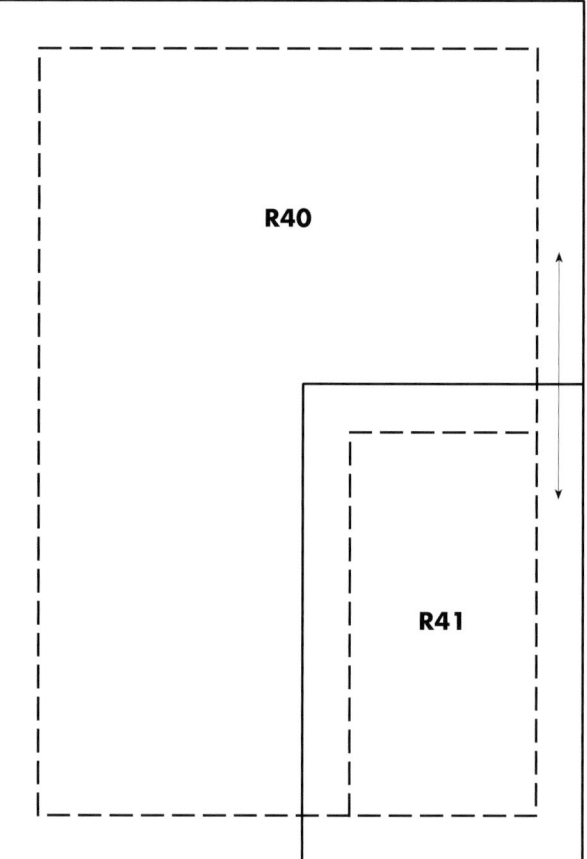

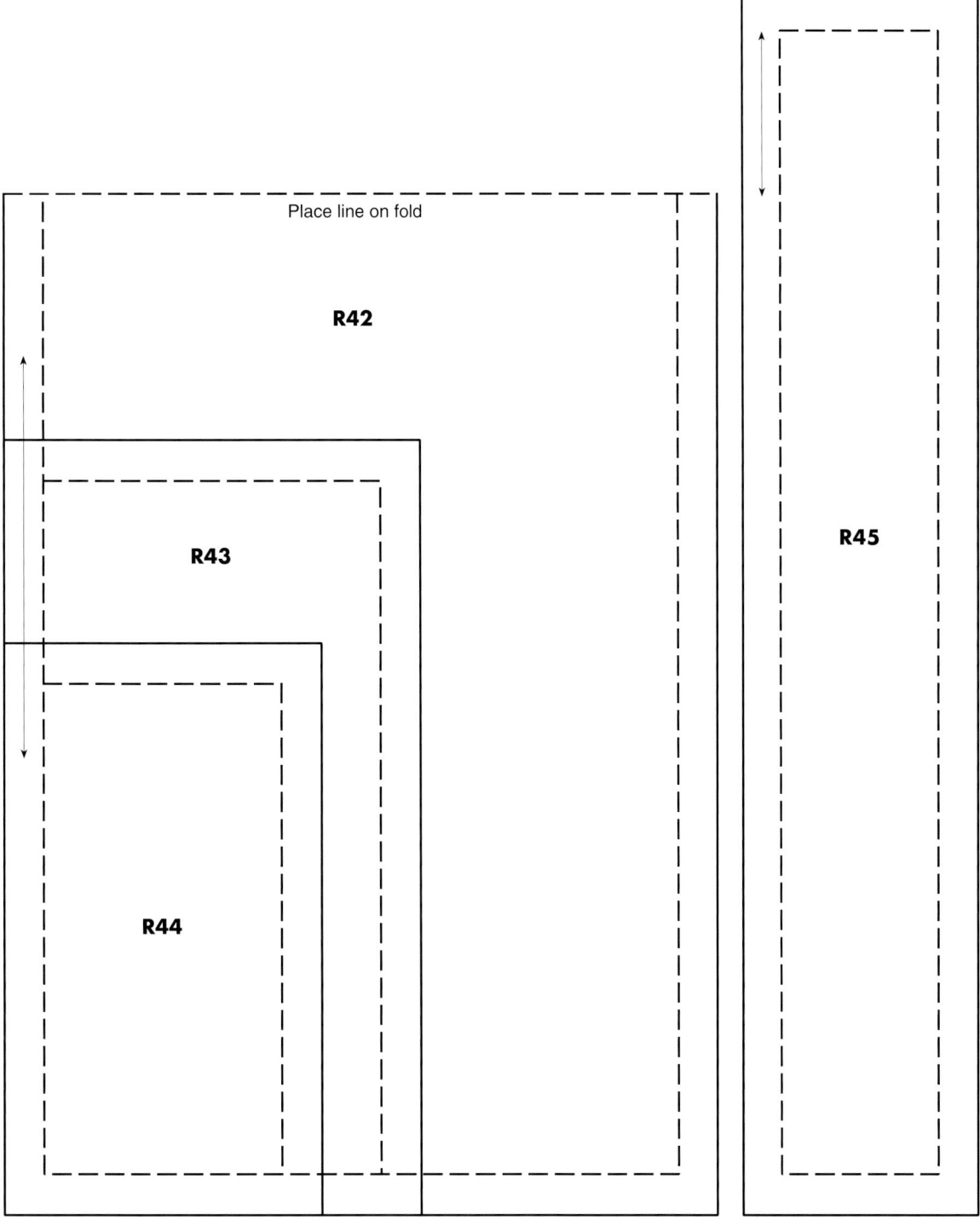

Place line on fold

R42

R43

R44

R45

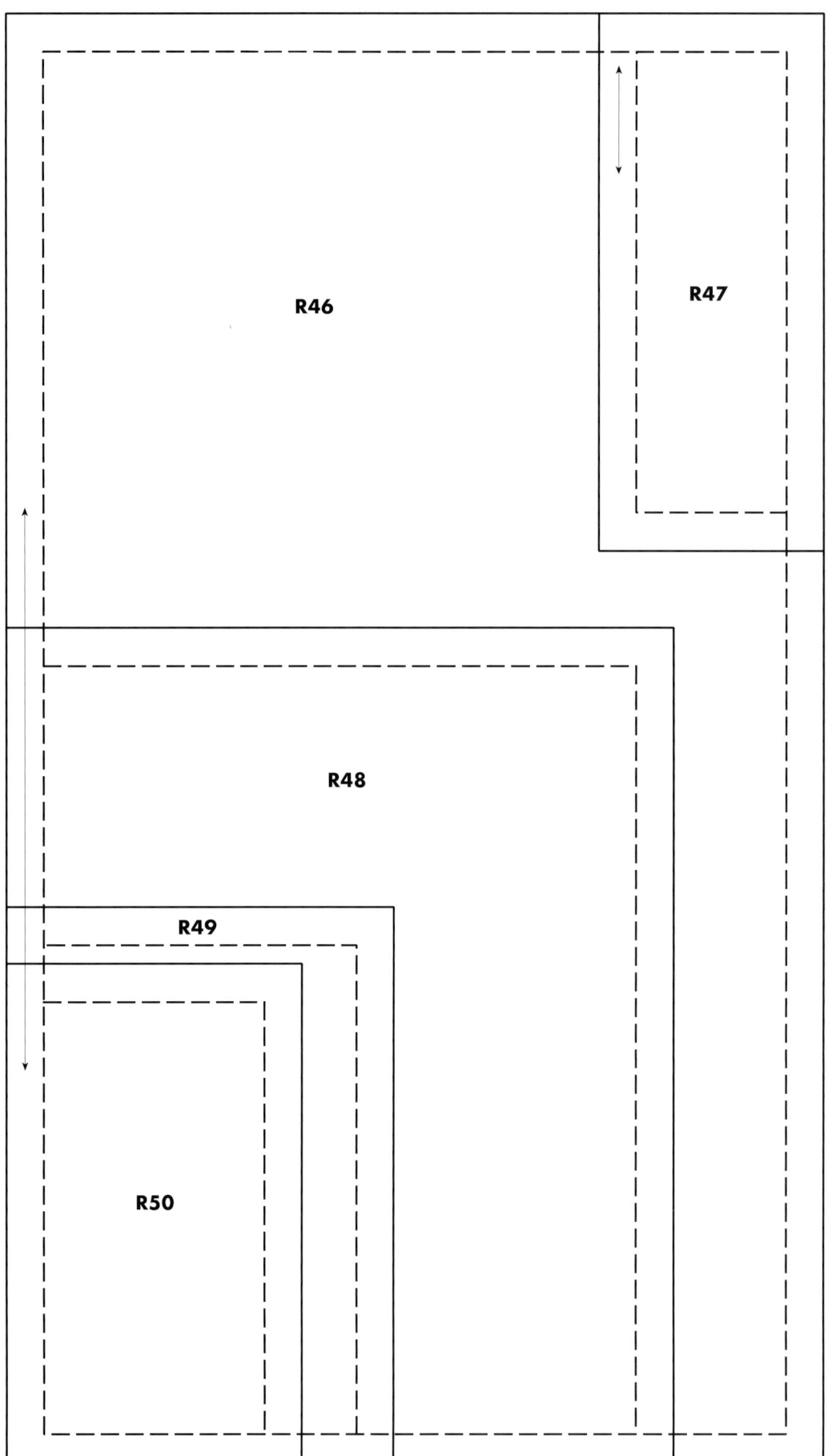

R46

R47

R48

R49

R50

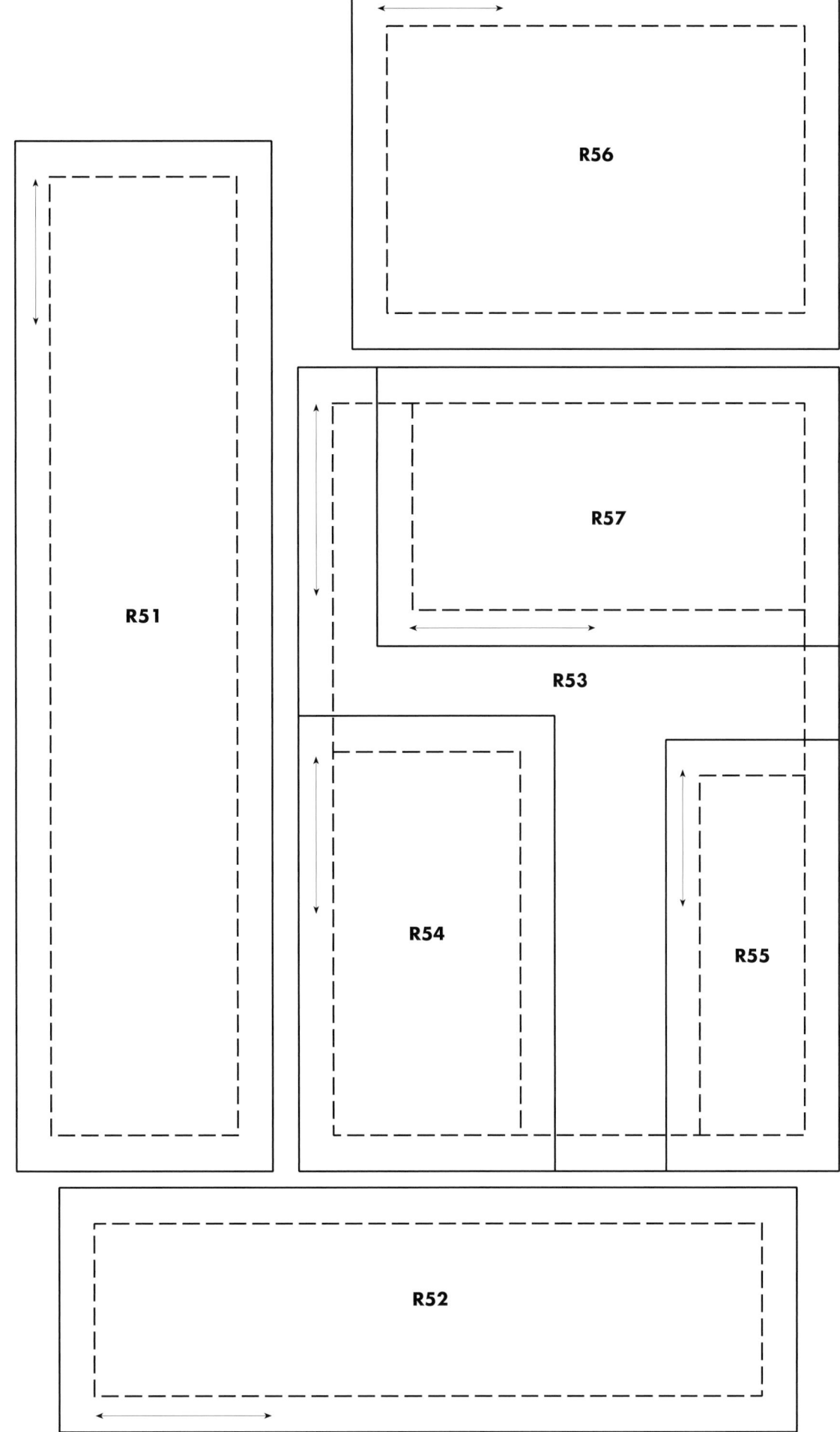

R56

R51

R57

R53

R54

R55

R52

145

SQUARE
TEMPLATES

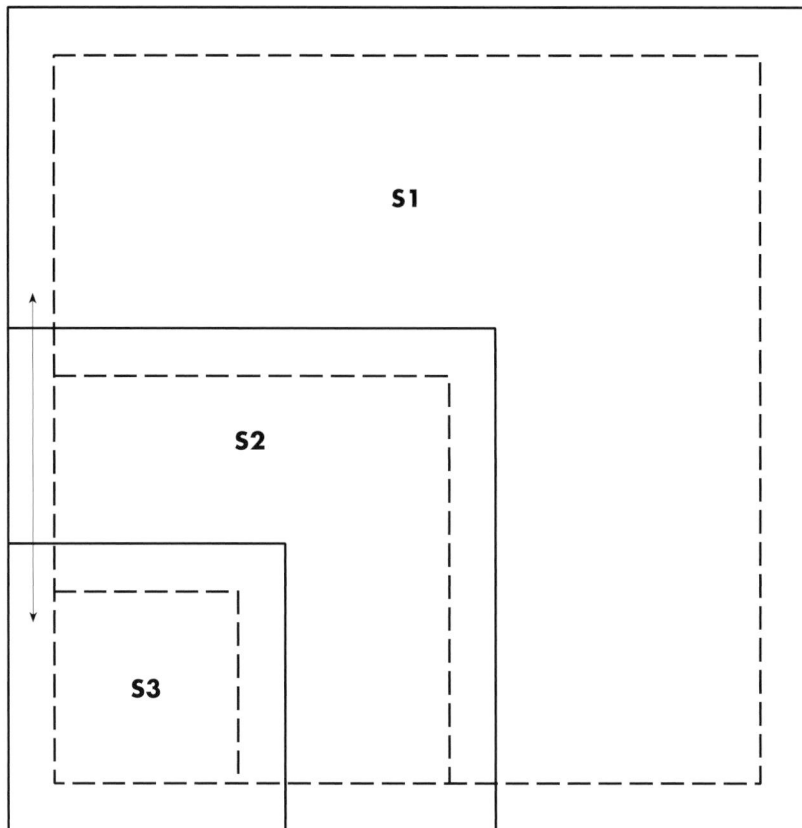

S1

S2

S3

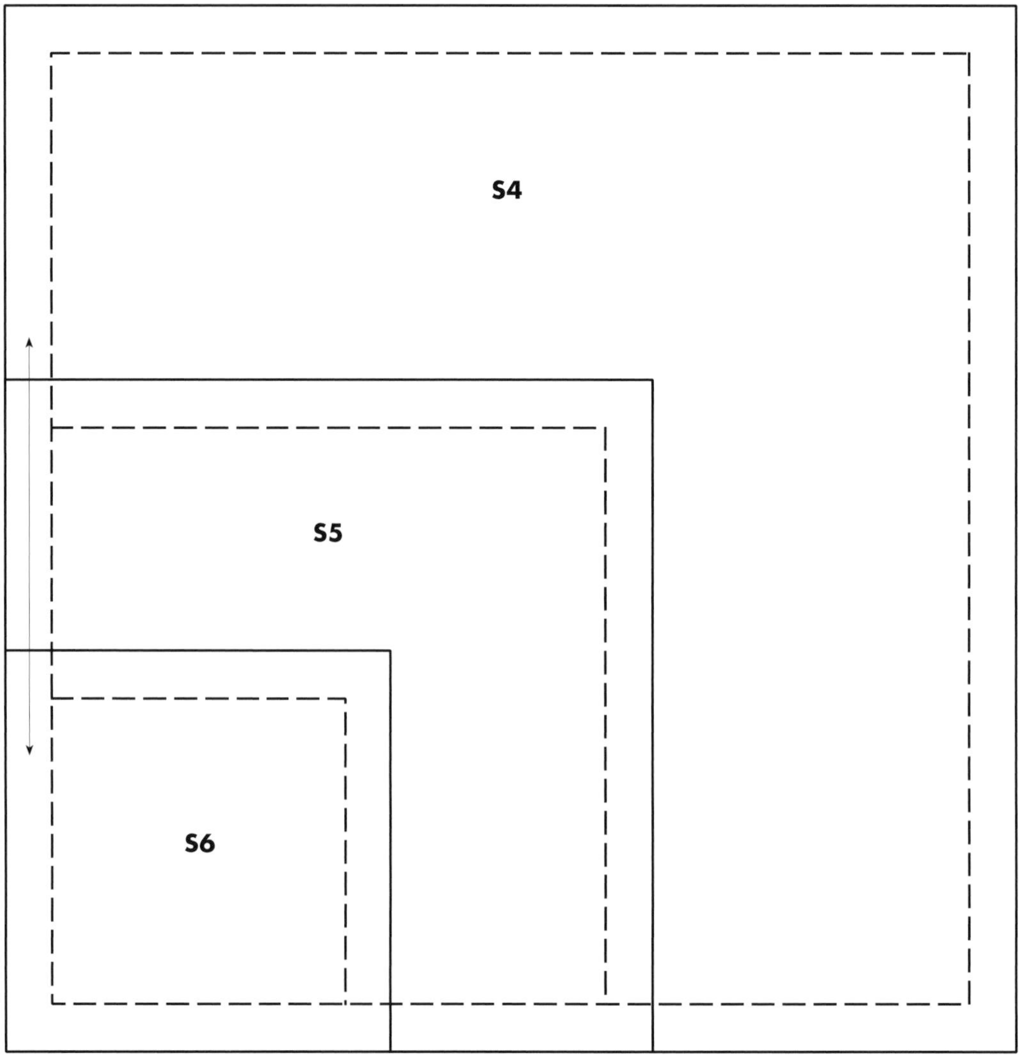

S4

S5

S6

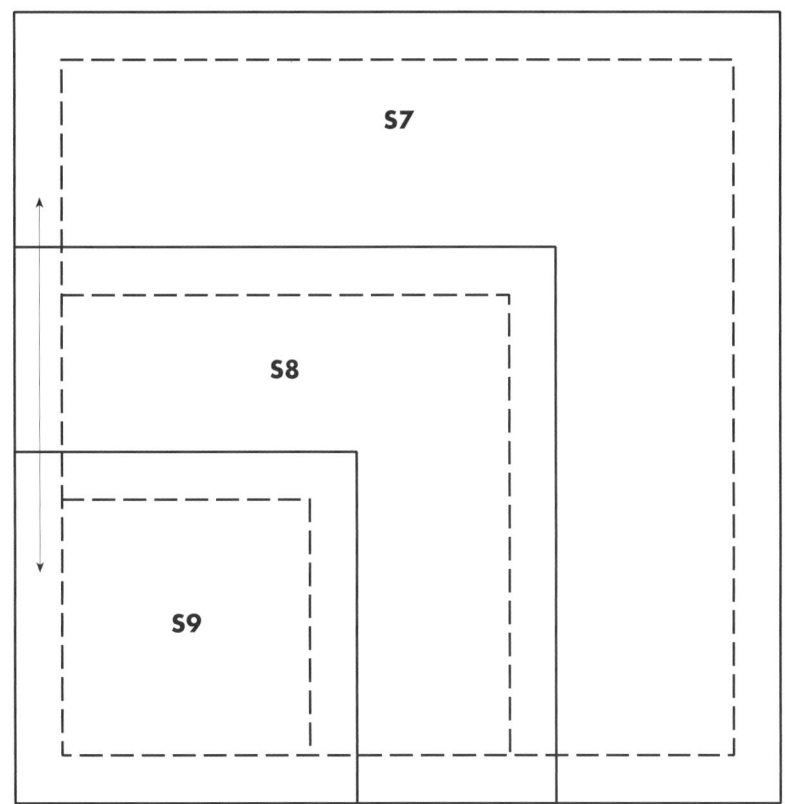

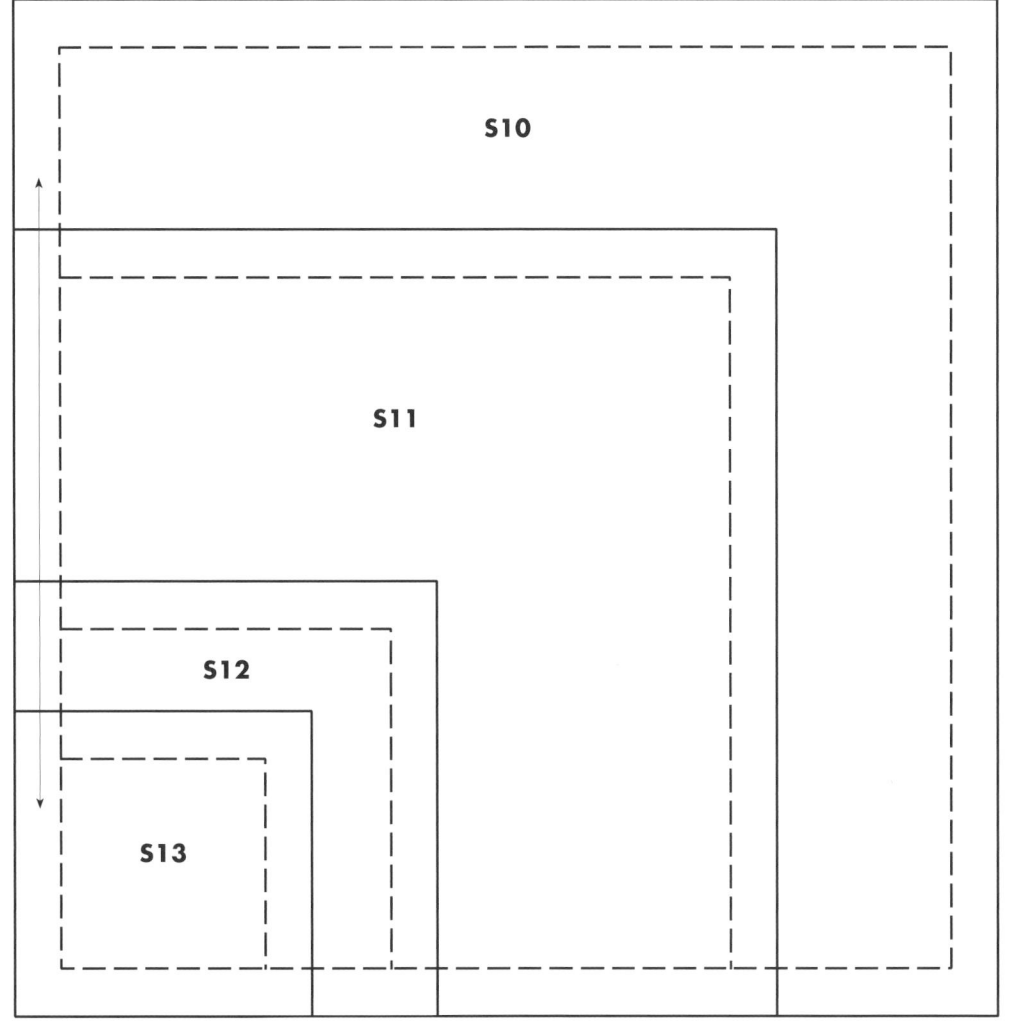

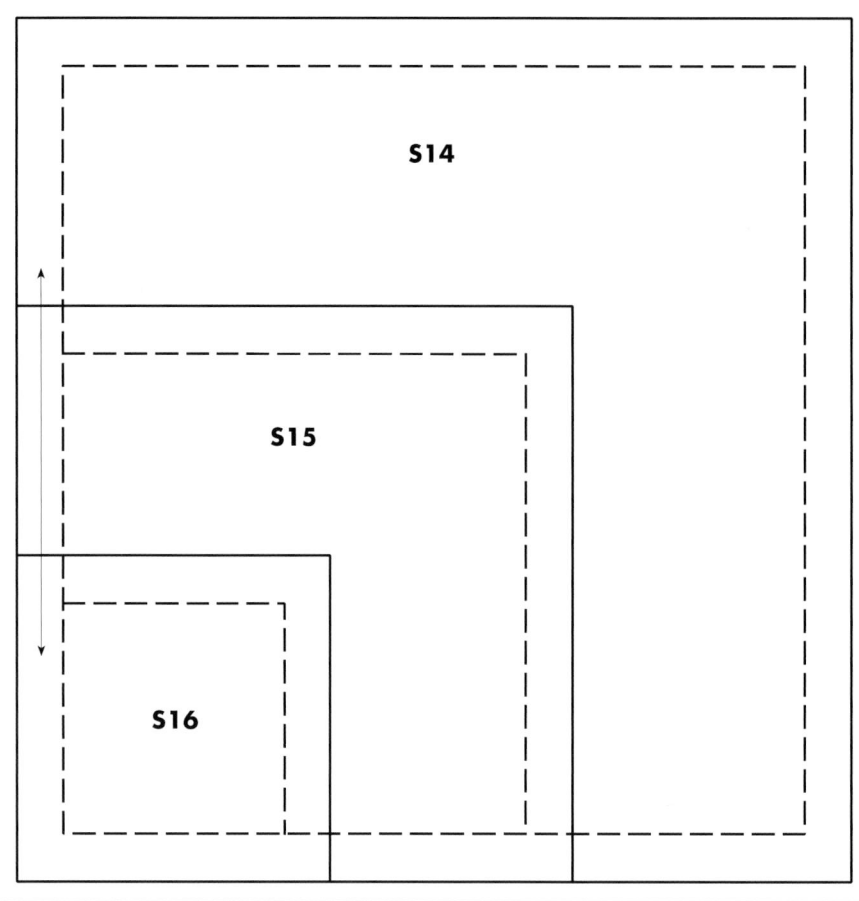

S14

S15

S16

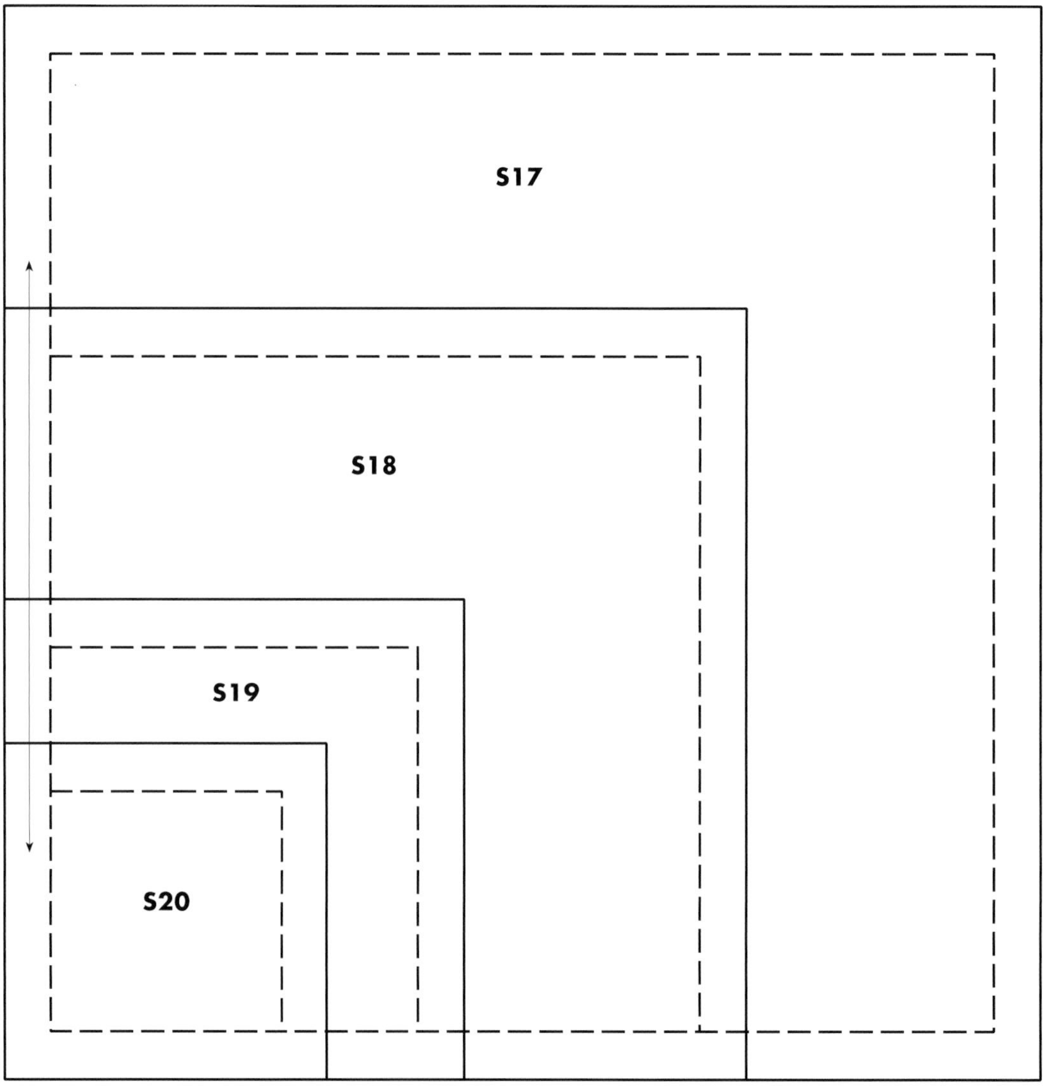

S17

S18

S19

S20

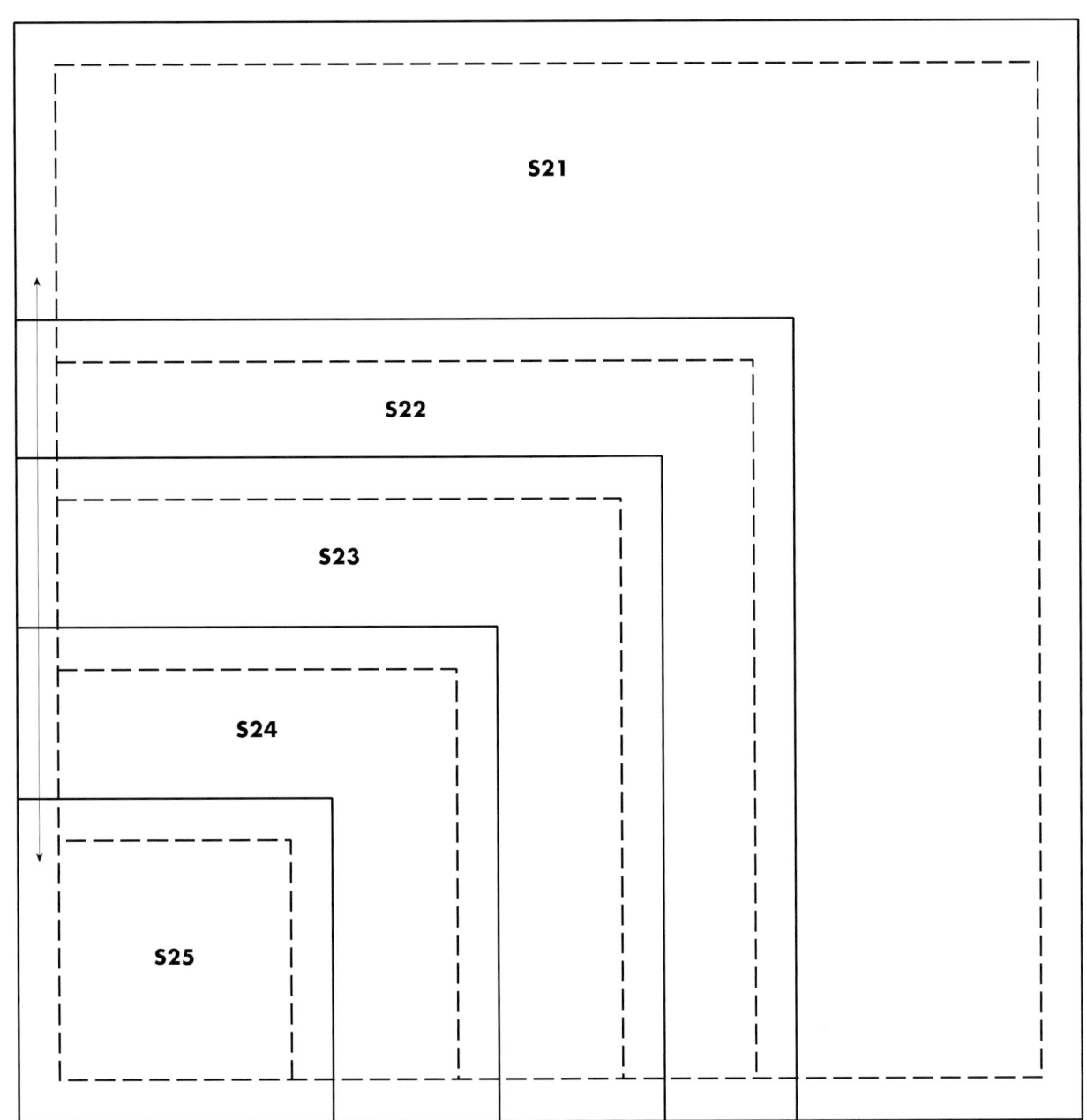

S21

S22

S23

S24

S25

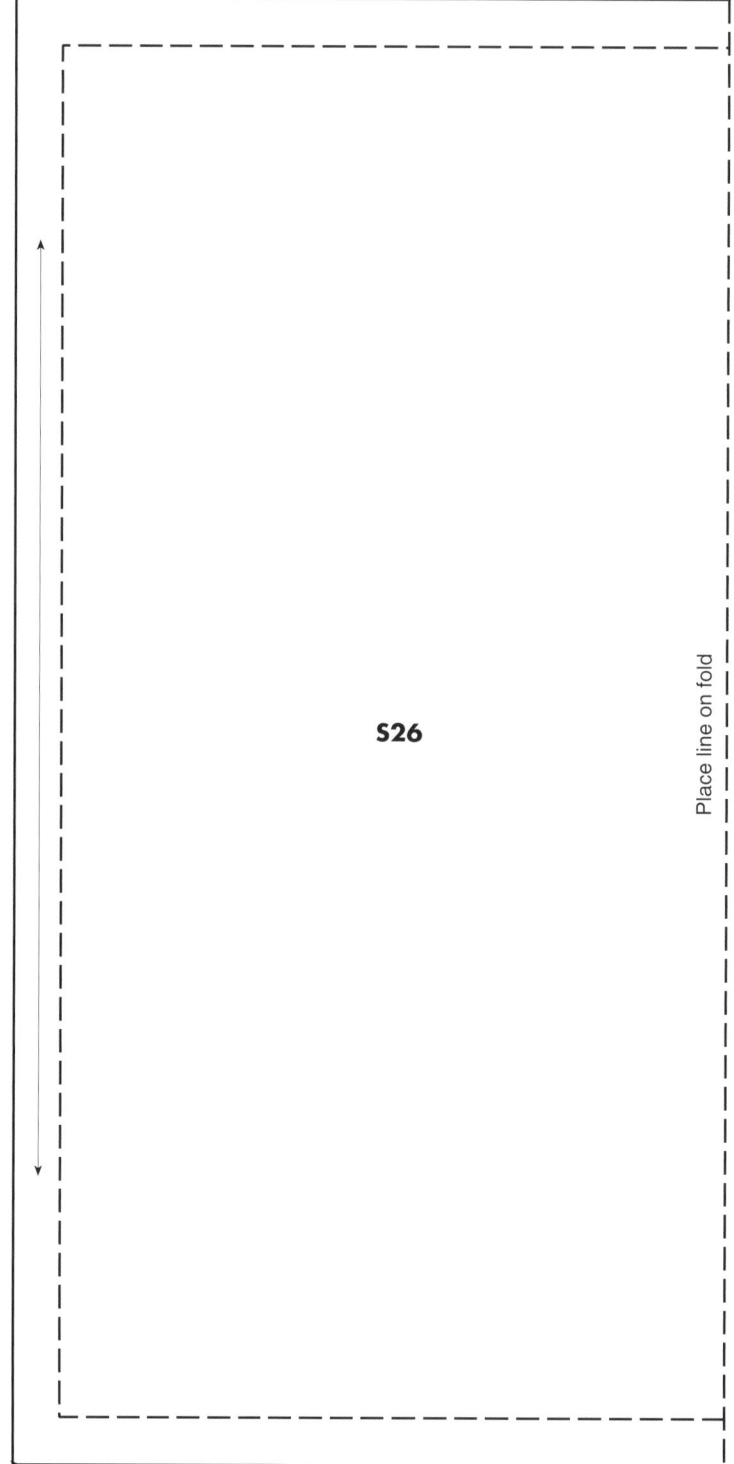

S26

Place line on fold

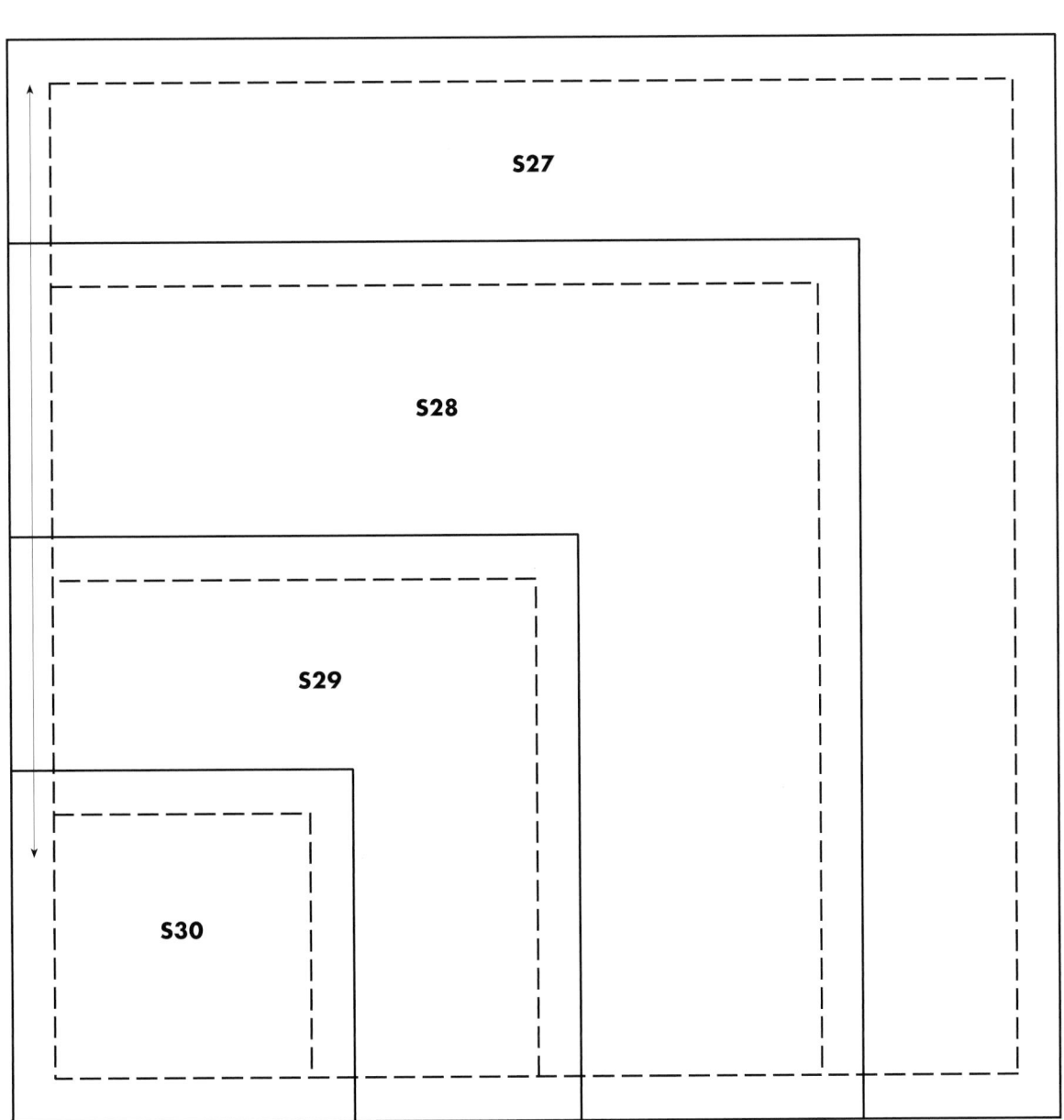

S27

S28

S29

S30

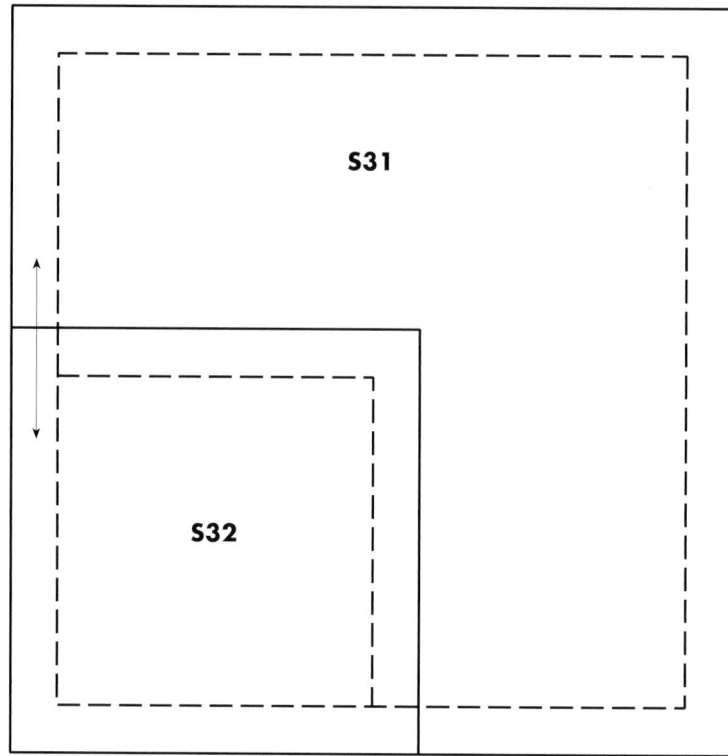

S31

S32

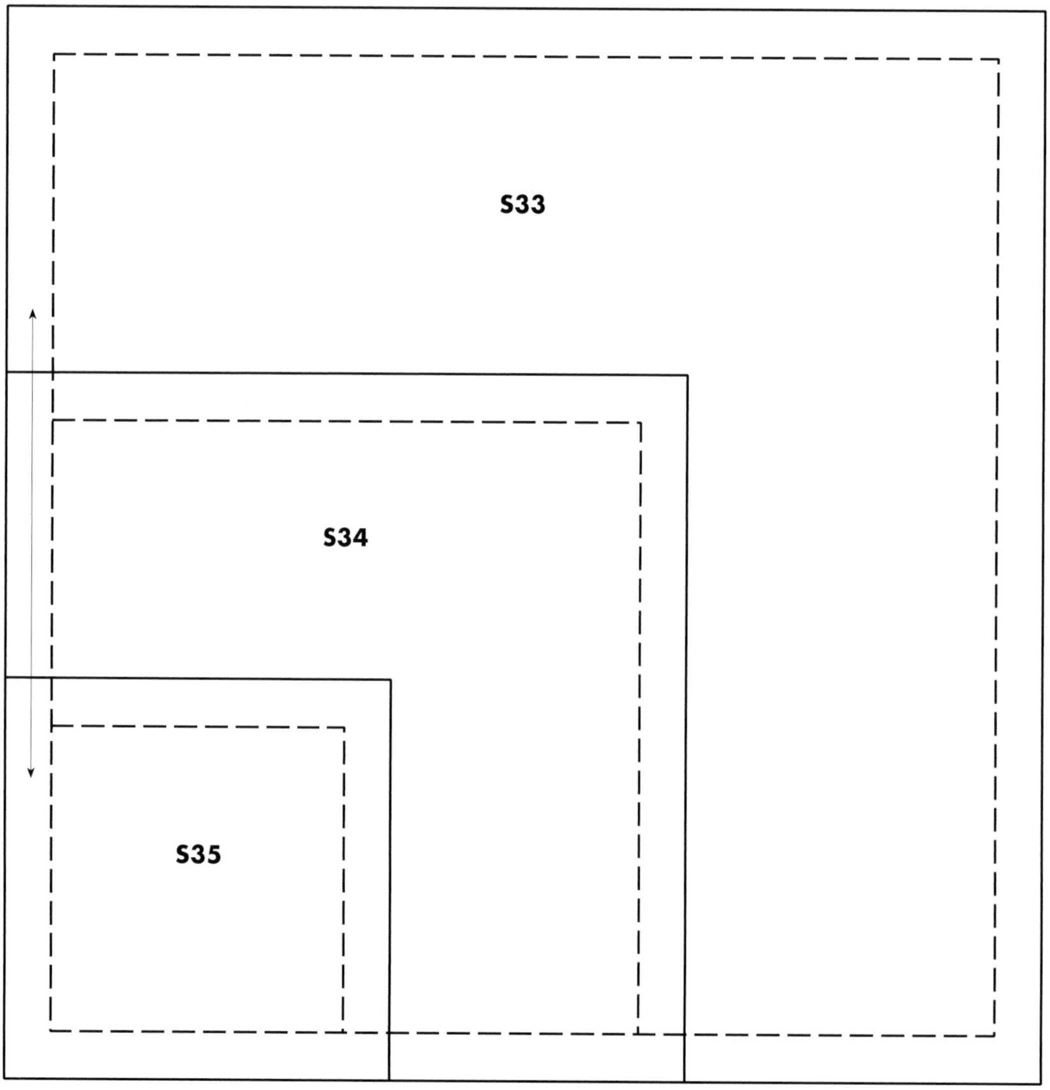

S33

S34

S35

TRIANGLE TEMPLATES

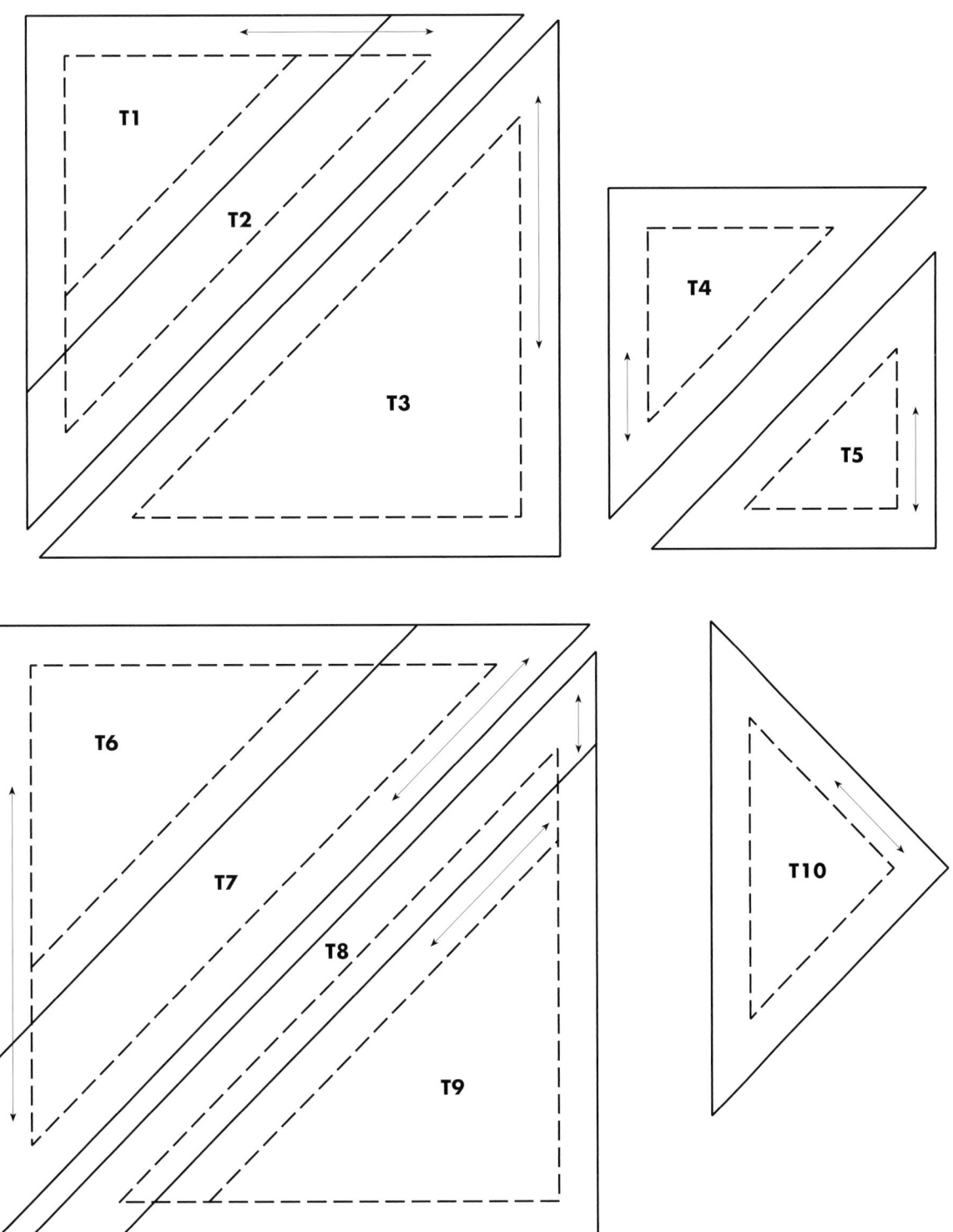

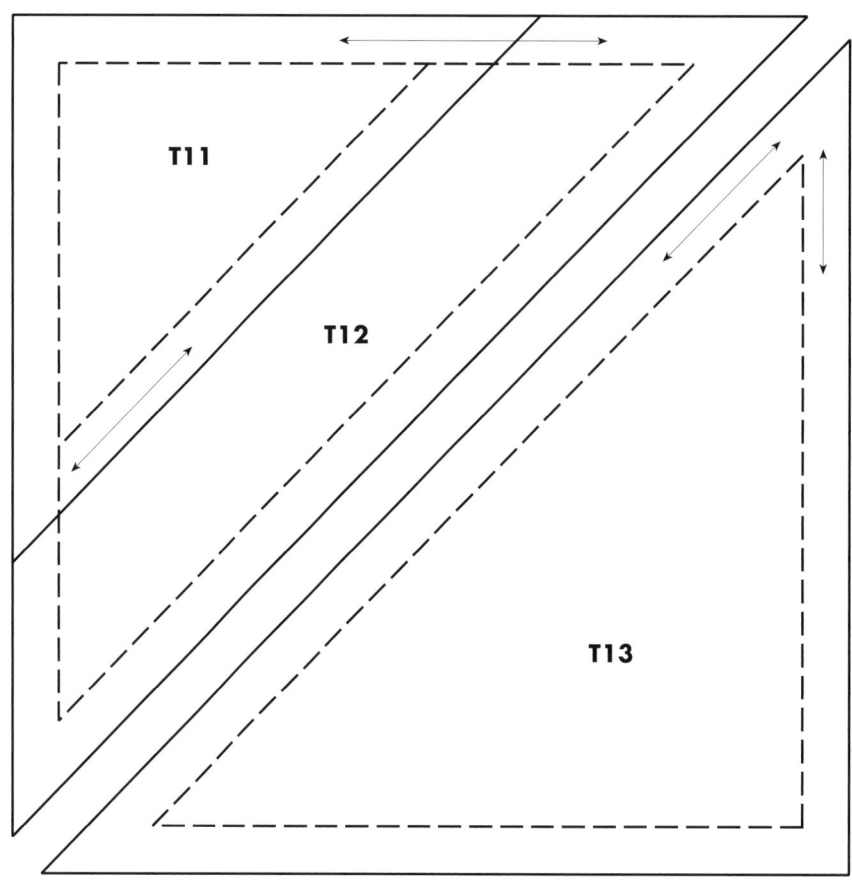

T11

T12

T13

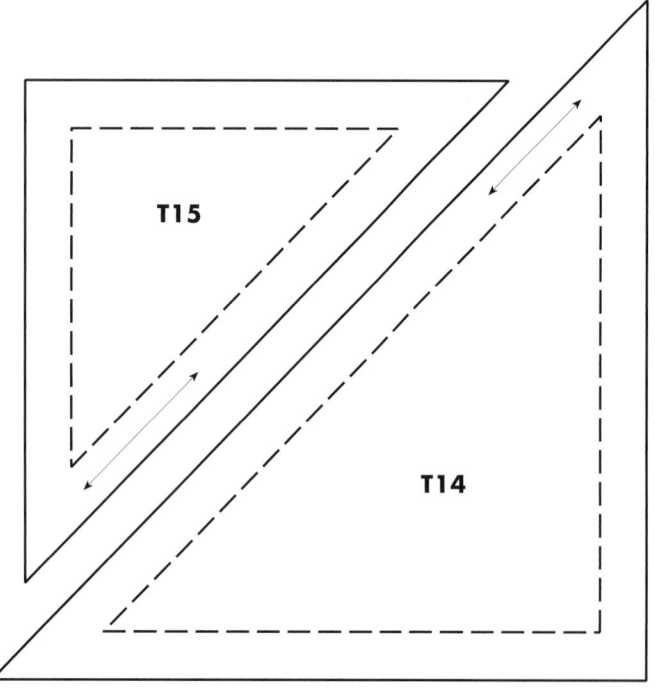

T15

T14

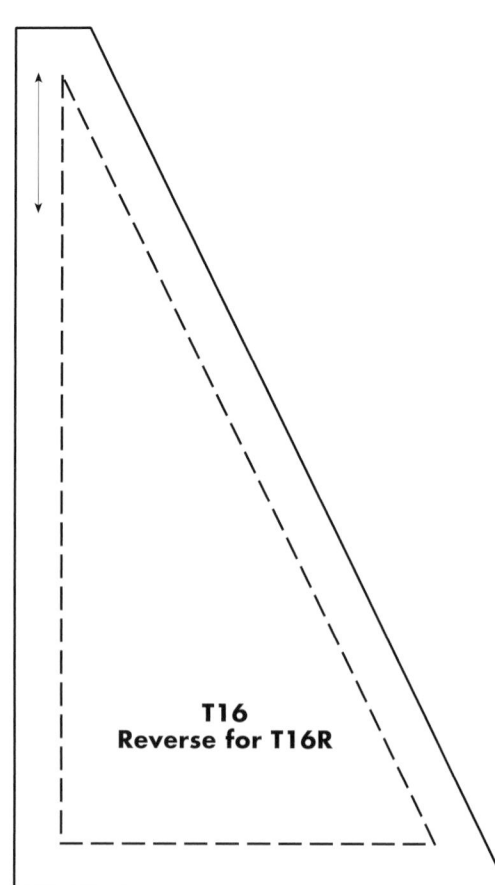

T16
Reverse for T16R

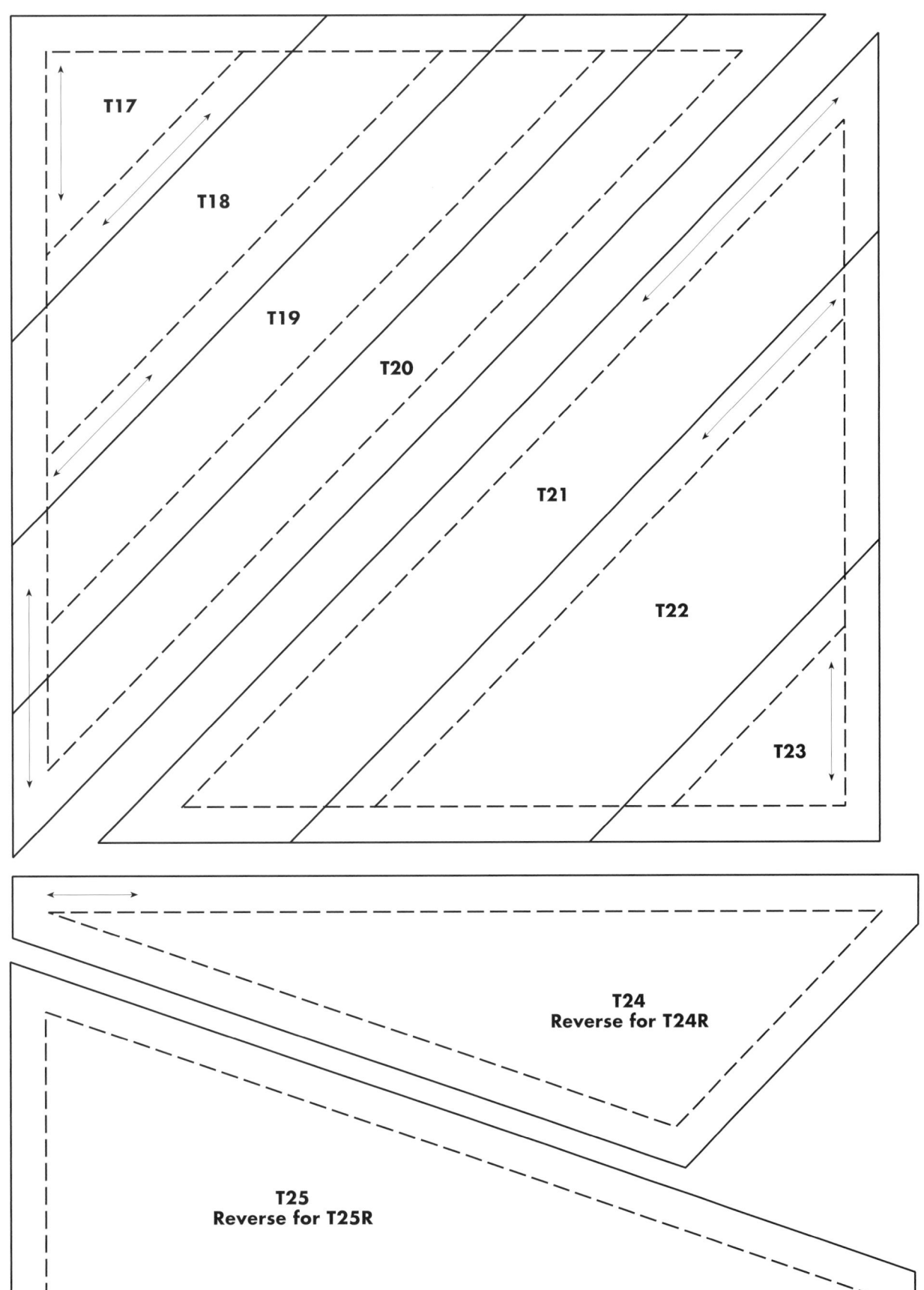

T17

T18

T19

T20

T21

T22

T23

T24
Reverse for T24R

T25
Reverse for T25R

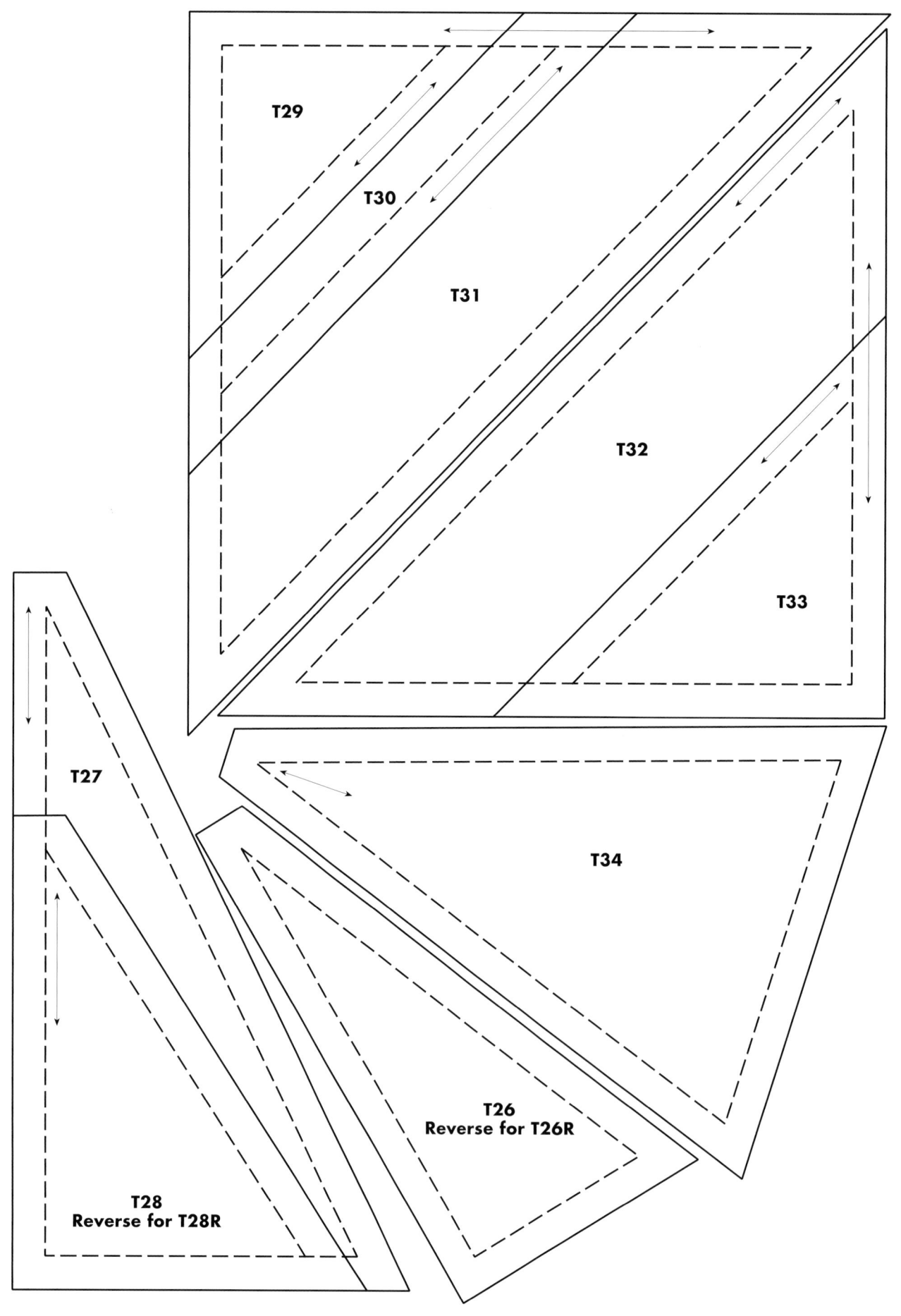

T29

T30

T31

T32

T33

T27

T34

T28
Reverse for T28R

T26
Reverse for T26R

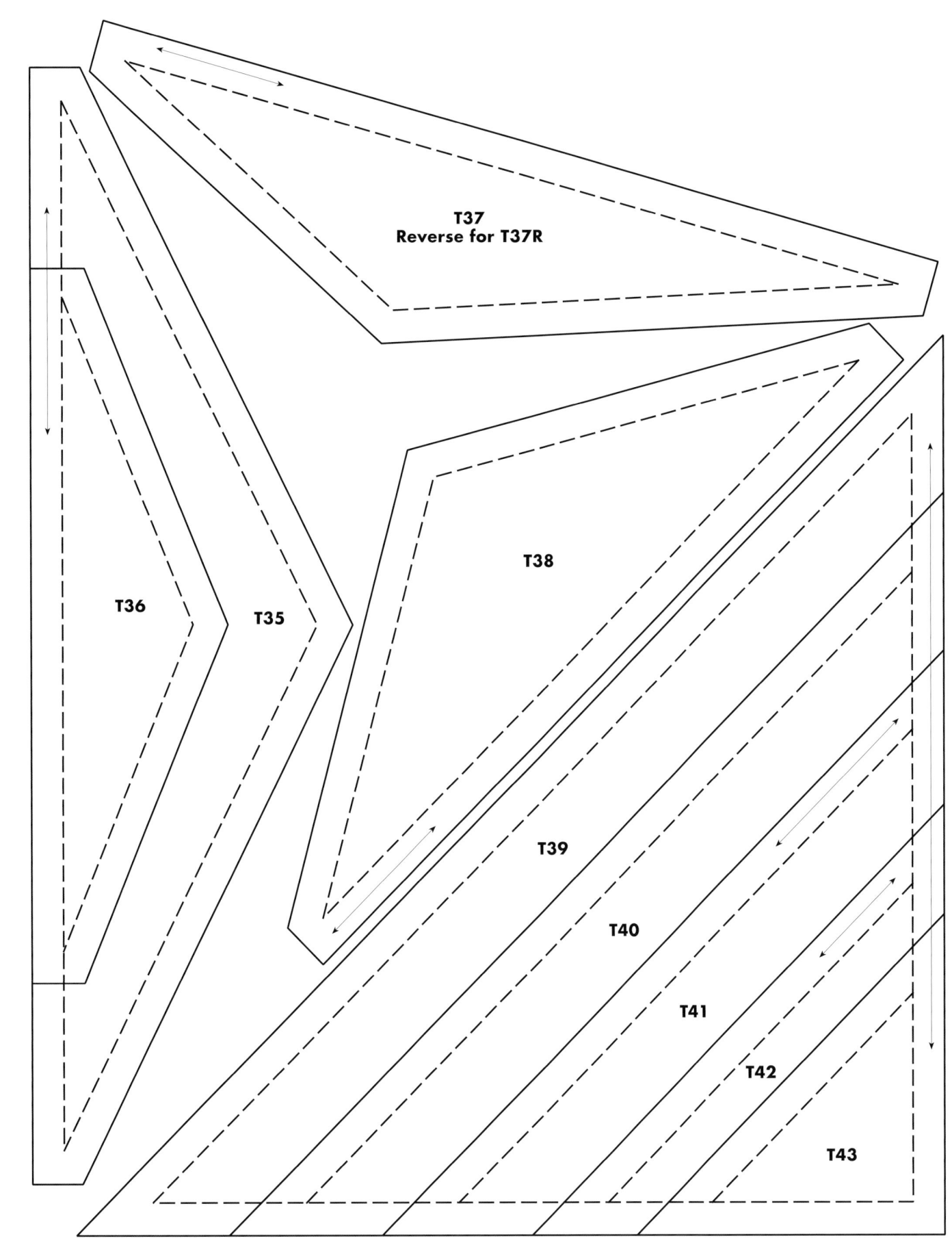

T37
Reverse for T37R

T36

T35

T38

T39

T40

T41

T42

T43

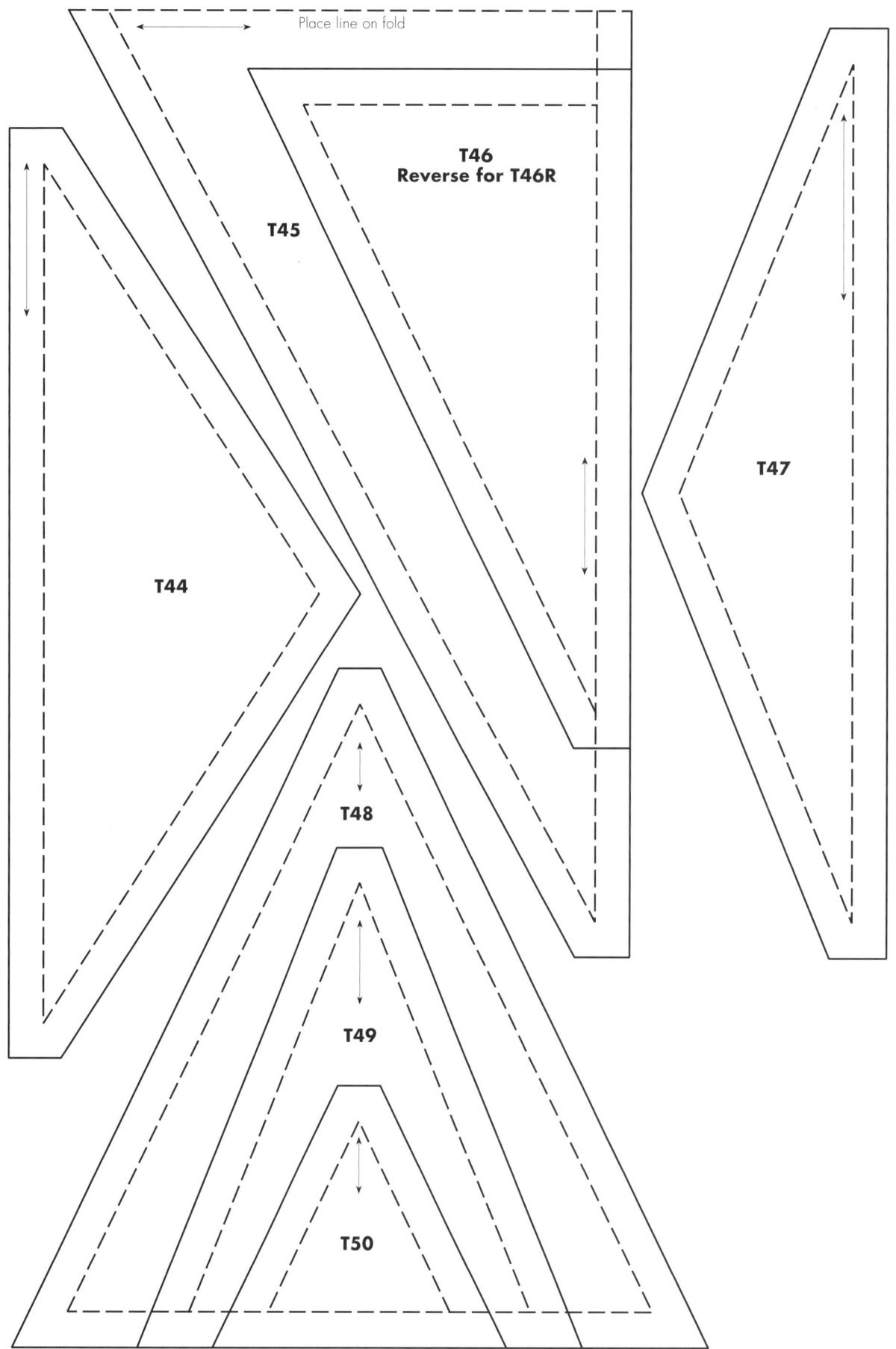

Place line on fold

T46
Reverse for T46R

T45

T44

T47

T48

T49

T50

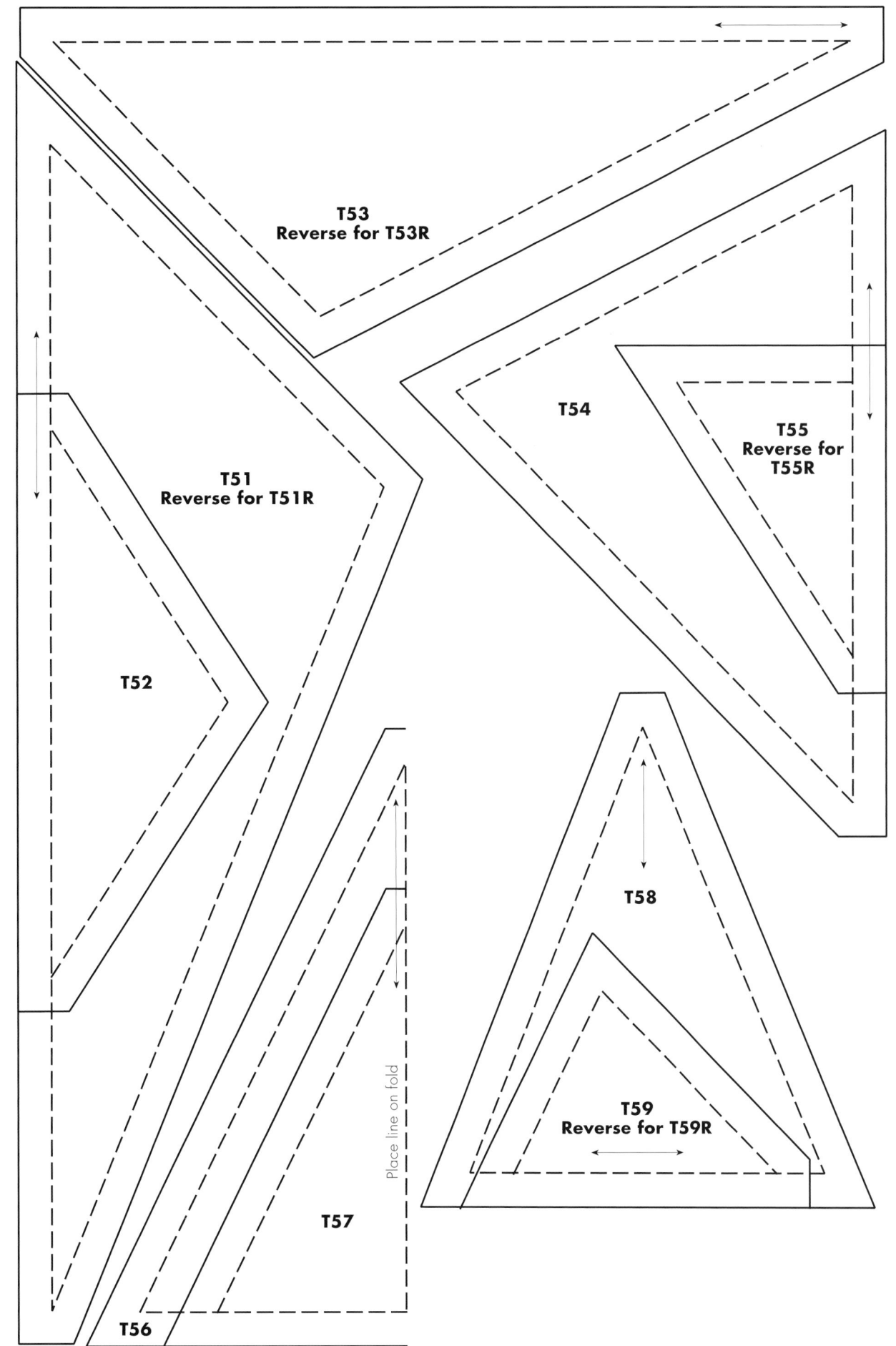

T53
Reverse for T53R

T54

T55
Reverse for
T55R

T51
Reverse for T51R

T52

T58

T59
Reverse for T59R

Place line on fold

T57

T56

159

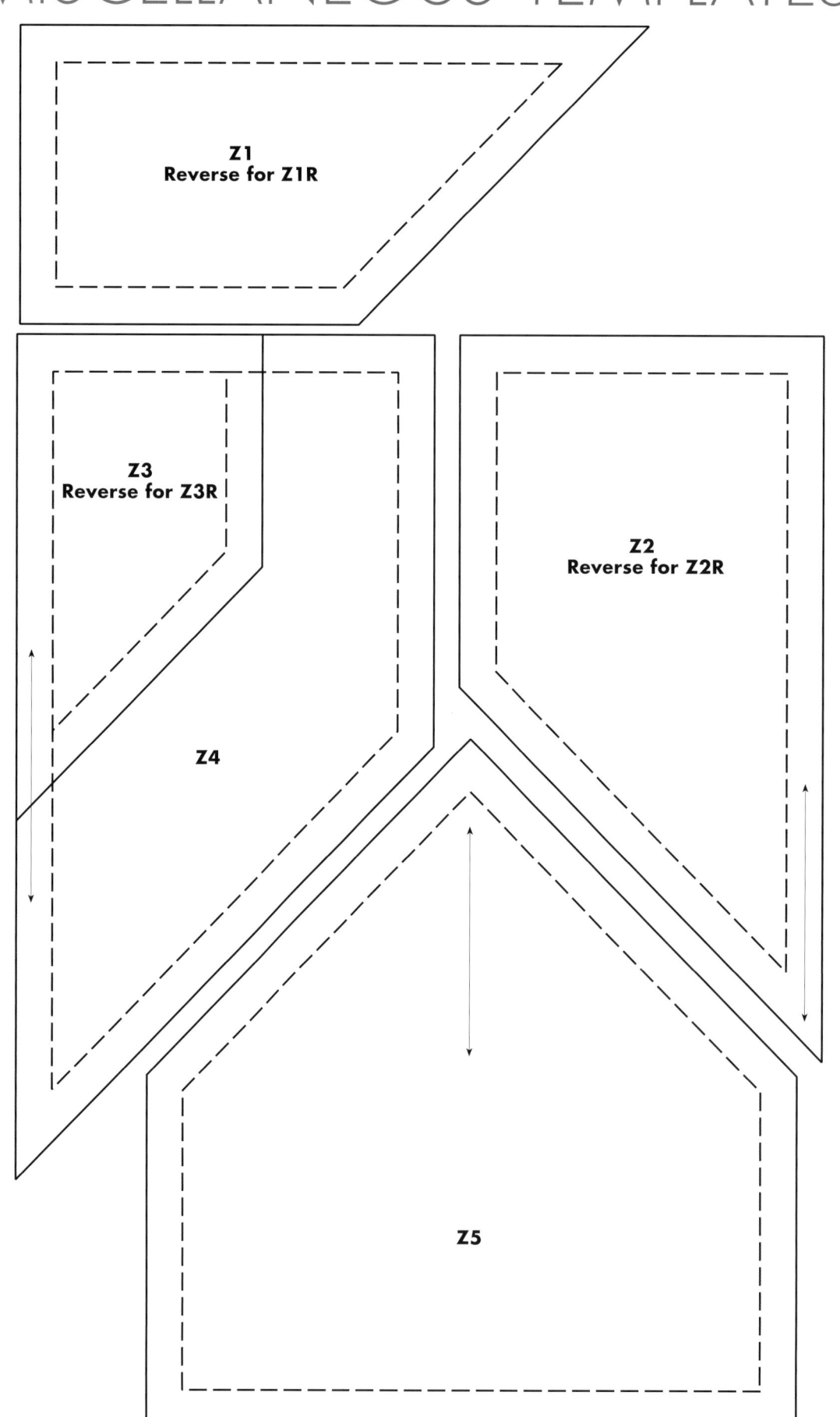

Z1
Reverse for Z1R

Z3
Reverse for Z3R

Z4

Z2
Reverse for Z2R

Z5

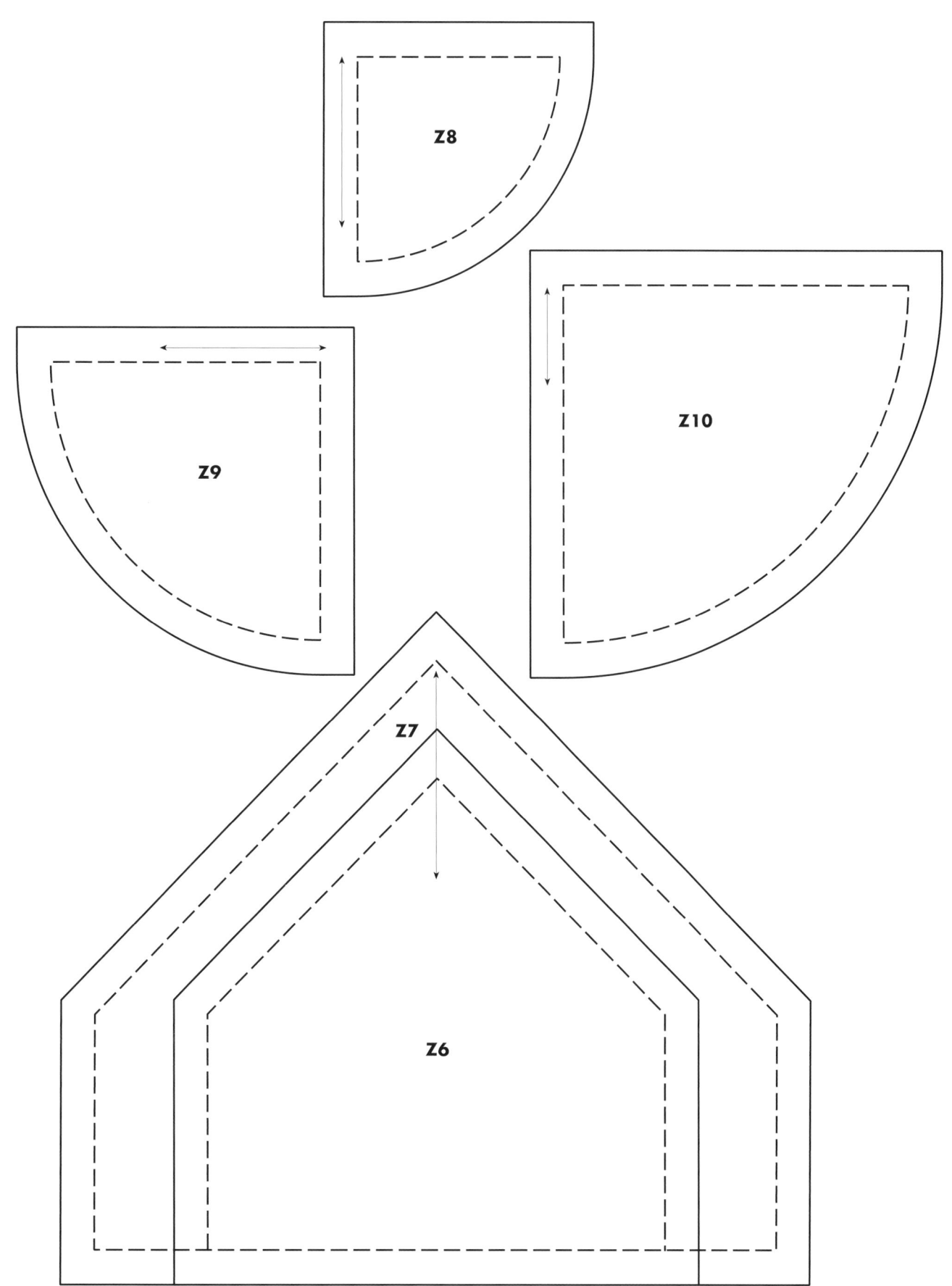

Z8

Z9

Z10

Z7

Z6

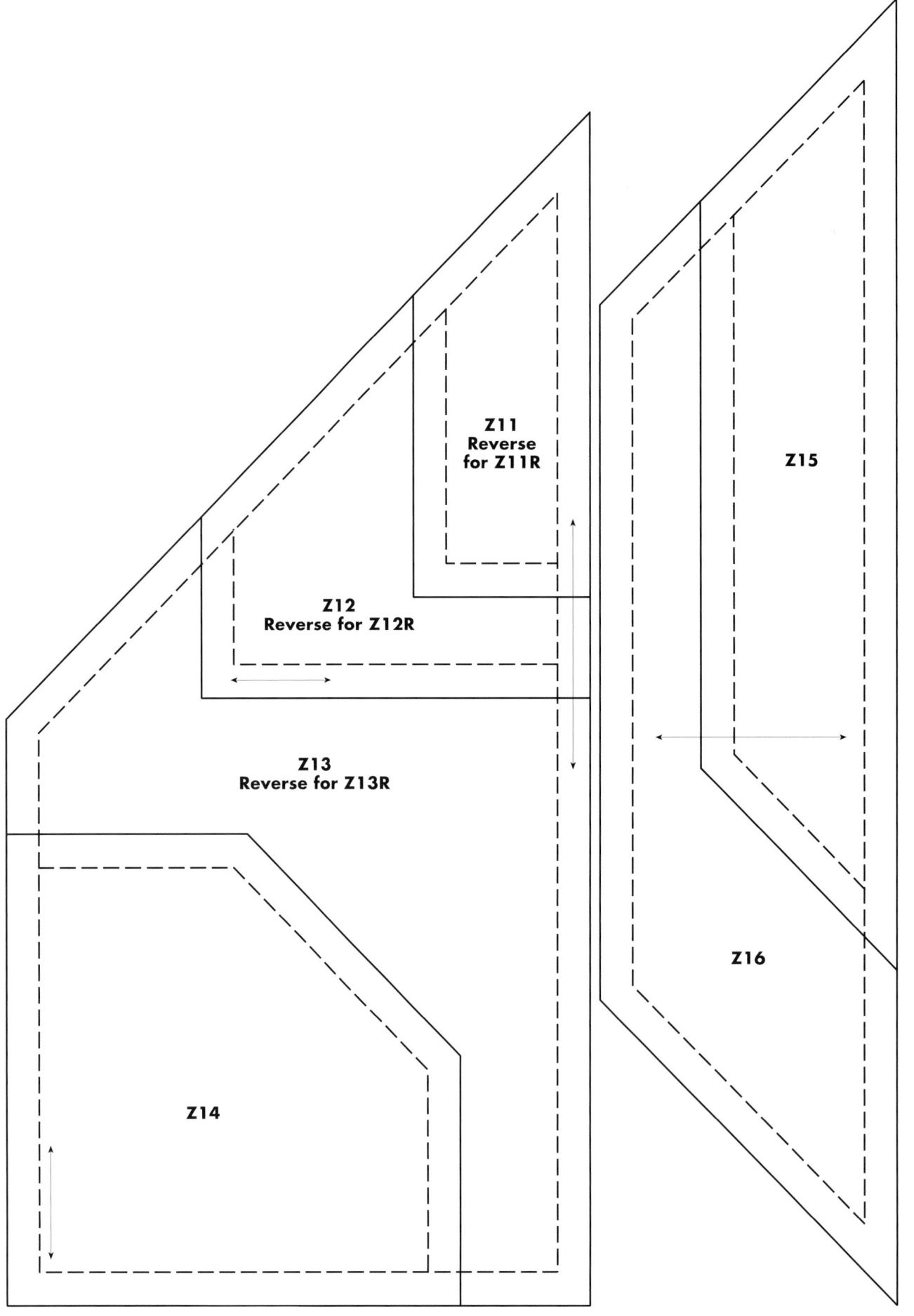

Z11
Reverse
for Z11R

Z12
Reverse for Z12R

Z13
Reverse for Z13R

Z14

Z15

Z16

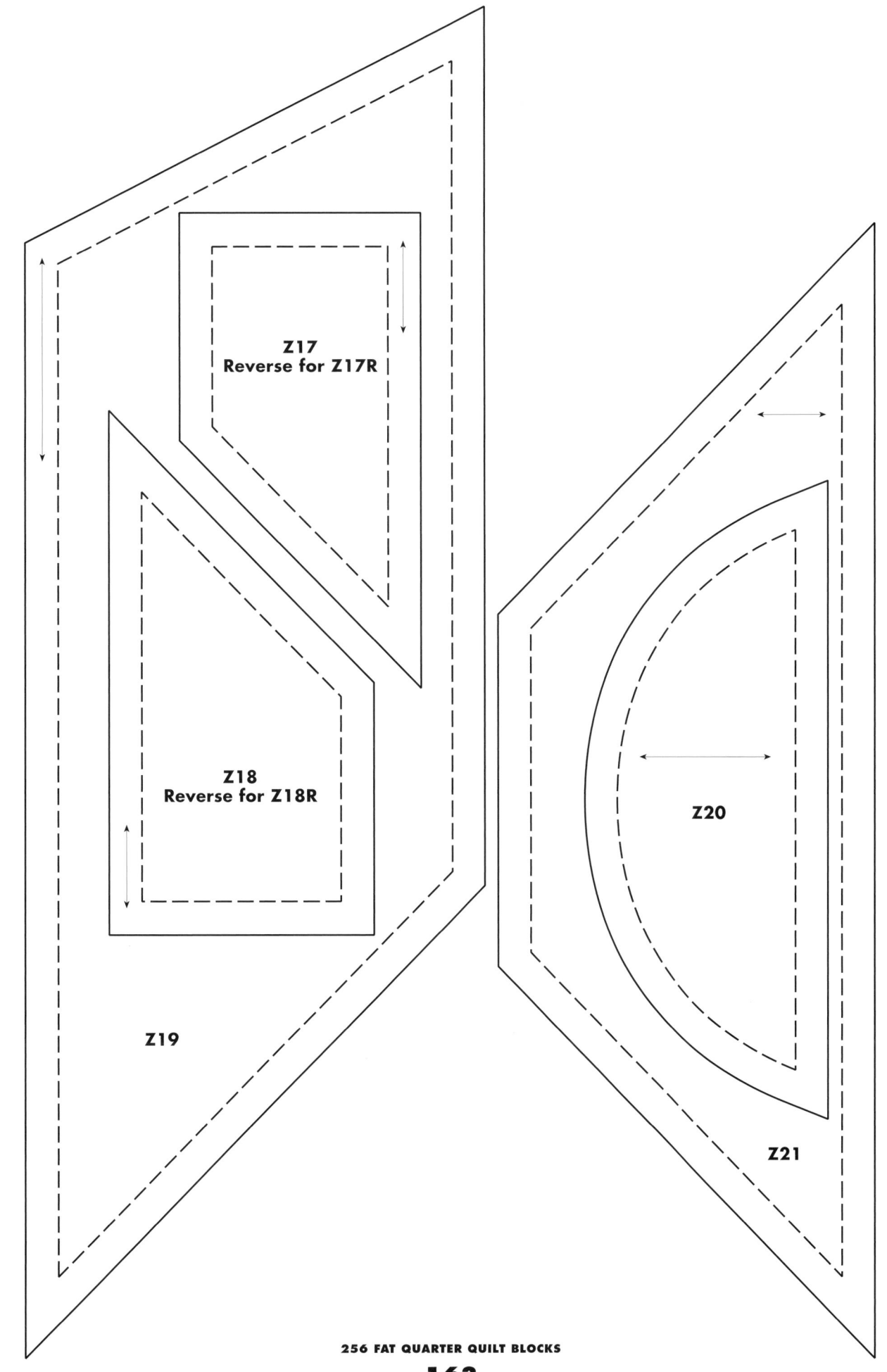

Z17
Reverse for Z17R

Z18
Reverse for Z18R

Z19

Z20

Z21

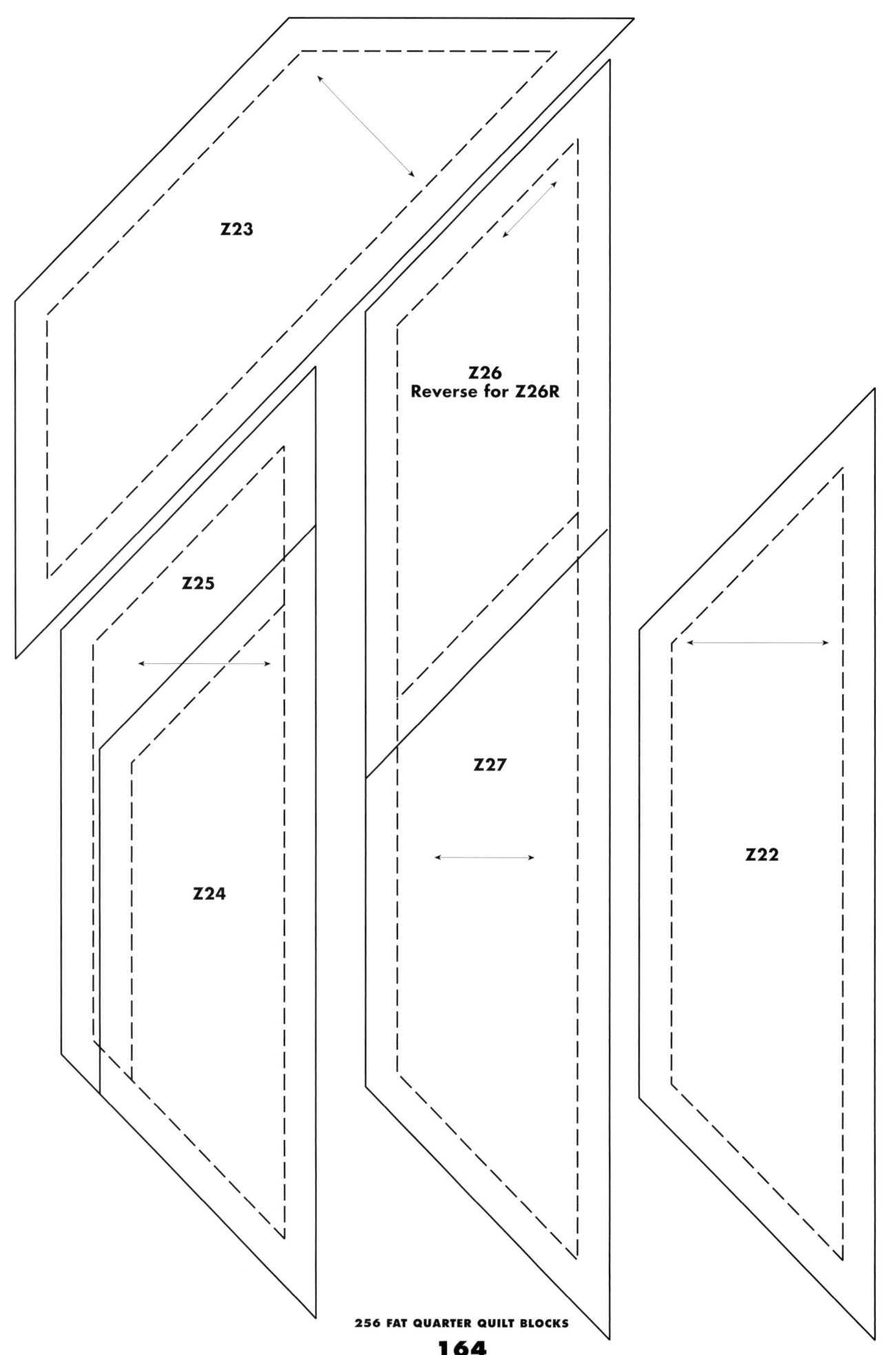

Z23

Z26
Reverse for Z26R

Z25

Z27

Z24

Z22

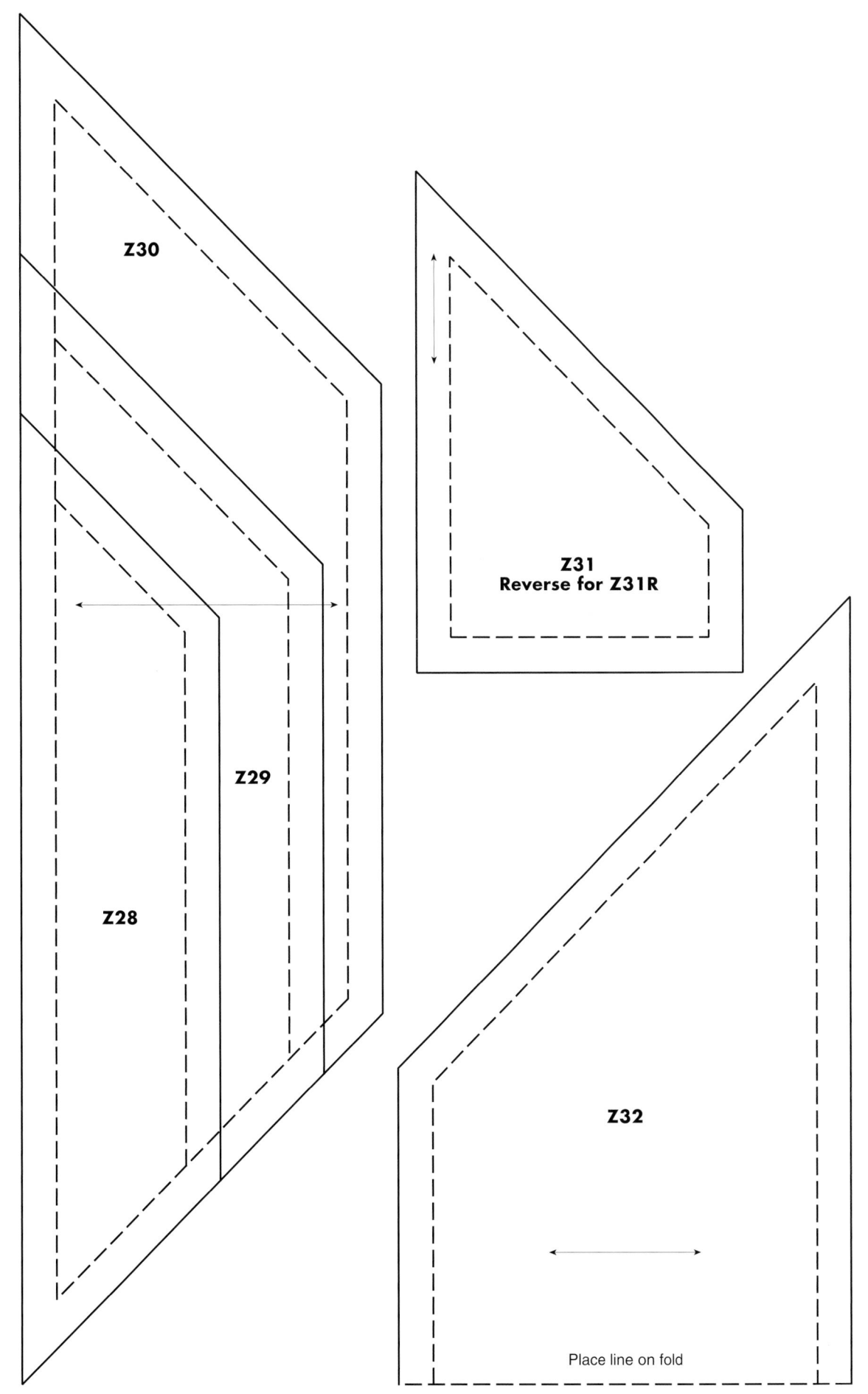

Z30

Z31
Reverse for Z31R

Z29

Z28

Z32

Place line on fold

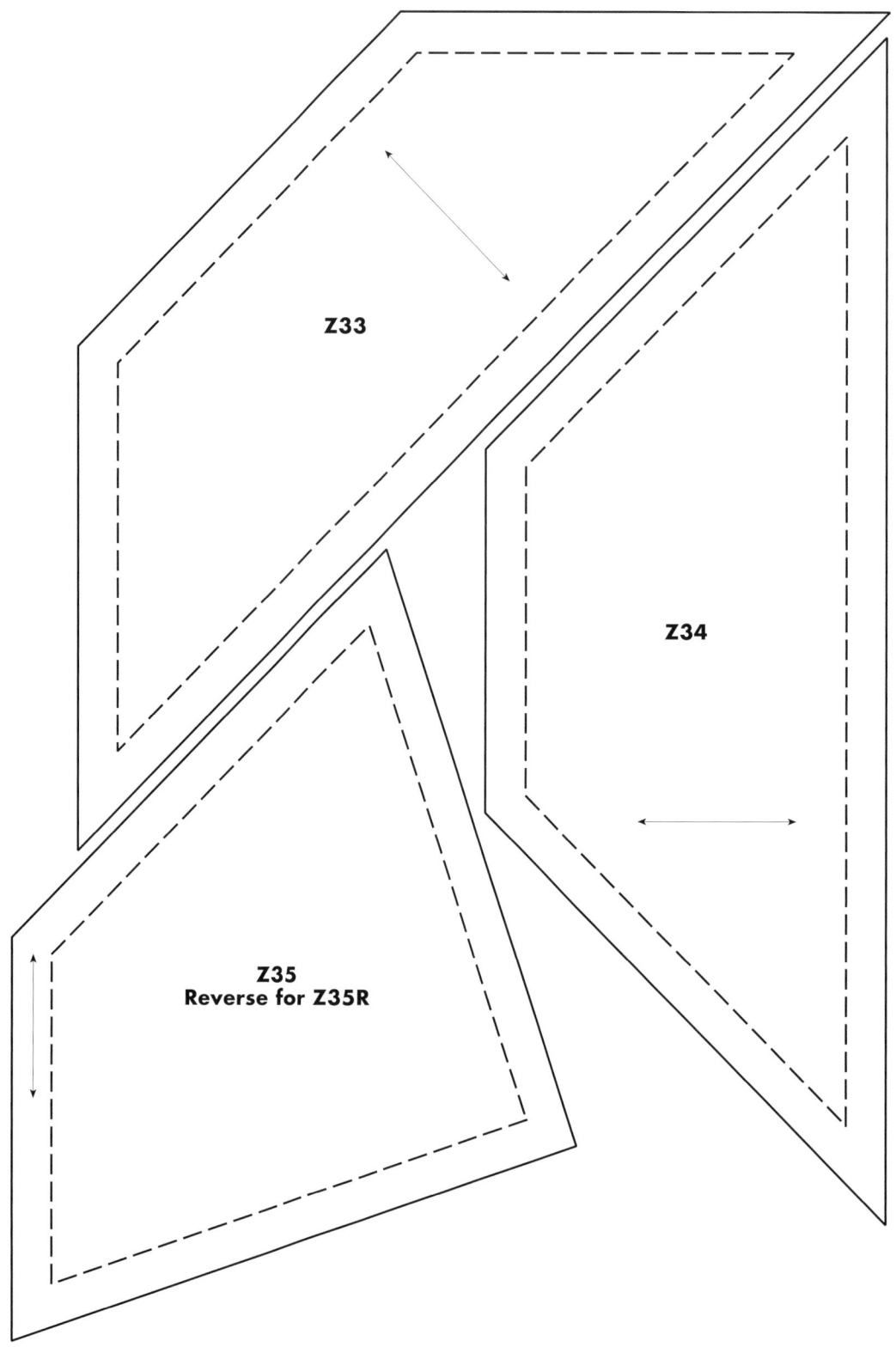

Z33

Z34

Z35
Reverse for Z35R

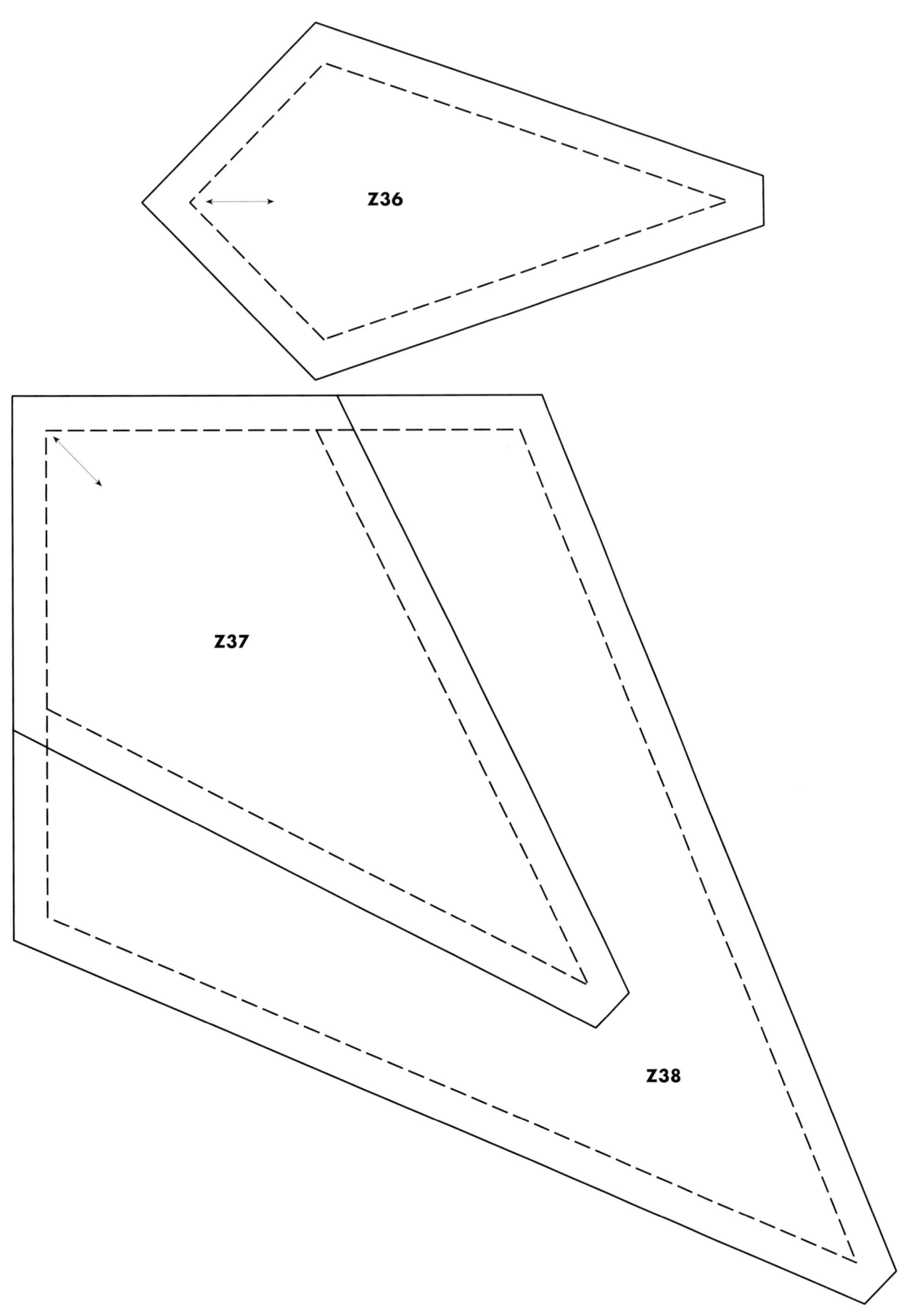

Z36

Z37

Z38

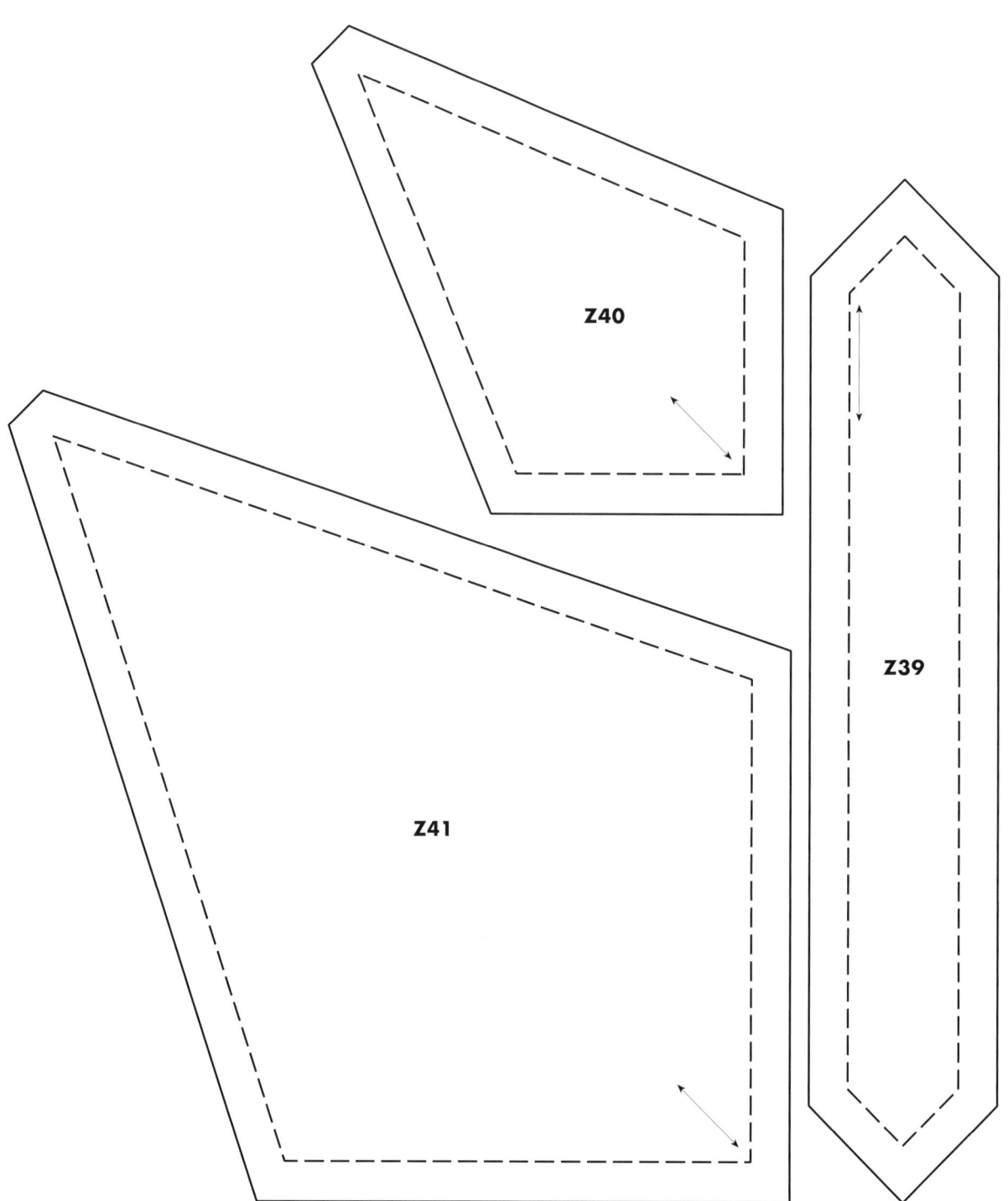

Z40

Z41

Z39

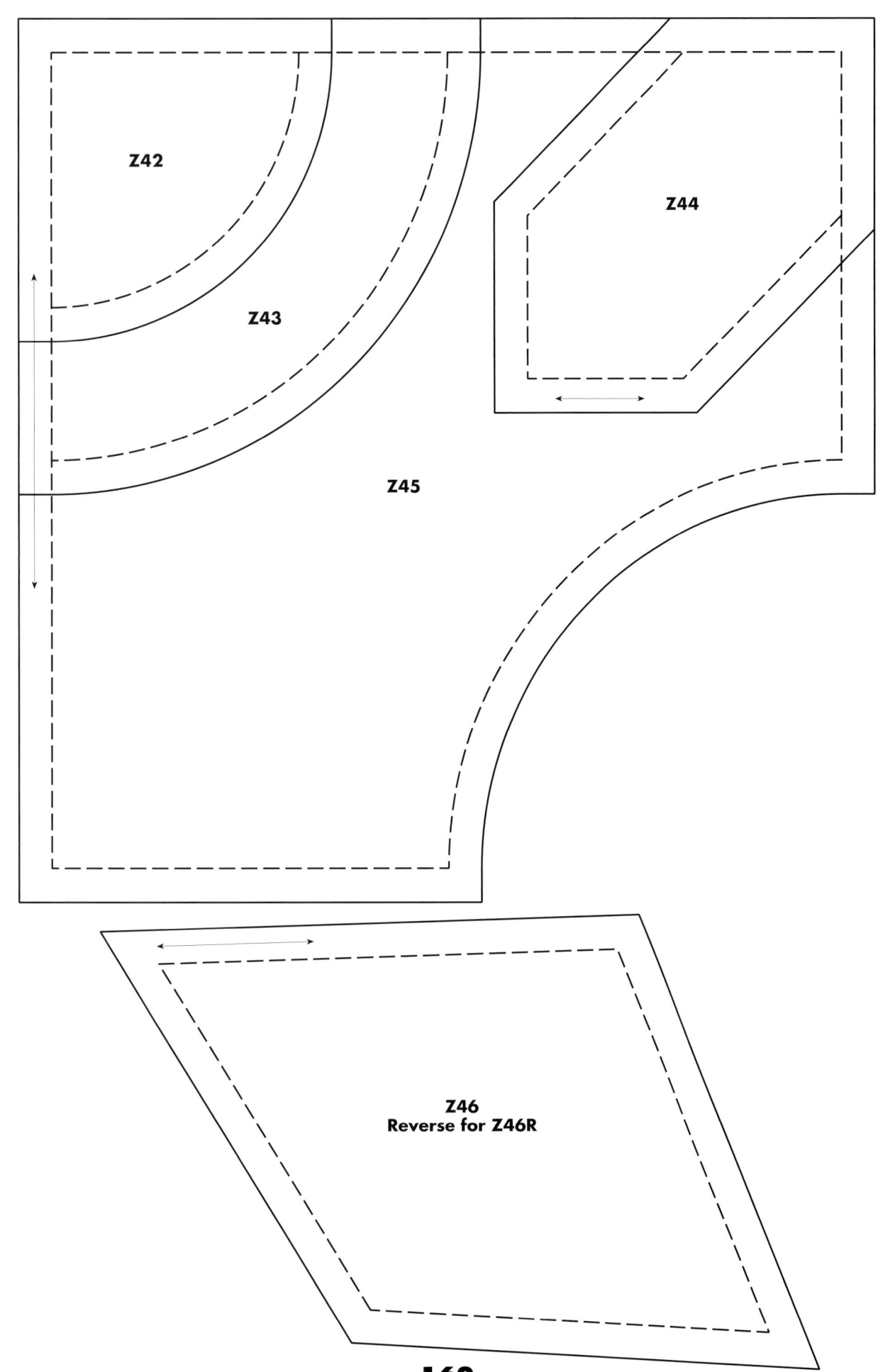

Z42

Z43

Z44

Z45

Z46
Reverse for Z46R

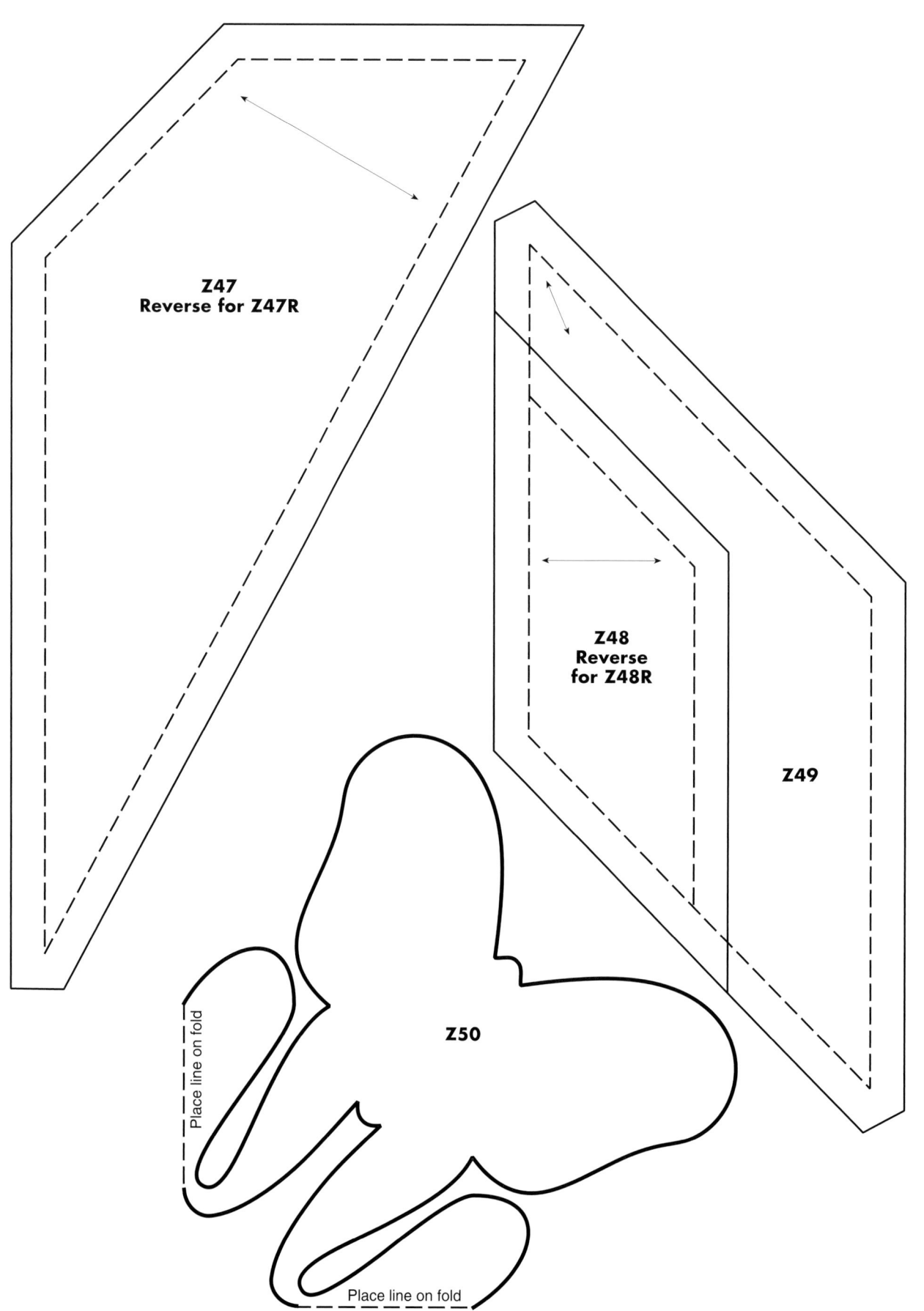

Z47
Reverse for Z47R

Z48
Reverse
for Z48R

Z49

Z50

Place line on fold

Place line on fold

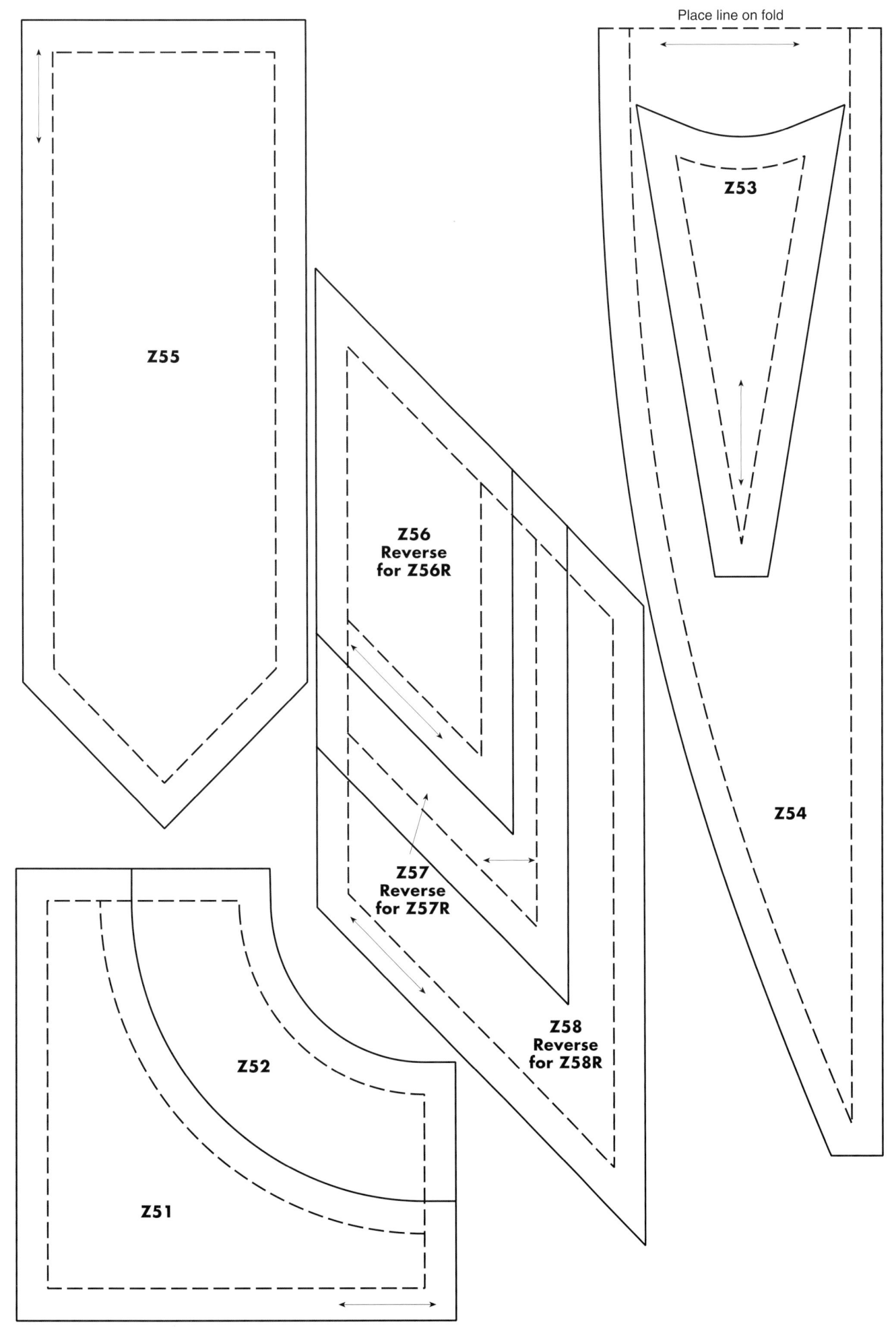

Place line on fold

Z53

Z55

Z56
Reverse
for Z56R

Z54

Z57
Reverse
for Z57R

Z58
Reverse
for Z58R

Z52

Z51

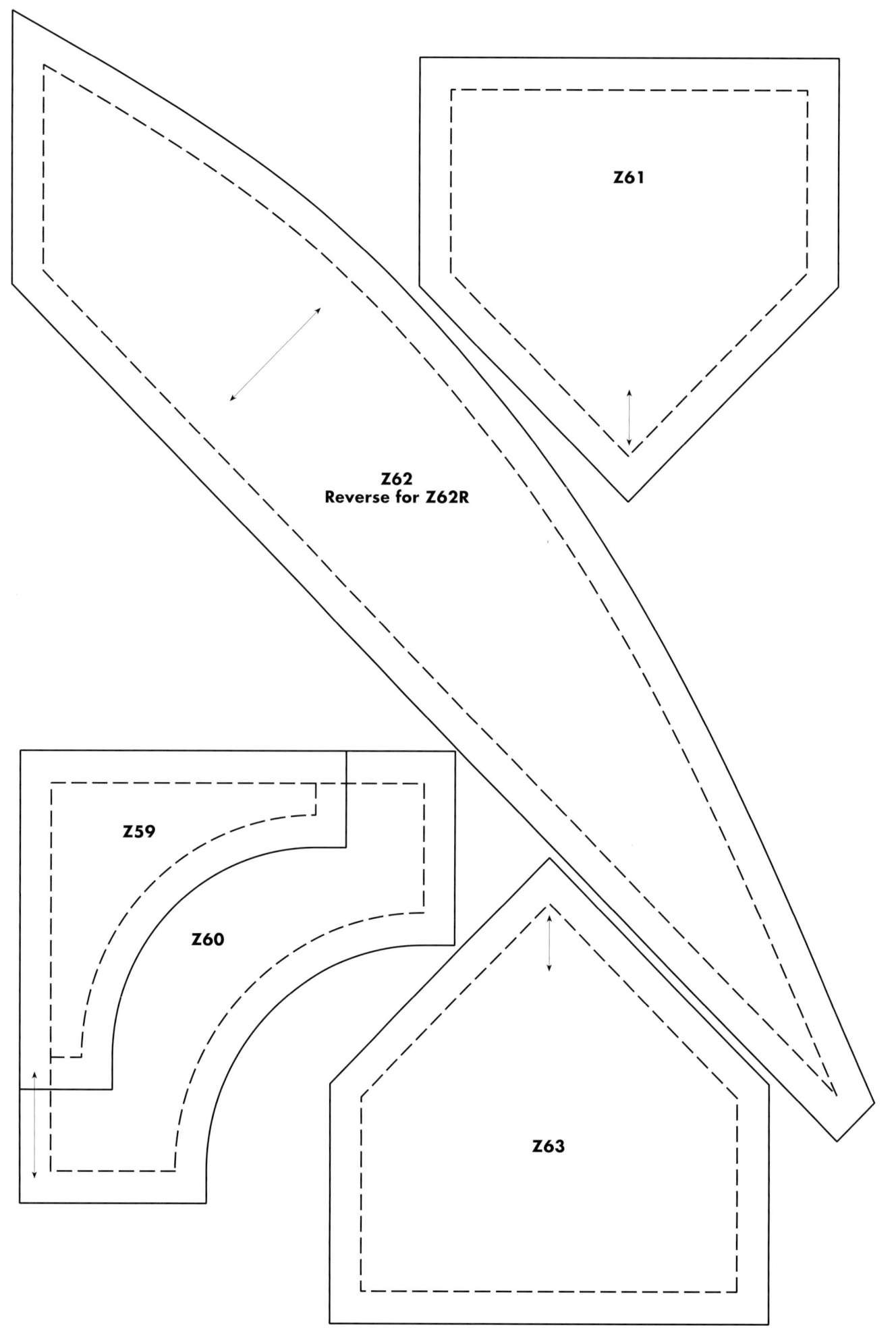

Z61

Z62
Reverse for Z62R

Z59

Z60

Z63

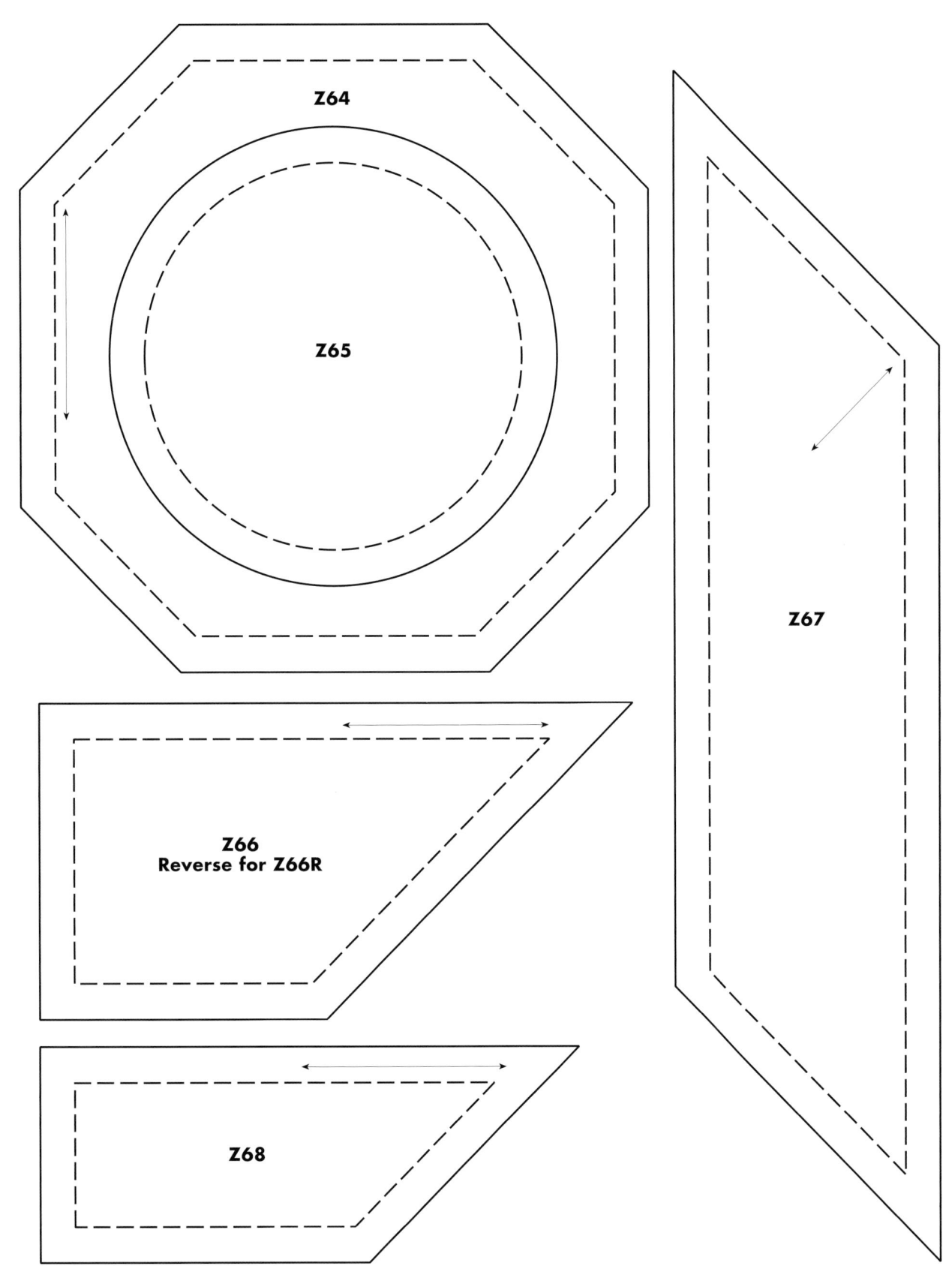

Z64

Z65

Z66
Reverse for Z66R

Z67

Z68

QUILT BLOCK INDEX

SPECIAL THANKS

We would like to thank the talented quilt designers whose work is featured in this collection.

Connie Kauffman
Golden Holiday Mat, 56
Pastel Pinwheels, 69
Patches of Sunshine, 62
Shining Star, 46

Toby Lischko
Diamonds Galore, 9
Midnight in the Garden, 66
Starry Lane, 18

Chris Malone
First Star, 16
Spring Garden Path, 59

Connie Rand
Golden Stars, 26

Judith Sandstrom
Primrose Cluster, 12
Sedona Illusions, 29
Tropical Butterflies, 43

Karla Schulz
Vintage Memories, 49

Julie Weaver
Beyond the Stars, 38
From the Heart, 64
Harvesttime, 32
Ice Crystals, 35
There's No Place Like Home, 22
Woven Threads, 52

FABRICS & SUPPLIES

Page 9: Diamonds Galore—Quilter's Cream Blend batting. Stitched on a Pfaff 2056 sewing machine and machine-quilted by Dolores Keaton.

Page 12: Primrose Cluster—DMC quilting thread and needles and Fiskars rotary-cutting tools.

Page 18: Starry Lane—Pfaff 2056 sewing machine used to stitch sample.

Page 22: There's No Place Like Home—Hobbs Thermore batting. Sample machine-quilted by Michelle Smith.

Page 32: Harvesttime—Fabrics from Moda's Seasons collection and Hobbs Thermore batting.

Page 38: Beyond the Stars—Hobbs Thermore batting. Sample machine-quilted by Michelle Smith.

Page 43: Tropical Butterflies—WonderUnder from Pellon, Fiskars rotary-cutting tools, DMC quilting thread and needles.

Page 46: Shining Star—Hobbs Heirloom cotton batting and Sulky cotton thread.

Page 49: Vintage Memories—Warm & Natural cotton batting.

Page 52: Woven Threads—Moda's Seaside Rose fabric collection and Hobbs Thermore batting.

Page 56: Golden Holiday Mat—Sulky Gold rayon thread and Hobbs Premium batting.

Page 66: Midnight in the Garden—Azalea Trail fabrics from P&B Textiles. Pfaff 2056 sewing machine used to piece the project.

Page 69: Pastel Pinwheels—Sulky Blendables thread and Hobbs Heirloom fusible cotton batting.

Metric Conversion Charts

Metric Conversions

U.S. Measurements		Multiplied by	Metric Measurement
yards	x	.9144	= meters (m)
yards	x	91.44	= centimeters (cm)
inches	x	2.54	= centimeters (cm)
inches	x	25.4	= millimeters (mm)
inches	x	.0254	= meters (m)

Metric Measurements		Multiplied by	U.S. Measurements
centimeters	x	.3937	= inches
meters	x	1.0936	= yards

Standard Equivalents

U.S. Measurement		Metric Measurement		
1/8 inch	=	3.20 mm	=	0.32 cm
1/4 inch	=	6.35 mm	=	0.635 cm
3/8 inch	=	9.50 mm	=	0.95 cm
1/2 inch	=	12.70 mm	=	1.27 cm
5/8 inch	=	15.90 mm	=	1.59 cm
3/4 inch	=	19.10 mm	=	1.91 cm
7/8 inch	=	22.20 mm	=	2.22 cm
1 inch	=	25.40 mm	=	2.54 cm
1/8 yard	=	11.43 cm	=	0.11 m
1/4 yard	=	22.86 cm	=	0.23 m
3/8 yard	=	34.29 cm	=	0.34 m
1/2 yard	=	45.72 cm	=	0.46 m
5/8 yard	=	57.15 cm	=	0.57 m
3/4 yard	=	68.58 cm	=	0.69 m
7/8 yard	=	80.00 cm	=	0.80 m
1 yard	=	91.44 cm	=	0.91 m

Embroidery Stitch Guide

Buttonhole Stitch

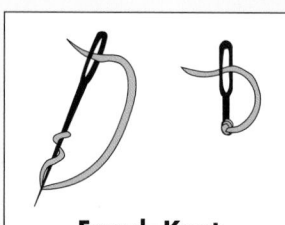

French Knot

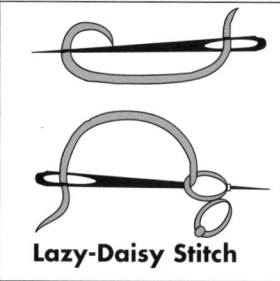

Lazy-Daisy Stitch

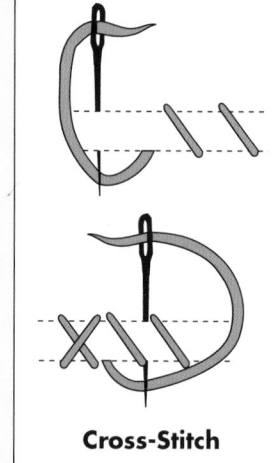

Cross-Stitch

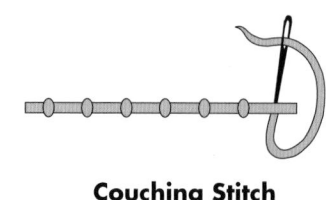

Couching Stitch

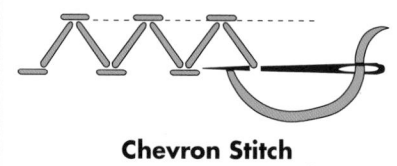

Chevron Stitch

Satin Stitch

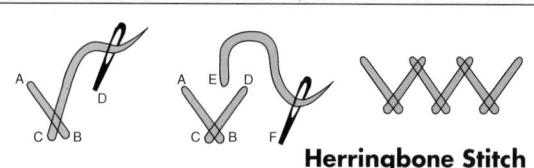

Herringbone Stitch

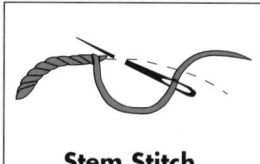

Stem Stitch

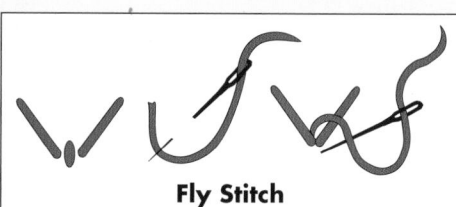

Fly Stitch

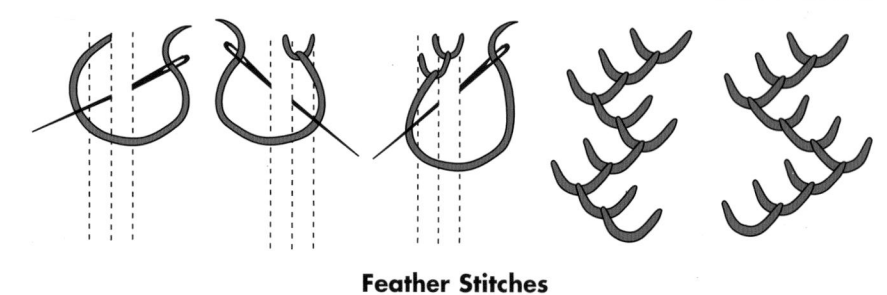

Feather Stitches

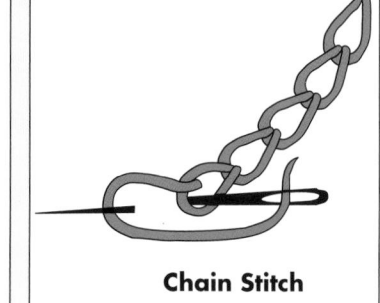

Chain Stitch